SISSY!

SISSY!

THE EFFEMINATE PARADOX IN POSTWAR US LITERATURE AND CULTURE

HARRY THOMAS JR.

THE UNIVERSITY OF ALABAMA PRESS
Tuscaloosa

The University of Alabama Press
Tuscaloosa, Alabama 35487-0380
uapress.ua.edu

Hardcover edition published 2017.
Paperback edition published 2019.
eBook edition published 2017.

Typeface: Avenir

Cover image: Based on an illustration by Ben Bolling
Cover design: David Nees

Paperback ISBN: 978-0-8173-5972-0

A previous edition of this book has been catalogued by the Library of Congress as follows:
Library of Congress Cataloging-in-Publication Data

Names: Thomas, Harry, Jr., 1977– author.
Title: Sissy! : the effeminate paradox in postwar US literature and culture / Harry Thomas Jr.
Description: Tuscaloosa : The University of Alabama Press, 2017. | Includes bibliographical references and index.
Identifiers: LCCN 2017004472| ISBN 9780817319632 (cloth) | ISBN 9780817391485 (e book)
Subjects: LCSH: Effeminacy in literature. | American literature—20th century—History and criticism. | American literature—21st century—History and criticism. | American fiction—20th century—History and criticism. | American fiction—21st century—History and criticism. | Men in literature. | Effeminacy—United States.
Classification: LCC PS228.E44 T56 2017 | DDC 810.9/353—dc23
LC record available at https://lccn.loc.gov/2017004472

This book is dedicated to all the sissies who survived to inspire and to all of those who didn't survive at all.

CONTENTS

PREFACE

My Own Effeminacy, A Brief History

This book argues that United States culture since the Second World War has had a paradoxical relationship to effeminate men and boys that we—as a nation—have both intensely hated and intensely loved them. While always acknowledging that American hatred of effeminacy is real and widespread, I attempt to shine light upon the other side of the paradox, revealing the less-often-acknowledged ways in which America has viewed effeminate men and boys as alluring, empowered, and empowering to others. It was only after writing this book that I realized how much my own personal relationship to (and feelings about) effeminacy mirrors the paradoxical arc that I highlight in the book. In the interest of making my own personal relationship to the subject matter of effeminacy clear, I want to outline some of the moments in my own life when (and where) effeminacy has left an indelible mark.

"Everyone stare at Harry," the lifeguard says. I am ten or eleven or twelve, away from home at sleepover camp. It is afternoon swim-in-the-lake time, and I am standing on the dock, leaning against its railing and waiting my turn to jump in. "Let's all look at Harry and the way he holds his wrrrrrrrrrists," the lifeguard continues. I hadn't been conscious of the way that I had been standing, but the lifeguard's elbows are bent so that his forearms are out in front of him, perpendicular to his body, and his wrists are bent so that his hands are perpendicular to his forearms, facing down. "Ooooooh, Harry just looooooooooooves to hold his wrists this way," the lifeguard says, affecting an over-the-top lisp so that "wrists" is transformed into something like "whists." My body knows that he is making fun of me long before my brain understands why he is making fun of me. I explode in the scarlet flush of humiliation as I realize that the other kids, the other guys, on the dock are following his instructions. They are all staring. They are all laughing. They are all bending their wrists and faux-lisping and laughing at me. Intellectually, I understand that I must have been standing there with one elbow up on the dock railing and wrist of that arm dangling limply. But why exactly this is a sin, why exactly it is an offense requiring my very public humiliation, is not clear to me. Later, the lifeguard—a thick, meaty guy whom I instinctually do not like but whom I instinctually understood to be a good example of what men are supposed to be—tells me that he was just looking out for me and that I should thank him for teaching me such an important lesson. The lesson, of course, was not to stand with limp wrists. Because only fags have limp wrists. And while at age ten or eleven or twelve it wasn't exactly clear to me what a fag was, it was unmistakably crystal clear that, whatever else a fag was, a fag was the absolute worst thing that a guy could be. Over the next many, many years, that lesson would be taught to me again and again and again: by my extended family, by my school, by my peers, by every show on television, and by every song on the radio. The lesson took so many different forms and was taught so relentlessly that it stopped even seeming like a lesson and began to feel like an unquestionable truth.

Fast-forward nine or eight or seven years. I'm 19. I'm gay. I'm out to one parent and most of my close friends. I've got a year of college in Atlanta under my belt. But the gay world remains largely theoretical to me, largely mysterious. My friends are well-meaning, but straight. I've yet to date a guy. In the upper-middle class North Florida world of my parents and their friends and the children of their friends who are my peers, there are no gay people except for the man who cuts my mother's hair. He is kind and funny and in retrospect I probably could have learned tons from him, but 19-year-old me recoils from him because he is a hairdresser and because I knew, instinctually, that men—"real" men like my father and the jock boys at school—would recoil from him. And I didn't want them to recoil from me. So even after I could admit to being gay, I continued to sincerely say sincerely terrible things, things that the adult me who will one day write this book is deeply ashamed of, things like, "Can't I just find a normal gay guy?" and "I'm gay, but I don't want to be a drag queen" and "I'm gay but not like *gay* gay." But despite the time and energy I put into thinking and saying objectively awful things like this, and despite the time and energy I put into worrying about whether I had a gay voice or a gay face or a gay walk (meaning, of course, a feminine voice or a feminine face or a feminine walk), it is a *gay* gay guy who rescues me from my own (largely self-imposed) loneliness and ignorance.

The Record Store Manager is a *gay* gay guy. Even in my North Florida late 1990s mental landscape where gay men didn't exist or were hairdressers to be ignored or AIDS victims dying young and quietly on weepy TV-movies-of-the-week, there is no doubt that the Record Store Manager is gay. Rail thin and bleached platinum blonde, he has large blue eyes, elfin facial features, and a silver hoop earing in each earlobe. He gesticulates wildly with his hands while he talks. He doesn't walk up and down the aisles of CDs so much as he levitates through them. Everything he does is a spectacle; once, when he gave himself a paper cut, he shrieked, "It's a stigmata!" and ran, arms flailing over his head, to the back of the store to find an adhesive bandage. To talk about music with him is to learn quickly how intense and passionate he is, to know that for him matters of musical taste are matters of life and death: The Pet Shop Boys and Belinda Carlisle and Pulp giveth life, whereas dumbed-down alt rock for frat boys taketh it away. That summer I am working part-time at a supermarket bakery, and the supermarket sits in the same strip mall as the Record Store Manager's record store. Once a shift, I take my mandated break, buy a Mango Snapple, and wander down to the record store to browse. I am utterly and completely terrified of the Record Store Manager but also drawn to him. I am simultaneously scared to be seen with him (lest people think we are alike in some way) and desperate for his approval. His record store is a mainstream corporate chain, and his income depends on selling Garth Brooks CDs to people whom he hates intensely. I long to be among the few he loves intensely. I am not entirely sure what club he belongs to, but I desperately want to be in it. Although I can't articulate this at the time, I know that there is a secret frequency that only the Record Store Manager can hear. I want him to teach me to hear it, too. I want him to yank me through the looking glass and show me the ropes, even as I am terrified to think of what I might find (out about myself) on the other side.

Somehow, someway, he does take me through the looking glass. Here is what I find on the other side: not fear and horror, not shame and loneliness. What I find is long talks, seminars in all but name only on which records to buy, which books to read, which clubs to go to, and what to expect when dating boys. These seminars are conducted on my breaks from the supermarket. Later they are conducted at the Record Store Manager's house. I am terrified to go there at first. What if he tries something creepy? But he does not try anything creepy. I've been raised and trained to hate and fear men like the Record Store Manager (men, I am beginning to understand, like myself), but he is nothing but kind and patient and giving and funny and lovely. We eat strawberry cheesecakes from the freezer section, using spoons to eat them right out of their little individualized tins as we watch Pet Shop Boys videos and he plays Dead or Alive albums that were only released in Japan. He becomes a friend and a mentor, and later when he is editing a local arts and entertainment paper, he gives me some of my very first published writing gigs, doing record reviews for new-at-the-time releases from über-gay acts like Erasure and Morrissey. And although it takes me longer than it should, ultimately I realize that fear and horror and shame and loneliness were lessons that the wider world had taught me, lessons that warped my brain until I (initially) saw the Record Store Manager as a threat. But he wasn't a threat. He was a gift. I'd been drowning, and he was a life raft.

Fast-forward twelve years. It is 2008, and I am an adult gay man horrified by the news of Lawrence "Larry" King, a gay 15-year-old boy who was shot and killed at his Oxnard, California, junior high school. King's murderer is a 14-year-old classmate (Cathcart). News stories of the event focus relentlessly on King's effeminacy, on the fact that he sometimes wore mascara and lipstick to school (Cathcart). This is insane, I think. How does lipstick become grounds for murdering a teenager? In trying to think through this, I read widely about men and masculinity and (homo)sexuality and think about maybe possibly someday writing a book saying something about some of those things. As a part of that process, I read James Dickey's 1970 novel *Deliverance*, and I become obsessed with a long passage in which Ed Gentry, the advertising executive who narrates the novel, notes that he works in an office building where he is surrounded by women. Even worse, from Ed's point of view, is that none of these women are women he wants to have sex with. He thinks that he wants to say to these women, "I am with you but not of you. But . . . I was of them, sure enough" (15). To fight off this feeling of being "with" and "of" women—which Ed experiences as an epic humiliation—Ed and his friends embark on a whitewater rafting trip where, as anyone who has seen the film version of *Deliverance* can tell you, they are attacked by mountain men and one of their number is anally raped. Ed and his friends flee the mountain men who hunt them and try to kill them before they can make it off the river. What strikes me about *Deliverance* is not the male-on-male rape so much as the fact that the "moral" of the story seems to be that being raped and hunted and almost killed and having to become a killer yourself is better than the oh-so-horrific fate of working in an office building with female co-workers. Having been friends with many women and having worked alongside many of them, this strikes me as remarkably insane. And yet Dickey's novel was a hit, and its film adaptation is considered a classic. Over lunch, I tell a friend, "I want to write a book about how much American men hate sissies. How scared they are by . . . the specter of the sissy!" My friend smiles and says, "*The Specter of the Sissy*, now there's a book title!" I nod in agreement, seeing my book take shape before me.

Fast-forward a few weeks or months. I am reading Michael Kimmel's groundbreaking *Manhood in America: A Cultural History* and having that sinking feeling that comes from realizing that what I thought was an original idea is actually a book that someone else already thought and wrote and published over ten years earlier. Kimmel's excellent study lays out the ways in which American men define themselves in opposition to effeminacy, and Kimmel himself uses the phrase "the specter of the sissy" to describe this animating fear of effeminacy (83). Feeling unoriginal, dumb, and utterly defeated, I throw myself a pity party. This pity party involves lots of video gaming and lots of watching of *RuPaul's Drag Race*, the genius reality competition show in which RuPaul Charles, America's most famous drag queen, presides over a competition to see which aspiring queen can successfully "Lip Synch For Your Life!" and snatch the title of America's Next Drag Superstar. Somewhere in the midst of medicating my grief with *Drag Race*, I stop and think, "Wait a minute. This show exists. RuPaul exists. In the same country where Larry King was murdered for being effeminate, RuPaul is a celebrity. RuPaul has a career. Has had a career since the 1990s! How is this possible?"

Those are the animating questions that drove the research and writing of this book: How is it somehow true that America both really, really hates sissies and really, really loves them? How can both of these things be true at the same time? How can effeminacy function culturally—as it has for me personally—as both a threat to be feared and avoided, and a fascinating, powerful off-ramp signaling a way to a different, better world? The story of America's hatred of effeminacy (represented in my own life by the lifeguard's mockery of my limp wrists) has been well told. Without ignoring it or downplaying its extreme (and often murderous) power, I have attempted, in the pages that follow, to map out the other half of the story, to show when and where post-WWII American literature and culture have looked on effeminate men as I looked on the Record Store Manager: as a fascinating, powerful figure who reminds us that the "rules" of heteronormative masculinity need not be either as strict or as meritorious as they might seem at first glance. Thus this project proceeds, broadly, from the perspective of both a queer studies that is interested in loosening rigid heteronormative sex/gender roles and from a feminist-influenced masculinity studies that names "the radical transformation of its object of study" as its "most desirable goal" (Adams and Savran 7).[1]

ACKNOWLEDGMENTS

I am listed as the sole author of this book, but this book has been made possible only because of the support—intellectual, emotional, and financial—that I have received from a great many people. I would like to thank Trudier Harris, Fred Hobson, John Kasson, Joy Kasson, Tim Marr, and Ruth Salvaggio for their insightful feedback on this project; John Howard for his intellectual generosity and help in seeing this book to print; Minrose Gwin for being the best mentor anyone could ask for, lending me her tremendous expertise as a thinker and a writer while always letting the project be my own; the members of my beloved "Americanist Writing Group"—Kelly Bezio, Ben Bolling, Angie Calcaterra, Ashley Reed, and Jenn Williamson—for thinking for me when I couldn't think anymore and believing in me when I no longer believed in myself; Elliott Caldwell, Clare Emily Clifford, Chris Coble, Brian Hare, Erika McVoy McCarthy, Meredith Raimondo, Molly Springfield, Ben Wise, and Maren Wood for their constant friendship and encouragement; my colleagues and students at Durham Academy's Upper School for providing me with an incredible professional home that demands I be my best self every day; my parents—Harry Sr. and Cecilia Thomas—for supporting me entirely in everything I have ever wanted to do and teaching me the values of honesty and hard work; and last but certainly not least, my partner, Joe Cawley, who reminds me every day that I have a home, both a physical space I share with him and a much more valuable place in his heart.

I would also like to thank everyone who helped with the production of this book: Ben Bolling, who provided an illustration that served as the inspiration for the book's cover; Harrison Haynes, who took my author photo; and several DA students—Alex Charles, Olivia Chilkoti, Austen Dellinger, Scott Hallyburton, Steven Kohl, Ian Layzer, and Thomas Owens—who helped me compile the index.

Finally, I would like to thank everyone I worked with at the University of Alabama Press: Dan Waterman for taking a chance on this book,

Vanessa Lynn Rusch for fielding my 10,001 anxious new author questions, and David Nees for his amazing work on the book's cover and interior design.

SISSY!

INTRODUCTION

SAYING "OH YEAH!" TO SISSIES: FASCINATING EFFEMINACY DEFINED

The nightclub is small, but it is packed with people wanting to see and celebrate sissies. Some fans are standing in front of the stage recording the show on their phones, while others, standing between the pool table and the arcade games, dance with such joyous, frenetic abandon that their bodies seem almost liquid. At the back of the stage, DJs spin the emphatic backbeat that has come to be associated with New Orleans bounce music,[1] the city's local mutation of rap music that is perhaps best described, by a musician who performs it, as "up-tempo, heavy bass, call-and-response type music that's party music and ass-shaking music" (Big Freedia, "Let's Bounce"). In front of the DJs, the two sissies this crowd paid to see spit lyrics over the music, their body language as confident as their words are fast and precise.

The performers are Katey Red and Big Freedia (pronounced "Free-dah"), both self-proclaimed sissies. And rather than hiding either their effeminacy or their homosexuality, the two sissies proclaim those features of their identity loudly, proudly, and vulgarly in their lyrics: "Big Freddie Kay Ready / We make it go down / We both suck dicks from all around / Rappin' at the DJs to make you go shake-shake / Everybody represent these two sissies" (Big Freedia, "Big Freddie Kay Ready"). Katey Red is a transgender woman who uses feminine pronouns but also claims the identity of sissy. Big Freedia (real name: Freddie Ross) is biologically male: six foot two, powerfully framed, deep-voiced, and fond of dressing in a mix of men's clothes and women's accessories (dangly earrings, long hair, big purses). Freedia also prefers she and her as pronouns. The song they are performing together is "Big Freddie Kay Ready" and in it, they engage in some of the call-and-response refrains that are a defining feature of New Orleans bounce music: "Katey Red is a—" goes the call, and the response is "dicksucker!" Similarly, the call "Big Freedia—" is met with the response "the dick-eater!"

This concert scene appears in a 2013 video profile called "Big

Freedia: The Queen Diva," made by taste-making Internet music magazine *Pitchfork*. In it, Katey Red and Big Freedia's very explicit and very explicitly effeminate performance inspires neither mockery nor panic. They are not laughed at or attacked. They are African American sissies loudly and quite explicitly expressing both their effeminacy and their homosexuality on stage, in front of a crowd that does not seem to be predominately gay or predominately African American. Their lyrics also link their homosexuality and their effeminacy, quite explicitly, to power and authority: "Get out the way / Get out the way / Dick-eater don't play! . . . You can take it how you want / 'Cause I'm a real-ass bitch" (Big Freedia, "Big Freddie Kay Ready"). And this audacious mode of self-presentation is greeted with fans' adulation; on record, the cheers that accompany the second half of their vulgar call-and-response exchanges are simulated, but when Katey Red and Big Freedia perform live, the cheers are very real indeed. As Freedia herself explains in another video produced by *Pitchfork* (where she is asked to explain how call and response sequences work in her live performances):

> I might say "A'han," and the girl [in the audience is] supposed to say "Oh yeah." I might say, "Them hoes," she's supposed to say "They mad." I'mma say "Your boy," she's supposed to say "I had." I say, "I made," and she say "My cash": "A'han / Oh yeah / These hoes / They mad / Your boy / I had / I made / my cash." And I might say "You better believe-ah" and everybody's supposed to say "Oh yeah!" "Big Freedia!" / "Oh yeah!" / "Queen Diva!" / "Oh yeah!" / "Dick Eater!" / "Oh Yeah!" / "You better believe-ah, The Big Freedia, The Queen Diva, The Dick Eater" and they're saying "Oh yeah! Oh yeah! Oh yeah! Oh yeah!" the whole time in the background. ("Big Freedia: Live at Public Assembly")

Watching the crowds in *Pitchfork*'s two videos of Big Freedia's performances—especially the dancers shaking themselves into ecstatic abandon in "The Queen Diva" documentary—it is easy to believe that everyone really is saying "Oh yeah!" the whole time, that everyone really is, as Big Freedia and Katey Red contend in their lyric, "representing these two sissies." This argument seems even stronger when one stops to consider the mainstream success that Freedia has experienced since 2010: a *New York Times Magazine* article focusing on her and Katey Red (Dee); a profile on *Late Night with Carson Daly* (*Last Call*); glowing write-ups of live shows on *Rolling Stone*'s website (Eddy); several documentary videos on *Pitchfork* ("Big Freedia Explains," "Big Freedia: The Queen Diva"); a touring slot opening for indie pop darlings The Postal Service (Ryder); a feature on NPR ("Big Freedia Lays Out"); a reality show on the FUSE cable network that has run for four seasons and counting (Plaisance); and in 2016 a prominent guest spot on pop superstar Beyoncé's single "Formation" (Beyoncé).

Big Freedia and Katey Red, and mainstream media's interest in them, are thus but one example of what I call fascinating effeminacy. Although it has taken many different forms at many different times and in many different contexts, fascinating effeminacy is the name I gave to modes of representation (actual or fictional) in which effeminacy—men and/or boys acting, dressing, behaving, moving, or otherwise conducting themselves in ways coded as traditionally feminine in their given time/place/culture—is presented and/or viewed as symbolic of some type of positive and/or desirable extra-normal quality or qualities. In this book, I argue that American literature and culture since WWII has a long tradition of representing effeminate men and boys as objects of adoration and fascination.[2]

If that claim seems ludicrous, it is because it contradicts a widely circulated and widely believed piece of conventional wisdom: the idea that America—and especially American men's—only reaction to effeminacy is fear and loathing. Vito Russo opens his renowned study of homosexuality in the Hollywood film *The Celluloid Closet* (1981, revised edition 1987) by summarizing this conventional wisdom about effeminacy and American culture. "Nobody likes a sissy," Russo writes. "That includes dykes, faggots, and feminists of both sexes. Even in a time of sexual revolution, when traditional roles are being examined and challenged every day, there is something about a man who acts like a woman that people find fundamentally distasteful" (4). This conventional wisdom—that America uniformly hates and loathes effeminate men (like Big Freedia) and trans women (like Katey Red)—has shaped a great deal of the mainstream media coverage of sissy rappers. While some of the better coverage of sissy bounce does place the music and its performers in the wider historical context of New Orleans's long-standing acceptance of gender nonconformity in its entertainment figures, most of the mainstream coverage of sissy bounce insists that sissy rappers are interesting precisely because the mainstream success and exposure they are experiencing is unprecedented for effeminate men and trans women. America liking Freedia and Red constitutes something new and unusual in American culture because, the unspoken assumption goes, everyone knows that America hates effeminacy. The *New York Times Magazine* profile of Freedia and Red (which does go on to place sissy rappers in New Orleans's historical context) even leads with this assumption. Its opening line is: "If 'gay rapper' is an oxymoron where you come from, how to get your head around the notion of a gay rapper performing in a sports bar?" (Dee). And this idea of newness—the assumption that sissy rappers are wholly new and different—is also echoed by Freedia herself. In an interview with NPR host Robert Smith, Freedia describes local bounce fans' initial reactions to sissy rappers by saying "that's when the game [of bounce music in New Orleans] totally switched, when me and Katey [Red] jumped in it, and yeah, we messed their heads up big time" ("Big Freedia Lays Out"). "Wait," asks Smith, "New Orleans has a rich gay culture. Was it unusual for two gay guys to be doing bounce music?" ("Big Freedia Lays Out"). Freedia then responds, "Um, 'cause it was a new music, a new sound. And New Orleans does have a rich gay culture, but that was something new for everybody" ("Big Freedia Lays Out").

Sissy! does not argue that Russo, the *Times Magazine*, and Freedia herself are wrong, only that their arguments are incomplete. On one hand, they are quite correct: American culture has a long and sadly all-too-rich tradition of hating effeminacy, and this tradition is ongoing. But their comments—and the work of many other scholars who have examined effeminacy—focus solely on America's hatred of effeminacy, and in doing so, they overlook America's paradoxically concurrent fascination with it. Russo is hardly alone in emphasizing only one end of effeminacy's paradoxical reception in US culture. Effeminacy, it seems, has a discipline problem: as an object of analysis it seems like a natural fit to many academic disciplines but has received a full and primary focus in none. And when effeminacy has been studied, scholars working on it have tended to emphasize how effeminacy is hated, at the expense of considering how effeminacy has also been figured as a source of desire, power, and/or transcendence of rigid, heteronormative sex/gender roles. Without denying or downplaying America's long (and painful and damaging) tradition of pervasive hatred of effeminacy, this book intervenes by arguing that that is only half of effeminacy's story in postwar American literature and culture. The neglected half of the story is fascinating effeminacy, and by shedding light on it, *Sissy!* aims to deepen scholarship's understanding of American culture's complex and contradictory relationship to effeminacy.

Big Freedia is an example of fascinating effeminacy precisely because her effeminacy is figured not as something shameful or negative but instead as something that grants her special abilities that gender-conforming people cannot access. Specifically, media coverage of Freedia consistently emphasizes how, in her live performances, she serves as the attention-demanding MC who ushers concertgoers into a participatory, sex-positive, body-positive space, a dance-induced joyfest. What Big Freedia does, says NPR host Robert Smith, "is roll into a town, set up in a club, and drive the audience wild. You can't just listen to Big Freedia, you have to be there to experience Big Freedia" ("Big Freedia Lays Out the Basics of Bounce"). The experience that Freedia creates at her shows is one in which the usually dominant hierarchies of gender, power, and middle-class respectability are upended in ways that her fans find empowering. In this space, Freedia herself serves as emcee, tour guide, and protector. "As attendance at even a few shows will tell you," explains Jonathan Dee in his *Times Magazine* article, "the eager and underserved audience for sissy bounce is clearly, overwhelmingly, women." Dee then goes on to quote Alison Fensterstock, a journalist who assembled and curated an oral and photographic history of New Orleans bounce music called "Where They At?" Explaining the appeal of sissy bounce to straight women, Fensterstock says, "There's like a safe-space thing happening. . . . When Freedia

[is] . . . singing superaggressive, sexual lyrics about bad boyfriends or whatever, there's something about being able to be the 'I' in the sentence. That's not to say that women can't like the more misogynistic [bounce] music too. I like it—some of it's good music. But it's tough to sing along about bitches and hos when you're a girl. When you identify with Freedia, you're the agent of all this aggressive sexuality instead of its object" (qtd. in Dee). Freedia, at her shows, creates a space where women can "perform an ecstatic act of physical aggression that is both exceptionally demanding and socially unacceptable in other contexts, at the behest of music that's ritualized and played at seemingly impossible tempos" (Dee). In other words, a recurring, key feature of Big Freedia performances is the fact that fans—most, but not all of them, female—come out of the crowd and dance ecstatically on or near Freedia, in the sexually suggestive, ass-shaking style known alternately as pussy-popping, p-popping, or twerking. As Freedia's DJ and manager, Rusty Lazer, describes it: "It's as if punk had been reinvented for women . . . the girls [in the crowd] literally push the dudes right out of the middle. It's just pure empowerment, physical aggression that's not spiteful or vicious" (qtd. in Dee). And not only does Freedia create this space—a joyous, raunchy, body-positive, sex-positive carnival atmosphere—at her shows, she also polices that space, ensuring that the (mostly) female fans who participate in it are not harassed by male concertgoers. "I think the girls like the gay rappers a lot because they feel safer," Lazer says. "You can get up in the front, you can dance for Freedia, you can work it for Freedia, but at the same time, if anybody comes up on you and gives you a hard time, Freedia's gonna be the first one—" (qtd. in Dee). "To defend the girl," Freedia says, finishing Lazer's sentence (qtd. in Dee). By creating a space where the "rules" of heteronormativity are temporarily suspended—gay men and trans women are front and center and speaking, all types of people can shake their asses, women's sexuality is praised not shamed, women's bodily autonomy is protected—Freedia's shows serve as a vivid contemporary example of fascinating effeminacy.

But fascinating effeminacy has a long history in postwar America, and while all types of fascinating effeminacy figure effeminacy as special in some way, they do not all figure it as special in the same way or special for the same audience. Like Freedia before him, the pianist and television star Liberace (discussed in Chapter Three) served up modes of effeminacy that primarily appealed to straight women, but Freedia's performances offer up the possibility of (gay male and straight female) sexual abandon, whereas many of Liberace's straight female fans adored him because they thought—improbable as it may seem to us now that Liberace's name is synonymous with campy gay excess—he presented a form of heterosexuality that was free from sexual threat. Offering up yet another type of fascinating effeminacy are the presentation, performances, and recordings of many rock musicians—from Little Richard to Prince to 1970s glam rock to 1980s hair metal—which frame effeminacy as a sign of intense, insatiable (mostly hetero-)sexuality.

Other modes of fascinating effeminacy are not particularly "about" sex at all. The sissy characters in the fiction of Carson McCullers and Truman Capote are children who do not possess adult sexual desire; they are presented as valuable because the difference created by their gender nonconformity enriches the otherwise drab small towns that they live in. And the truth-telling queens of James Baldwin's *Giovanni's Room* (1956) depict effeminacy as an external sign of the internal courage it takes to live openly and honestly in a homophobic world that is often cruel and hypocritical. In other times and places, effeminate men and boys have been depicted as quasi-mystical beings with healing powers (Tony Kushner's *Angels in America* [1992–93]), nearly magical helpers inherently skilled in hair, makeup, and fashion styling (a legion effeminate men on reality TV shows, of which "Mr. Jay and Ms. Jay" from *America's Next Top Model* and Tim Gunn from *Project Runway* serve as good examples), and warriors who wield the witty barbs and cutting insights of campy humor as their swords and shields (think of Truman Capote's recurring role as a late-night talk show guest, Paul Lynde's long run on *Hollywood Squares*, or the shade-throwing queens of director Jennie Livingston's *Paris Is Burning* [1990], to name but a few). These examples are hardly exhaustive. Nor are they all necessarily "good" examples from a feminist/queer-positive point of view. But they do serve to demonstrate the wide and rich variety of ways in which

American culture has, contrary to popular and scholarly conventional wisdom, adored effeminacy.

THE EFFEMINATE PARADOX, PART 1: THREAT

Although this study focuses on fascinating effeminacy, it is important to remember that in postwar US culture, effeminacy is always framed paradoxically. Although *Sissy!*'s argument focuses heavily on the fascinating side of that paradox, it is crucial to remember that the other side of the effeminate paradox—threat—is always also operating. The exclamation mark in the title of this book is meant to be deliberately and provocatively ambivalent, in reflection of the hybrid, paradoxical status that effeminacy is frequently assigned. The exclamation mark can be read as indicative of the anger behind a grievous insult ("You worthless sissy!"), but it can also be read as an indication of wonder and fascination (as in "Sissy that walk!" a phrase drag queen/musician/television personality RuPaul Charles uses on his hit TV show *RuPaul's Drag Race* to indicate that a drag queen's walk is substandard precisely because it is not effeminate enough). But by pointing out that effeminacy has often been portrayed as either threatening or fascinating, I do not mean to suggest that representations of effeminacy may be *only* threatening or *only* fascinating. The reading of effeminacy in postwar US literature and culture that I am proposing here is not either/or, but rather both/and: effeminacy is often portrayed as having a mix of threatening elements and fascinating elements.

Take, for example, the Boy Scouts of America and Liberace. A good example of effeminacy being viewed as threatening, the Boy Scouts were founded in the early twentieth century as a corrective to widespread concerns that urban living would weaken and sissify (white, middle-class) boys. Liberace, of course, is a good example of fascinating effeminacy: his extremely effeminate mannerisms and gaudy Las Vegas live performances earned him millions over the course of a career that ran from the late 1940s until his death in 1987. The Boy Scouts saw effeminacy chiefly as a threat; they were in fact founded to ward off effeminacy, to prevent it from ever coming to be. But we do not fear things that do not grab our attention, even if our attention is grabbed only in an alarming way. Clearly, the Boy Scouts saw effeminacy as a threat, but it was a threat they were fascinated with, a threat fascinating enough that it served as their raison d'être. Likewise, millions of Liberace's adoring female fans found him fascinating in a positive way—caring, emotionally attentive, attractive but sexually nonthreatening—but his brand of extremely effeminate masculinity was new to them precisely because it was unfamiliar. And its unfamiliarity led many heterosexual men to see Liberace's effeminacy as threatening to mainstream mid-century standards of masculinity (which demanded that men be emotionally stoic, and sexually dominant/aggressive). Thus, representations of effeminacy in postwar US literature and culture are almost always positioned on a spectrum, a continuum with total threat on one side and total fascination on the other. Individual representations of effeminacy are positioned at different points along this continuum; many emphasize effeminacy's threat while others play up its fascination. But no single representation of effeminacy sits entirely at one end or the other; we are always fascinated by effeminacy because, on some level, we find it threatening. And vice versa: we are always threatened by effeminacy because, on some level, we find it fascinating.

While acknowledging that representations of effeminacy in postwar American literature and culture exist on a continuum with pure threat at one end and pure fascination at the other, I want to explore the "end points" of this continuum. I use the phrase "end points" tentatively since, as I have said, effeminate representation almost always contains some mix of both threat and fascination. That said, it is still useful to examine what the extreme "ends" of this representational continuum look like and how they have tended to function.

The first of these discursive modes, representations that emphasize effeminacy as threat, is well illustrated in a small passage from the second edition of Michael Kimmel's *Manhood in America: A Cultural History* (2006). Writing about the definition of manhood in the United States at the end of nineteenth century and the beginning of the twentieth, Kimmel says: "Most terrifying to men was the specter of the sissy. . . . by the last decade of the century the term had come to mean weakness, dependency, and helplessness—all the qualities that men were not. The sissy was outwardly feminine in demeanor, comportment, and affect. If manhood is defined by courage, generosity, modesty, dignity, wrote Rafford Pyke in his 1902 diatribe against sissies in *Cosmopolitan* magazine, then the sissy was 'flabby, feeble, mawkish . . . chicken-hearted, cold, and fearful.' . . . 'Real men, Pyke argued, 'laugh at him,' while women rightfully shun him, as he causes a general 'moral nausea' among observers, 'a vague yet insurmountable feeling of malaise'" (83).

Effeminacy is defined here, explicitly, as a man being "outwardly feminine in demeanor, comportment, and affect," but it also carries other, clearly implied meanings: to be a sissy is to be the opposite of a man. Working backwards from the provided definition of a man, we can infer that a sissy is cowardly, selfish, immodest, and undignified. Kimmel also goes on to say that by the 1920s, "Homosexuality hovered like a specter over anxious parents, who were convinced that effeminacy in young boys was a certain predictor of adult male homosexuality" (*Manhood* 135).[3]

Sissies are thus seen as either proto-homosexuals or homosexuals. This implied meaning adds to the visible provocations of effeminacy (a man appearing feminine in demeanor, comportment, and/or affect), and in total, we can say that the sissy is a walking scandal of sorts, a lurid spectacle. Effeminate men make a scene of themselves, and this scene is pathetic and abnormal; it evokes "moral nausea" in onlookers. Note that the presence of onlookers is assumed in the archival sources that Kimmel cites: sissies cannot pass without notice or attention because their existence signals that something is badly amiss in US culture. Sissies are problems that require the intervention of skilled experts: Dr. Alfred Stillé, former president of the American Medical Association, claimed, in 1947, that "a man with feminine traits of character, or with the frame and carriage of a female, is despised by both the sex he ostensibly belongs to, and that of which he is at once a caricature and a libel" (qtd. in Kimmel, *Manhood* 83). Late nineteenth- and early twentieth-century American anxieties about the effeminizing effects of urban living and increasingly corporatized labor are what caused the sissy to be cast as a pathologized social type, one that—as Kimmel and many others have noted[4]—sparked the concerned intervention of not just journalists and medical doctors, but also psychologists, sociologists, and many amateur "boy workers" such as Scout Masters. The Boy Scouts were, in fact, founded in the hope that contact with fresh air and the outdoors would help (white, middle-class) American boys fend off what Kimmel calls "the specter of the sissy," so that they could grow into healthy, virile men who could defend America and father its next generation. In this, Boy Scouts are one of many, many American institutions designed to ensure the production of appropriately masculine American boys by fending off "the specter of the sissy," a force which is pathetic when it occurs in individual men, but which could be disastrous if allowed to take hold nationwide.

This is the most common and widely circulating concept of American effeminacy: representations that stress effeminacy's threatening nature (although, embedded within that threat there still remains a fascination: in this conception, effeminacy is important enough that the head of the American Medical Association needs to weigh in on it). Other masculinity studies scholars have articulated similar conceptions of effeminacy, ones in which the threat of being shamed for effeminacy functions as a disciplinary mechanism that controls the behavior of all men, straight and gay. After extensive field work observing male high school students, C. J. Pascoe defines masculinity as "a form of dominance usually expressed through sexualized discourses" (5); attaining masculinity means demonstrating mastery and competence, and to fail to demonstrate mastery and competence is to assume "the most unmasculine position . . . a fag position, in which a boy is weak, penetrated, and lacking in mastery over his and others' bodies" (23). But because masculinity is a process, fag "is not necessarily a static identity that attaches permanently to a certain (gay) boy's body; rather, it is a fluid identity that boys struggle to avoid, often by lobbing the insult at others" (22). That is, the epithet *fag* (and the identity it connotes) is as much about non-normative gender performance as it is about sexuality and functions, among the groups of young men Pascoe observed, like a proverbial hot potato: an individual man or boy experiences it as an unwelcome and potentially damaging foreign object that has been lobbed at him and which he is furiously eager to get rid of, by pawning it off on someone else and thus proving that it never truly belonged to him in the first place.

The subject position produced by the disciplinary mechanism of effeminacy—whether we call that position *fag*, *queen*, *queer*, *sissy*, or something else altogether—is, therefore, not a fixed and unchanging identity, but a more fluid position, a mode of being that men can be placed into and to which they have some degree of ability to move out of. And it is the constant fear of lapsing into, or being forcibly assigned to, this denigrated fag/effeminate position that allows effeminacy to be used as a disciplinary mechanism. Men will do a great deal to avoid being placed into or seen as inhabiting a fag/effeminate position. An effeminate gay male character in Mark Merlis's novel *An Arrow's Flight* (1998) explains the disciplinary power of effeminacy by arguing that nations are able to send young men off to die in wars precisely because those young men's refusal to fight would be seen as effeminate: "You can't defy them [hegemonically masculine men], even your defiance just tells them they're the real men. It's all a big circle and they fence you inside it the minute you're born. They look between your legs and sign you up. So when you're big enough they can send you into this war that isn't going to end next week. . . . Guys will go on bleeding in the mud as long as they can just be picked. Please don't leave me out" (363).

Sociologist Peter Hennen also highlights the disciplinary nature of effeminacy with his term the "effeminacy effect," by which he means the way in which effeminacy functions as a threat that controls the behavior of men in a given culture (9–13). The effeminacy effect is what pushes some men toward modes of masculinity viewed as (hetero) normative and what sustains those modes as normative throughout a given culture. In Hennen's view, the effeminacy effect is both deeply pervasive and intensely powerful in US culture, even, or perhaps especially, amongst gay men—the very group likely to be assumed, in popular stereotype, to be both effeminate themselves and welcoming of effeminacy.

Examples of representations that stress effeminacy as the threat in

American literature and culture are tremendous in number and range; they run from the seemingly trivial to the literally deadly. For example, in *Love and Death in the American Novel* (1960) Leslie Fiedler argues that a man's flight from effeminacy is the quintessentially American story. Natty Bumpo, Ishmael, Huck Finn, and the other American literary protagonists that Fiedler discusses are young white men in desperate flight from civilization, which they perceive as hell-bent on feminizing them. Fleeing this dreaded fate, Fielder's protagonists run to the sea or out to the frontier, where they experience deep homoerotic bonding with older, darker men. This idealized state that American protagonists escape to is "the homoerotic fable" (349), but Fiedler is sure to specify—in a note on his own work, included in the second edition of *Love and Death*—that he "wanted it to be quite clear that [he] was not attributing sodomy to certain literary characters or their authors" (349). In other words, Fiedler's critical position is this: Yes, Jim and Huck shared a homoerotic love while they were out there alone together on their raft. But don't worry, this was an "innocent" homosexuality. You don't have to be grossed out by imagining them actually having gay sex. The homophobic implication of Fiedler's work is, of course, that sexually consummated male-male pairings are "guilty." Damned if they do and damned if they don't, Fiedler's American literary protagonists will surely be feminized if they remain at home, but they will also become feminized (and "guilty") if they physically consummate their love for one another and become homosexuals. Effeminacy—brought on by an apparently infectious feminine civilization on one side and by "guilty," sexually active homosexuality on the other—forms the nightmarish outside that surrounds and encloses Fiedler's definition of American literature.

Russo sees a similar dynamic of effeminacy-loathing in American film and argues that from the very earliest days of American cinema, "Men of action and strength were [depicted as] the embodiment of our culture, and a vast mythology was created to keep the dream in constant repair. Real men were strong, silent, and ostentatiously unemotional. They acted quickly and never intellectualized. In short, they did not behave like women" (5–6). The sissy was thus "used onscreen and off, as both scapegoat and weapon" (Russo 31); sissies in film served as a negative example, their sometimes monstrous and sometimes comical failed manhood served to shore up the real man's successful, heroic masculinity.

And contrary to conventional wisdom, while US lesbians and gay men have gained greater visibility and societal acceptance in the second half of the twentieth century, these changes have not necessarily meant an end to US cultural anxieties about effeminacy. As Eve Kosofsky Sedgwick points out, the American Psychiatric Association's 1973 decision to no longer classify homosexuality as a mental illness might have signaled an increasing acceptance of homosexuality, but it explicitly did not indicate a wider acceptance of effeminacy; the same *Diagnostic and Statistical Manual of Mental Disorders* "that, published in 1980, was the first that did not contain an entry for 'homosexuality,' was also the first that *did* contain a new diagnosis, numbered (for insurance purposes) 302.60: 'Gender Identity Disorder of Childhood'" ("How to Bring Your Kids Up Gay" 156, emphasis Sedgwick's). Effeminacy as the threat is, as I have said, widespread in US culture and has been for a long time. Fiedler, Russo, and Sedgwick draw attention to but three examples of many.[5]

Again, this existing work on effeminacy as a disciplinary mechanism/threat is not incorrect. Nor are its accompanying observations that effeminacy is culturally constructed, meaning that what exactly constitutes effeminacy will shift from time and place and be inflected by a given culture and time period's conceptions of race, class, and nationalism.[6] But while the conclusions of this scholarship around effeminacy as threat are correct, they do not tell effeminacy's complete story.

THE EFFEMINATE PARADOX, PART 2: FASCINATION

The other, lesser-known side of the effeminate paradox, fascinating effeminacy, is well described in a selection from E. Patrick Johnson's *Sweet Tea: Black Gay Men of the South, An Oral History* (2008). Stephen (no last name given) is the youngest of the black gay men that

Johnson interviews for the book. Born in 1982 in Atlanta, Georgia, Stephen was raised in Tuscaloosa, Alabama. During their interview, Johnson asks Stephen if he knew of the existence of any other gay people as he was growing up, closeted, in Tuscaloosa. Stephen responds in the affirmative:

> I had never met them. I had never seen them. But I had always heard about them: sissy Mickey and sissy Greg. That was their names . . . . I couldn't point them out anywhere, but that's how everybody knew them. The girls were going [over to where sissy Mickey and sissy Greg lived] to get their hair done, the guys were known sometimes to on [sic] over there and getting [sic] favors done. . . . I had never seen them before. This was just some myth, some mythical creatures [laughter]. . . . Everybody knew that they may be sissies, but don't fuck with them because they will cut you. [Laughter] Because they are crazy. . . . And, they just took on this like larger than life thing. . . . I was just intrigued the way they could sort of be integrated [into small town life] and sort of not. . . . I have no idea who sissy Mick is or sissy Greg is. [Laughter] But that was their names, and they were two project queens. [Laughter] It's true. It's true. (517)

Note that sissy Mickey and sissy Greg command an audience even when they are not literally present. Stephen has never met them, never seen them, and yet all the same, sissy Mickey and sissy Greg remain legendary to him. Stephen "had always heard about them"; the phrasing indicates that he cannot remember a time when he did not know about them. In Stephen's mind sissy Mickey and sissy Greg are "some myth, some mythical creatures" who are "sort of" integrated into the normal, day-to-day life of the community and "sort of not." In some ways this mirrors the threatening conception of sissies invoked by Kimmel's archival sources: sissies are otherworldly, not fully of the community, and their presence creates a ruckus.

But the similarities between the two conceptions of effeminacy end there. In the sissy-hating archival materials that Kimmel cites, sissies make a pathetic spectacle, one that invokes moral nausea in a viewer. In stark contrast, the sissies that Stephen describes are people that you "don't fuck with" because "they are crazy" and "they will cut you." Sissy Mickey and sissy Greg are implied to be homosexual (Stephen mentions them after Johnson asks a question about sexuality, not gender presentation), but they are hardly spineless figures who cower at the thought of physical exertion or the threat of physical violence. Instead, they are known to wield physical violence themselves. Far from being pushovers, they are powerful figures, not be crossed. They stand outside of middle-class conventionality in many ways: via their gender presentation (they are so effeminate that "sissy" has become permanently attached to their names), their presumed level of mental health (they are "crazy"), and their social class (they are "project queens"), but this outsider status also makes them fascinating and imbues them with power that generated an awed respect in Stephen when he was closeted (more tightly bound to middle-class, heteronormative definitions of what is acceptable).

Stephen's comments also indicate that sissy Mickey and sissy Greg are needed in the community of Tuscaloosa because they provide certain services that are presumably unavailable elsewhere or at least not available with the level of quality that sissy Mickey and sissy Greg can provide. To women, the sissies provide hair styling (women go "over to get their hair done"). To men, Stephen says, they provide "favors." Stephen does not specify the nature of these "favors," but they are presumably sexual. We have very limited evidence with which to understand these alleged encounters between the sissies and the allegedly "normal" guys who visit them for sexual favors, and so it is impossible to definitively read the play of issues such as sexual identity, sexual behavior, consent, reciprocity, and power dynamics in these encounters. That said, the point remains that Stephen's description of the sissies includes a sexual element, one that implies that sissy Mickey and sissy Greg marshal a kind of fascinating sexual allure in addition to being perceived as people not to be trifled with. The tropes of fascinating effeminacy present here are clear in Stephen's description of these "larger than life" sissies. The enactment of this particular mode of effeminacy also renders a subject not quite real, or as Stephen says, "sort of" in the community that surrounds them, and "sort of not."

Nor are sissy Mickey and sissy Greg isolated examples. The parallels between them and the sissy rappers from New Orleans described at the start of this introduction should be obvious. But one can go much further back in American history and still find fascinating effeminacy. The 1920s and '30s were particularly good decades for it in the United States. Russo—complicating his own previously cited claim that everyone hates a sissy—says that in Hollywood films of the 1920s and '30s sissies were often portrayed as "fun," "a refuge of nonconformity," and "a lurking reminder of an alternative truth" (32). And historian George Chauncey describes the "pansy craze" that took hold of New York nightlife during Prohibition so strongly that by "1930–31, clubs with pansy acts became the hottest in town" as ostensibly straight tourists crowded speakeasies where male entertainers performed effeminate characters onstage (314). But perhaps the most well-known example of effeminacy as fascinating spectacle is the long and successful career of Wladziu Valentino Liberace, the extremely effeminate pianist whose legions of adoring fans knew him best by his last name only. From the late 1940s until his death in 1987, Liberace had Americans tuning into his various television programs and attending his famous live shows in Las Vegas; by the mid-1950s, he was earning a million dollars a year (Pyron, 162). And as New Orleans's sissy rappers and the other examples of fascinating effeminacy in popular culture discussed earlier indicate, the popularity of effeminacy as the fascinating grotesque certainly did not end with Liberace.[7]

EXPLAINING THE PARADOX: THE GROTESQUE

Simultaneously hated and loved, effeminacy never goes unremarked in postwar US literature and culture. But how can both of these things be true? The answer lies in the grotesque, the representational mode that is routinely used to portray effeminacy. But what exactly is the grotesque? Wolfgang Kayser, in his *The Grotesque in Art and Literature* (1957, English translation 1963), notes that the word *grotesque* is ultimately derived from the Italian, where it was first used to describe a decorative style of painting that came to light during late fifteenth century archeological excavations. According to Kayser, grotesque painting was both ornamental and unreal. Grotesques were marked by impossible and fantastic forms: humans with animal heads, delicate flower stems supporting heavy columns, and mergers of the human and the vegetable. Thus, in art historical terms, the grotesque is "something playfully gay and carelessly fantastic, but also something ominous and sinister . . . [it is] the face of a world totally different from the familiar one—a world in which the realm of inanimate things is no longer separated from those of plants, animals, and human beings," a world which depicts "the monstrous fusion of human and nonhuman elements" (Kayser 21, 24). At the conclusion of his study of the grotesque's long history in nineteenth- and early twentieth-century art (visual, literary, and musical), Kayser emphasizes the grotesque's power to disturb, suggesting—in all capital letters, no less—that "THE GROTESQUE IS THE ESTRANGED WORLD," that its subject matter is everything that a dominant culture excludes or ignores (184).

In his *Rabelais and His World* (1965, English translation 1968), Mikhail Bakhtin also emphasizes the grotesque's connection to that which shocks, appalls, and offends. Tracing the roots of the grotesque back to medieval European peasant culture, Bakhtin says that grotesque art is inherently subversive and anti-hierarchical. This is because grotesque art, for Bakhtin, has a strong "material bodily principle, that is, [it emphasizes] images of the human body with its food, drink, defecation, and sexual life" (18). Grotesque art is art that represents the grotesque body, and the grotesque body, unlike the classical body of Greco-Roman art, is a body that transgresses its own bounds by spitting, eating, vomiting, urinating, defecating, masturbating, and/or fornicating with other bodies. The grotesque body is the body that will not behave, a body that is always transgressing the limits of politeness.

Leonard Cassuto, in his *The Inhuman Race: The Racial Grotesque in American Literature and Culture* (1997), also stresses the grotesque's relation to borders and the transgression of them. Looking primarily at representations of race in American literature before the twentieth century, Cassuto argues that the "grotesque has a peculiar disruptive power" (8). This "disruptive power" is the ability to be both threatening and alluring, and it arises from the hybridity of grotesque figures: neither fully human nor fully thing/object, grotesque representations are disturbing because they defy easy categorization and "categorization is the way in which human beings know the world and organize it" (8). Whether the "disruptive power" of the grotesque is a revolutionary or a reactionary force is a matter of great debate; theorists of the grotesque have disagreed tremendously over its ultimate sympathies. Kayser and Mab Segrest have both argued that the grotesque reaffirms the status quo by allowing the ostensibly normal to confirm their sense of superiority by gawking at the ostensibly abnormal. On the other hand, Bakhtin and Patricia Yeager have both argued that certain types of grotesque art provide a means to critique prevailing norms.

And so a short working definition of the grotesque must necessarily highlight these five features: the grotesque is an interdisciplinary style (it occurs in both visual art and textual art); it is concerned with the non-normative human body; it focuses on both the tensions and the pleasures produced by hybridity; its overall effect on readers/viewers can be both alluring and revolting, often both at the same time; and its overall relationship to the status quo has been a subject of great debate.

In discussing the grotesque in relation to depictions of effeminacy in US literature and culture since 1940, I want to stress the issue of hybridity. Effeminate boys and men are often depicted in terms of the grotesque precisely because their bodies are perceived as being hybrid, a blend of male biology and feminine dress, behavior, affect, and/or mannerisms. Instead of a combination of the human and the inhuman (say, a human body with dog's head), effeminate men are seen as grotesque because they take human features that are not supposed to intermingle (the masculine and the feminine) and transgressively combine them in one body, which thus reads as impossible, inhuman. As Kayser says, the grotesque involves "the fusion of realms we know to be separated" (185); effeminate men are thus grotesque because they short-circuit heteronormativity's claim that the masculine and the feminine are two separate, never-overlapping fields.

This makes "effeminate man" a distinct category from "trans." Sissy indicates a contrast in one's gender identity (man) and one's outward gender expression (marked as feminine in a given culture/time/place). Trans, on the other hand, indicates a contrast between the biological sex one was assigned at birth (male or female) and one's authentic gender identity (man or woman). If the so-called "logic" of heteronormativity assumes that gender identity corresponds directly to gender expression (so that a person who understands themself to be a man would "naturally" assume/perform a masculine gender role), the sissy complicates that "logic" by insisting that a man can—and can want to—assume/perform some or even many modes of gender expression that are coded as female. In contrast, because transwomen are women, full stop (whose outward gender expression might be masculine, feminine, or any point in between), I see them as being related to—but distinct from—the sissies who lie at the heart of this book's analysis. Having said that, I must acknowledge that this very book opens with a discussion of an artist—Katey Red—who identifies as both trans and sissy. It is difficult and dangerous to make assumptions about identity categories precisely because people are deeply complex. Katey Red reminds us that "sissy" and "trans" are—like all identity markers—subjectively interpreted and applied categories. Without intending to disrespect or diminish Katey Red, this study does generally presume that sissies are men and boys who identify as male (in terms of gender identity) and whose gender expression is coded as feminine in their culture. This means that "sissy" is related to but nevertheless distinct from "transwoman," wherein female gender identity does not align with the biological sex the transwoman was assigned at birth.

The type of hybridity that both disturbs and captivates is precisely the kind of hybridity that the sissy is guilty of embodying. He is biologically male, but exhibits allegedly femininely coded traits (concern for neatness and external appearance, emotional sensitivity, etc.). This same type of threatening hybridity is also true of the queen, who is the adult sissy. For example, John Rechy's *City of Night* (1963) is a novel about male-male hustling. But even in this novel—written by a gay man and populated with sexual outlaws of all types—the characters in the book reserve their highest levels of scorn for men who dress like men while talking and acting effeminately. As one character says, he "dislike[s]" effeminate men because they are "neither men nor women" (230). Rechy's narrator—himself a gay male prostitute—agrees with this statement wholeheartedly. Even drag queens get more respect in the novel, because their clothing and styling (long hair, makeup, dresses, high heels) seem to match their gendered behavior (lusting for butch men, longing for a man to marry them) in a way that is not true of effeminate men. Although drag queens are biologically male, in day-to-day, non-sexual interactions they both appear female and behave in feminine ways. Thus, Rechy's narrator does not see them as grotesquely hybrid; for him, drag queens (whose external appearance, when they are in drag, matches their external appearance and comportment) are neither as threatening or revolting as effeminate men, who mix masculine dress with feminine behavior.

Other examples of effeminate men being described in grotesquely hybrid terms include George "Bubber" Kelly in McCullers's *The Heart Is a Lonely Hunter* (1940), a young boy who plays with rifles but is nonetheless called a "sissy" by neighborhood boys after he expresses his desire for "a real pretty [costume] made out of all different colors. Like a butterfly" that he could wear to school each day and "dance around" in (140); and Kevin Sessums, who in his memoir *Mississippi Sissy* (2007), realizes that his own effeminacy terrifies his athletic father and causes his father to ask, "*What kind of creature is this? This is a part of me? Flesh of my flesh? Why don't you want to go out and play like the rest of the boys? . . . Why do you want to sit inside laughing with the women all the time? Must you laugh with the women?*" (7, emphasis Sessums').

In attempting to add "the effeminate paradox" to existing masculinity studies scholarship and in suggesting that the grotesque, as a representational mode, can help to explain the paradox, my goal is not to somehow resolve the effeminate paradox (in fact, I am skeptical about that it ever could be resolved) or to suggest that scholars should focus on one side of it or the other. Instead, I argue that we need to be cognizant of the ways in which effeminacy is always paradoxical, always hybrid, always teetering between revolting audiences and fascinating them, sending them running for the hills and yet also singing a siren's song that beckons them to step closer to a different world, one in which old and familiar systems of classification and hierarchical power arrangements loosen, rearrange themselves, or are scrambled into joyous non-recognition.

Some (though not all) modes of fascinating effeminacy are empowering precisely because they frame effeminacy as a door through which people can glimpse a different world, one in which sex/gender roles need not necessarily be bound to the demands of heteronormativity and in which definitions of both masculinity and femininity can be freer, more fluid, and more inclusive than they are in the "real" world from which these representations originate. One such example is John Henry West—the six-year-old sissy boy in Carson McCullers's *The Member of the Wedding* (1946)—declaring that, in an ideal world, "people ought to be half boy and half girl" (338). Another is found in James Baldwin's *Giovanni's Room* (1956), where the only character capable of both the wisdom and courage to defy the sexist and homophobic dominant culture is an effeminate queen named Jacques, who tells David, the novel's self-loathing protagonist, to let go of his fear of being perceived as effeminate and to love his male partner without shame: "Love him . . . love him and let him love you. Do you think anything else under heaven really matters?. . . you can give each other something which will make both of you better—forever—if you will not be ashamed, if you will only not play it safe" (57). Later in the century, Mark Doty invokes fascinating effeminacy when he reflects on his childhood as "a little ridiculous, heavy little sissy" in *Firebird: A Memoir* (1999). When an elementary school teacher indulges Doty's effeminacy by letting him dance in front of his class to a recording of Igor Stravinsky's *Suite from the Firebird*, Doty enters into an ecstatic state and is transformed, becoming "power and authority. . . . the firebird after all. . . . a heavy little boy no longer weighted, without limit, hardly held to earth at all" (81–82). In this moment, young Mark is no longer bound by the shame that he had previously felt because he "can't be who they [his parents and his classmates] want, [and because] that they do not want who he is [an effeminate boy]" (82).

These examples—and others like them, discussed throughout this book—demonstrate the existence of a discursive tradition in which fascinating effeminacy can function in a way that is empowering and positive from the point of view of both queer studies and feminist-influenced masculinity studies. Yes, threatening effeminacy is the most frequently occurring trope in postwar US literature and culture's representation of effeminacy, and yes, in that capacity, it does function as a disciplinary mechanism leveled at men. But effeminacy is also a mode of gender performance embraced and performed by individual men, a gender performance that is routinely figured as queer in relationship to mainstream US culture and standards of masculinity. And as José Esteban Muñoz argues, "Queerness is a structuring and educated mode of desiring that allows us to see and feel beyond the quagmire of the present" (1). And so in a world where the present reality for many people who are queer—in terms of gender presentation, sexuality, and/or both—is one that is filled with ridicule, silencing, violence, erasure, and/or death, effeminacy's ability to gesture, even if only imaginatively, to new worlds is crucially important. Muñoz argues that queerness, when encountered aesthetically, gestures to new futures. I would modify his argument slightly and say that US literature and culture already have a tradition of fascinating effeminacy as a means of transport not so much to a better future but as a way to sidestep into a kind of queer alternate reality: less a way of imagining a utopian future and more a means of envisioning a decidedly different (and better) present. That is, the queer utopias Muñoz imagines are not always merely potential or always just out of our reach, ahead of us in time. Some portrayals that emphasize effeminacy as the fascinating grotesque remind us that queer (in all the positive sense of that word) potentiality is already amongst us, already suggesting ways in which the present can be (or may already be) different from the heteronormative status quo. This is precisely why effeminacy is so routinely rendered as the grotesque; it signals other worlds, other ways of being—and that is both threatening to those already in power and alluring to those dissatisfied with, or victimized by, the status quo.

WHY THESE EXAMPLES?

Sissy! focuses on this postwar US literature and culture because the paradoxical representation of effeminacy has been central to many US cultural debates during this time period, and therefore also central to much US literary and cultural production. It is in post-WWII America that middle-class straight white men really begin, en masse, to find their hegemony in American culture challenged and critiqued. They return home from the war to find women working outside the home (and present in increasing numbers in previously all-male institutions such as higher education), African American veterans demanding equal treatment from the country they'd risked their lives defending, and the increasing visibility of gays and lesbians. All of this social upheaval means that the meaning of manhood—and by extension the meaning of effeminacy—was up for grabs, open for redefinition.

Historians of gay and lesbian identity, including John D'Emilio and George Chauncey, have argued that WWII was a transformational force in the formation of gay and lesbian identities. While other historians (most notably John Howard) have qualified and complicated some of their major claims, I remain convinced of the soundness of D'Emilio and Chauncey's basic claims about the war as a force that took young Americans away from small towns and familial surveillance and put them in contact with other men and woman who felt same-sex desire in the same ways they did. The formulation of gay and lesbian identity—and later, the formulation of political movements for gay and lesbian equality—are tremendously important for any project on effeminacy, because effeminacy is so routinely linked to male homosexuality. The steadily increasing cultural visibility of openly gay men in the second half of the twentieth century has only added to cultural anxieties about the shifting nature of US masculinity.

Beginning this project in 1940 (rather than 1945, the technical beginning of postwar America) also allows me to fully include America's first literary generation of openly queer writers: Carson McCullers (born 1917), Truman Capote (born 1924), James Baldwin (born 1924), and Gore Vidal (born 1925), almost all of whom began publishing in the

1940s.[8] This generation of queer writers is an ideal starting point for an examination of effeminacy in US literature because while the views of these authors are by no means uniform, issues of sexuality and gender nonconformity are (to greater and lesser degrees, depending on the author) central preoccupations of their work.

Finally, 1940 also makes sense as a starting date for this project because in *Gay New York* (1994), historian George Chauncey demonstrates that the middle decades of the twentieth century saw a shift in the ways in which Americans understood the relationship between same-sex desire and gender identity. Chauncey's claim is that, beginning in the late 1930s, American culture experienced a "reorganization of sexual categories and the transition from an early twentieth-century culture divided into 'queers' and 'men' on the basis of gender status to a late twentieth-century culture divided into 'homosexuals' and 'heterosexuals' on the basis of sexual object choice" (22). That is to say, in the pre-World War II gay world that Chauncey maps, men (particularly working class men) could have sex with other men and still be understood to be "normal" so long as they undertook the supposedly "active" role in same-sex relations and maintained a "masculine" gender performance in their day-to-day lives. Chauncey claims that this shift in thinking about sexual behavior and gender identity began in the late 1930s and intensified during and after World War II, until homosexual/heterosexual eventually became "the hegemonic sexual regime in American culture" (23). I contend that it is this "hegemonic sexual regime" that colors so much of our contemporary understandings of both effeminacy and so-called "successful" or "real" masculinity. It thus makes sense to begin the project at a point when the regime change Chauncey describes was settling into place.

As a starting point, 1940 also allows this project to begin its analysis at a time when the definition of effeminacy that is still in widespread use today—a man dressing, acting, and/or behaving like a woman, which is almost always read as an indicator of homosexuality—was firmly in place. For example, the Rodgers and Hammerstein musical *Carousel*, which debuted on Broadway in 1945, contains a song called "Soliloquy," in which carnival worker Billy Bigelow expresses his feelings about being an expectant father. Imagining that his unborn child might be a boy he can name Bill Jr., Billy imagines the kind of boy his son will be and sings that "His mother can teach him / the way to behave, / But she won't make a sissy out o' him— / Not him! / Not my boy! Not Bill" (Rodgers and Hammerstein 94). The sentiment expressed in this song—that mothers were to blame for the creation of effeminate sons and that an effeminate boy was extremely undesirable—was in widespread circulation in US culture by 1940. It is this notion of effeminate men and boys as shameful and problematic that so many of the texts discussed in this book attempt to counter, revise, or openly reject.

In other words, Billy Bigelow is clearly no lover of effeminacy, but he's also not the only voice in the debate. To be sure, the discursive tradition of fascinating effeminacy has circulated, in US literature and culture, less widely and less loudly than the tradition that emphasizes effeminacy as threat. But circulating less widely is not the same as never having existed at all. There is a long-standing minority tradition of fascinating effeminacy in postwar US literature and culture, and its empoweringly queer possibilities lie in wait, anticipating the day when scholarship about effeminacy might catch up to—and mirror—the passion, outrage, sensational scandal, and rich complexity that effeminacy itself has already created in the second half of the twentieth century.

Although fascinating effeminacy offers a dizzying array of potential examples to discuss, I selected the specific examples highlighted in this book's later chapters because they demonstrate particularly intense or noteworthy examples of fascinating effeminacy, examples that have proved to be the basis of enduring, oft-repeated tropes about effeminacy in U.S. literature and culture. That is to say: the particular modes of fascinating effeminacy explored in later chapters are modes that give postwar US literature and culture particular character types that recur throughout the postwar period and across a wide range of media. That is why each of this book's chapters is organized around a particular type of fascinating effeminacy.

Chapter One, "The Sympathetic Sissy: Carson McCullers, Truman Capote, and Fascinating Effeminacy in Postwar US Literature," explores early literary efforts to rewrite dominant cultural narratives about US boyhood and effeminacy. Reading three novels from the 1940s—McCullers's *The Heart is a Lonely Hunter* (1940) and *The Member of the Wedding* (1946), and Capote's *Other Voices, Other Rooms* (1948)—I argue that they constitute the beginning of fascinating effeminacy in canonical US literature. This chapter begins with an overview of late nineteenth and early twentieth-century discourses of white male American boyhood, and the anxieties about sissy boys that accompanied those discourses. After making the case that the sissy boy was a heavily pathologized type (routinely portrayed as a threat to America) by the start of the 1940s, I turn to the novels and examine their differing, deeply sympathetic representations of sissy boys. I argue that McCullers and Capote are both sympathetic to gender nonconforming children and that their representations of sissy boys rewrite dominant cultural narratives about American boyhood by casting effeminacy as a phenomenon that enlivens and enriches the standard, heteronormative world of active men and passive women, which, in contrast to the modes of effeminacy presented in their novels, seems grim, colorless, boring, and oppressive. In giving postwar US literature the template for the Sympathetic Sissy child, McCullers and Capote anticipate figures such as the character Kurt Hummel from the TV series *Glee*, as well the memoirs of sissy childhood discussed in Chapter Five.

McCullers and Capote both write about effeminate boys; by not writing about the onset of puberty and adult sexual desire, they can imply that their sissy boy characters will grow up to be gay, without ever having to definitively say so or to explore what a combination of effeminacy and adult homosexuality might look like. But Chapter Two, "The Straight-Acting Gay Man versus the Truth-Telling Queen: Gore Vidal, James Baldwin, and Gay Men's Debates about Effeminacy," reads two novels that directly confront the questions of effeminacy's value and relationship to male homosexuality. Both Gore Vidal's *The City and the Pillar* (1948) and James Baldwin's *Giovanni's Room* (1956) feature protagonists who try desperately to de-couple male homosexuality from its associations with effeminacy. Typologically, the protagonists of both novels are what contemporary gay culture would call the Straight Acting Gay Man, the gay man who appears and acts masculine, and who takes pride in differing from heteronormative straight men only in terms of his sexual object choice. Vidal's novel—which is often called the first openly gay male novel in America—embraces effeminacy as threat and suggests that it is better for a gay man to be a murderer than a queen; Baldwin, on the other hand, critiques the Straight Acting Gay Man, suggesting that his protagonist David's obsessive investment in maintaining an "immaculate" masculinity untainted by femininity is a primary source of the violence and tragedy that he inflicts on himself and on others. Furthermore, Baldwin places this critique of David firmly in the mouths of Truth-Telling Queens, effeminate gay male characters that David himself has scorned. Baldwin thus employs discourses of fascinating effeminacy and suggests—contrary to what his protagonist believes—that it is effeminate gay men, not straight-acting ones like David, who are truly brave. Read together, these novels dramatize debates about effeminacy and homosexuality that continue to be fought within gay male communities (Straight Acting Gay Man is, in fact, a term from the 1990s that I retroactively apply to Vidal's novel). They demonstrate how gay men were in no way free from the fears about effeminacy that haunted their heterosexual counterparts in the postwar period and show that debates about whether effeminacy should be seen as threat or fascination have been central to gay male literary fiction from its earliest stages.

While Chapter Two is concerned with gay male debates about the meaning and value of effeminacy conducted among gay men, Chapter Three—"'I [Heart] Boys Who Sparkle': Straight Female Fandom and Fascinating Effeminacy"—turns to moments where heterosexual women have embraced effeminacy and even seen it as sexually compelling. The chapter focuses on what I call Boys Who Sparkle: effeminate men and boys who are seen, by their straight female fans, as tremendously desirable precisely because they present an alternative to typical, heteronormative modes of masculinity. The term "Boys Who Sparkle" is inspired by Stephenie Meyer's *Twilight* saga (2005–2008), her best-selling human-girl-meets-vampire-boy romances. My reading of Meyer's *Twilight* novels focuses on Edward Cullen, the very effeminate but very heterosexual vampire boy who serves as the idealized love object/

perfect boy for Bella, the female protagonist of the novels. Having defined "Boys Who Sparkle" using Edward as a contemporary model, the chapter then turns backward in time and makes the case that the Boy Who Sparkles is an enduring and recurring mode of fascinating effeminacy, one most prominently on display in straight female fandom of boy bands such as *NSYNC and such performers as Justin Beiber. I make this argument through an examination of the stage and television career of the pianist Liberace (1919–1987), America's most famous Boy Who Sparkles. (Although Liberace was a gay man whose name today is nearly synonymous with effeminate homosexuality, many of his adoring straight female fans read him as heterosexual, and I read his persona as such.) Finally, the chapter looks at the extremely gender-bifurcated receptions that both Liberace and Edward generated amongst viewers and readers and takes those differing reactions as an occasion to argue for a revision in current theories of the grotesque, one that pays greater attention to the role that the viewer or the reader of a given image or text plays in deciding which mode of the grotesque any given text, image, or performance will be seen as enacting.

From Boys Who Sparkle capable of driving their fans wild with excitement, Chapter Four, "Amplifying the Paradox: Effeminacy in the Age of HIV/AIDS," turns to the HIV/AIDS epidemic and examines how it intensified both halves of the effeminate paradox, presenting effeminate men as either plague-bearing Typhoid Marys or nation-mending Healing Queens. In Randy Shilts's best-selling nonfiction novel *And The Band Played On* (1987), for example, effeminate men are figured as irresponsible, uncontrollably promiscuous plague-carriers. Shilts blames the introduction and spread of AIDS in America on "Patient Zero," whom he reveals to be an extremely effeminate French Canadian gay male flight attendant named Gaëtan Dugas. In Shilts's narrative, Dugas knowingly spreads HIV/AIDS because his narcissism (which Shilts explicitly links to his effeminacy) makes him unable to be celibate. Thus, effeminacy, in Shilts' account, is not just threat; it has literally become murderous. But in stark contrast to Shilts's monstrous portrayal of effeminacy, Tony Kushner frames effeminacy as magical in his epic two-part play *Angels in America* (1992–1993). Kushner's effeminate male characters take Baldwin's Truth-Telling Queens to an entirely new intensity. Entertainers and nurses and prophets, Kushner's Healing Queens do more than just speak truth to a single individual; the magical powers that some of them possess are vital to Kushner's vision of revitalizing the American dream in the face of mass death from AIDS and the deadly selfishness of Reagan-era America. Finally, if Shilts' and Kushner's work represent, respectively, the amplification of the threatening effeminacy and fascinating effeminacy tropes, then another type of AIDS fiction aims to short-circuit the paradox altogether. Sarah Schulman's novel *Rat Bohemia* (1995) is my example of this unusual mode of AIDS fiction that aims to portray effeminacy as value-neutral and un-grotesque, neither threat nor fascination.

Although the HIV/AIDS epidemic is by no means over, the literary representations of it that I examine in Chapter Four end in 1995. Chapter Five, "'The Sissy Triumphant': Fascinating Effeminacy Goes Mainstream," concludes the book by taking its discussion of the effeminate paradox up to the present. I argue that while both ends of the effeminate paradox remain alive and well in early twenty-first century US culture, fascinating effeminacy is now more mainstream than it ever has been before. First, I look at a nonfiction genre that I call "the sissy memoir," which is prose autobiography that deals, in some significant ways, with an effeminate boyhood. I read three sissy memoirs—Mark Doty's *Firebird: A Memoir* (1999), André Leon Talley's *A.L.T.: A Memoir* (2003), and Kevin Sessums's *Mississippi Sissy* (2007)—and argue that the genre uses one end of the effeminate paradox (fascinating effeminacy) to redeem the pain caused by the other (threatening effeminacy). That is, while the authors of sissy memoirs make it clear that childhood effeminacy often leads to bullying from peers and parental disappointment, they also insist that an effeminate childhood leads to an adult life gifted with special abilities, insight, and imaginative possibilities. This is why they are, to paraphrase Doty, Triumphant Sissies. Whereas many of the previously discussed fascinatingly effeminate types discussed to this point are rare—the Sympathetic Sissies I discussed are fictional, Boys Who Sparkle exist largely in the realm of performance, and both Truth-Telling Queens and Healing Queens require extraordinary courage in order to do their work—the Triumphant Sissy is real: honest about his scars, but alive, kicking, and fabulous. This chapter then closes with a demonstration of how the popular (and controversial) It Gets Better Project, a web-based initiative to combat LBGTQ teen suicide, replicates the sissy memoir's triumphant message about effeminacy. I look at President Barack Obama's It Gets Better video, which paints a picture of queer life that is remarkably similar to that of the sissy memoir: a painful queer childhood becomes, later in life, a fabulous queer adulthood.

Although effeminacy does not always equal male homosexuality—Vidal's Straight-Acting Gay Man demonstrates many gay men's visceral rejection of effeminacy, and the greatly coveted emotional sensitivity and physical nonaggression of Boys Who Sparkle prove that effeminacy can be heterosexual—conventional wisdom tightly links the two in postwar US literature. And so as homosexuality becomes more and more acceptable in mainstream US culture and queer thinkers and activists worry about what might be lost in a shift to "homonormativity," what is the fate of effeminacy? Must it, too, lose its edge as moves into the mainstream? My Conclusion, "Our Makeup Is Terrible, but I Love You Anyway": Why Fascinating Effeminacy Matters in the Twenty-first Century, argues not necessarily. Through an analysis of *RuPaul's Drag Race*, I argue that fascinating effeminacy contains radical potential that can undercut or lessen some of the pitfalls of both hetero- and homonormativity.

In his sissy memoir, Doty writes that "the queer boy's dynamic" is to be "simultaneously debased and elevated," to be both "the rejected boy, inside the unloved body" and also "the sissy triumphant, enraged, jeweled by an elegant crown of his own devising" (106). Doty's statement works on three levels: Doty is writing specifically about his own life, his own circumstances and upbringing, but the duality that he articulates might in fact serve as a manifesto for this book (hence my use of part of the above quotation in the title of Chapter Five). I argue that some representations of effeminacy contain radical potential, that they hold queer potential, that they gesture to new worlds by reminding us that alternate models of thinking about (and organizing) sex and gender roles are already in our midst. Through their use of fascinating effeminacy, they suggest that effeminacy might be a means of accessing power and pleasure, new modes of being and heightened imaginative possibilities. These representations of effeminacy show us that difference doesn't always have to mean threat or malady or panic; it might also mean something better.

ONE

THE SYMPATHETIC SISSY

CARSON MCCULLERS, TRUMAN CAPOTE, AND FASCINATING EFFEMINACY IN POSTWAR US LITERATURE

In a 1901 newspaper article titled "The Boyhood of Sissie," Adam Beaseley expresses affection for "the beautiful barbarism of little boys," but admits that he himself fell short of this ideal and was, instead, a "sissie," a "Sunday School monstrosity" (qtd. in Grant 835). Physically weak, timid, and often sickly, Beaseley condemns his own "mysterious mania for revery and for books" and suggests that his childhood was flawed because he was not more physically active and combative (qtd. in Grant 835). A 1902 article in *Cosmopolitan* magazine by a writer named Rafford Pyke declared that real men "laugh" at the sissy while women shun him because of the "moral nausea" he invokes (qtd. in Kimmel, *Manhood* 83). Nor was social stigma the only hardship effeminate boys faced: in the early decades of the twentieth century, they were increasingly made the targets of psychological and medical intervention designed to reduce or end their effeminacy. For example, historian Julia Grant highlights the case of Tom, a three-year-old boy who was diagnosed as a sissy in the early 1930s by both his father and clinicians at Chicago's Institute for Juvenile Research. After Tom's father's "bullying" of his own son failed to "make him more of a man," Tom was separated from his parents and "placed in a children's institution for a period of three months" in the hopes of stopping his effeminate behavior (Grant 840).

The above anecdotes are by no means unique. The discourses of boyhood and manhood that they articulate—both explicitly and implicitly—are perfectly representative of a view of American boyhood that began at the end of the nineteenth century and continued to thrive and grow in popularity in the first four decades of the twentieth century. In this view, American boys (here almost always assumed to be white and middle class) are inherently wild, rambunctious, boisterous, physically active, strong, and brave. They like playing outdoors, getting dirty, and fighting with one another. They are not interested in nice clothes, book learning, or the fine arts. They do not want to be cooped up inside, and they shun excessive displays of emotions that might make them seem vulnerable. All that boys are, naturally, is masculine. All that they shun is feminine. In fact, being a boy means shunning the feminine. Any boy who does not—or cannot—shun the feminine is, by definition, a failed or flawed boy, a sissy. This is the usual story, the story of effeminacy as threat: there are real boys and sissies. Real boys are valued and seen as natural. Sissies are pathologized and seen as a problem to be treated or cured.

But this chapter isn't about the usual story. It is about the birth of a new story, an alternative schema for assigning value to American boys. This new story is about the introduction of fascinating effeminacy into US literary fiction. This chapter examines three novels published in the 1940s in which sissy boys are valued: Carson McCullers's *The Heart Is a Lonely Hunter* (1940) and *The Member of the Wedding* (1946), and Truman Capote's *Other Voices, Other Rooms* (1948). These novels rewrite dominant US cultural narratives about effeminacy by recasting it as a positive phenomenon that enlivens and enriches the standard, heteronormative world of active men and passive women, which seems grim, boring, and oppressive in contrast to fascinating effeminacy.

McCullers's sissy boy characters come to bad ends in the novels in which they appear, but she consistently portrays their diminishment and death as a communal loss. So while her sissy boys either conform to heteronormative gender roles or die, McCullers always insists that their communities are worse off for having forced change or death upon them. And in *Other Voices, Other Rooms*, Capote takes the time-worn adolescent male coming-of-age novel about a boy becoming a man and transforms it into the story of a boy finding both identity and power as he moves from boyhood into an adult homosexuality that Capote strongly equates with femininity. In these novels effeminacy is not lack or failure or horror or monstrosity. Instead, these novels emphasize effeminacy's ability to fascinate. Their portrayal of effeminate boys highlights what Mab Segrest, writing about McCullers several decades later, has called "vitalizing differentness" (25).[1] That is, in these novels, effeminacy is a force that is different, but whose difference is necessary to the community's health.

This is what makes McCullers's and Capote's effeminate characters Sympathetic Sissies. For both authors, effeminacy is vital because it enlivens an otherwise dull and drab heteronormative world; it fascinates precisely because it conjures up the impossible. Effeminate boys and men bridge the barrier that is supposed to exist between the masculine and the feminine, a barrier that, according to the discourse of the dominant culture, is supposed to be ironclad and impenetrable. In embodying that which is supposed to be impossible, effeminate boys and men expand what Alan Sinfield has called "the boundaries of the plausible," the conditions of discursive possibility that form the limits of subject formation in a given culture at a given time (31). That is, the gender presentation of effeminate boys and men demonstrates that the boundaries of what is possible in selfhood are not as narrow as their observers had perhaps been brought up to believe. The novels discussed in this chapter argue that effeminate boys and men are valuable precisely because their effeminacy functions as a kind of living fantasy, one that expands the limits of what is known to be possible in terms of embodied gender presentation. This expansion can literally save lives, and, thus, these novels depict the shaming, silencing, and/or death of effeminate boys and men as a grave loss for their communities.

Now, a few words of clarification: I do not mean to suggest that the novels I discuss below suddenly brought about a wholesale revolution in US culture or that they changed the way that the majority of Americans viewed, and reacted to, effeminate boys and men. They quite clearly did not: sissy-hating is an old and robust tradition in the United States. It long pre-dates the novels discussed in this chapter and has continued to exist long, long after them. I am not telling a story of wholesale regime change here; I am not arguing that McCullers's and Capote's use of fascinating effeminacy suddenly and wholly replaced the discursive conditions of effeminacy that preceded them. Rather, what I want to suggest is that the three novels examined here form the beginnings of a minority discursive tradition in US literature, one often overshadowed by the dominant discourse of effeminacy as threat, but nevertheless existing alongside it in some form or another since 1940. So while the novels discussed here certainly did not alter mainstream perceptions of effeminacy in the United States, they did model a new representational strategy, a way of insisting that effeminate men and boys had value, possessed worth, and did not deserve cruel rebuke, physical harassment, or death simply by virtue of being effeminate.

AMERICAN BOYS: SAVAGE AND "REAL," NOT SISSY

By 1940, the year that McCullers published her first novel, *The Heart Is a Lonely Hunter,* American discourses about boys and boyhood were already deeply entrenched in a real boy/sissy binary. This binary developed out of—was, in fact, a solution to—a paradox faced by white middle-class men in the late nineteenth century.

According to historian Gail Bederman, white middle-class American men living in the later decades of the nineteenth century and the early decades of the twentieth faced a dilemma. On the one hand, popular discourses of manhood insisted that the true sign of manhood was what Bederman calls manly restraint, the ability of a man to exercise self-control and mastery over his own passions. According to Victorian-era discourses of masculinity, a white, middle-class man who achieved self-control "gained the strength, as well as the duty, to protect and direct those weaker than himself: his wife, his children, or his employees" (Bederman 12). But city life and increasingly corporatized male labor (where cooperation, rather than rugged individualism, was key, and labor was more likely to be intellectual than manual) was likely to produce too much self-restraint and make a generation of American men who were weak, innervated, and effeminate. These effeminate men would be crippled by neurasthenia—a disease that doctors do not recognize today, but which turn-of-the-century American medicine took very seriously—which made men "like an undercharged electric battery. . . . lack[ing] in adequate power" (Bederman 85). The men "most in danger of developing neurasthenia were middle- and upper-class businessmen and professionals whose highly evolved bodies had been physically weakened by advances in civilization. . . . civilization's demands on men's nerve force had left their body positively effeminate" (Bederman 87).[2]

G. Stanley Hall (1844–1924), a professor of pedagogy and psychology, proposed a solution to this paradox, and it is Hall's solution that leads to the development of the real boy/sissy binary. Hall believed in the theory of recapitulation. Scientific orthodoxy at the time, recapitulation theory held that an "individual would follow the developmental path its forebearers took. . . . As a child or young animal matured, it precisely repeated the evolutionary path its ancestors had taken, from the most distant protozoan upward" (Bederman 92). Hall combined recapitulation theory with the dominant racist ideology of the day, which suggested that whites and blacks were separate species, and that the white race was more evolved and civilized than any other. Thus, in Hall's model of adolescent development, young white boys passed through various stages of primitive barbarism before they became fully evolved and civilized—but not *too* civilized—white male adults.

To Hall, young white boys were, literally, at the same state of evolution as adult, non-white "savages," and so asking young white boys to act or be otherwise was foolish, since they were simply incapable of it. It was also dangerous, in Hall's view, to try to suppress the energy and boisterousness of the stage of childhood savagery that young white boys passed through because it was necessary that American white boys retain a measure of savage strength and vitality as they matured into civilized men. Without this reserve of savage vitality, white American boys would grow up and become weak, effeminate neurasthenics. Hall thus gave lectures and wrote newspaper columns about the dangers of female teachers smothering the primitive savagery of young white boys. He chided (female) teachers for disciplining the rowdy behavior of young boys, behavior that Hall understood to be a "reliving of primitive emotions" that functioned "as a sort of vaccination process. . . . reliving their ancestors' primitivism would allow boys to carry a weakened case of 'savagery' in their systems and thus give them the primitive masculine strength to avoid neurasthenic breakdown and overcivilized effeminacy" (Bederman 97). Without social and educational systems in place to support and encourage this vaccinating period of childhood savagery, Hall feared that American white boys would become weak, effeminate American white men and that the white race would fall from its place at the top of civilization. In Hall's model of childhood development—which met with resistance early on but eventually became very popular—it was right for boys to be loud, unruly, physically active, aggressive, and competitive. Rather than trying to control or stop these behaviors, adults should encourage them.

The unspoken assumption of Hall's model is that boys who were not naturally loud, unruly, physically active, aggressive, and competitive were, by definition, a problem. The term that came to be applied, over the course of the late nineteenth and early twentieth century, to these problematic boys was, of course, "sissy." The Boy Scouts—founder Robert Baden-Powell's *Scouting For Boys* was published in 1908—were just one group formed to combat these anxieties about the supposed sissification of boys and young men; the purpose of these groups was to get boys outside, to put them in nature and force them into rugged play which would ostensibly fend off the ostensibly weakening and corrupting effects of effeminacy.[3]

This real boy/sissy binary, and the value judgments inherent within it, was circulated in a variety of ways. Texts played a huge part. As Kenneth B. Kidd has shown, there was an entire industry of "boyology," in the final decades of the nineteenth century and the early decades of the twentieth, a proliferation of "descriptive and proscriptive writing on boyhood across a variety of genres" (1). These genres include what Kidd calls the "Bad Boy" book, a genre whose greatest popularity he dates from 1876, with the publication of Mark Twain's *Adventures of Tom Sawyer*, to about 1916, with the publication of Booth Tarkington's *Penrod and Sam*.[4] These novels celebrate the real boy as a type: "the Bad Boy author declares boyhood's independence from all things feminine" (Kidd 52). Bad Boy books thus stress the complete and total separation of boys and anything deemed to be feminine. For example, Henry A. Shute's 1902 *The Real Diary of a Real Boy* went through sixteen editions by 1914; the story of "a rambunctious and pugilistic" eleven-year-old, the novel depicts "the model boy who obeyed his mother and exemplified Christian forbearance" as being distinctly less desirable than "the little 'tuff' who narrates the diary" (Grant 834). Shute's text and others like it reflect the fact that "boy culture. . . . curbed the expression of tender, vulnerable emotions" while it simultaneously "stimulated aggression and encouraged [male] youngsters to vent their physical energy" (Rotundo 45). In other words, Bad Boy novels repeatedly make it clear that real boys are physical active, even violent, boys who relentlessly shun the feminine and, as Leslie Fiedler has famously argued, light out for the territories *Huckleberry Finn*–style in order to avoid the tyrannical, civilizing influence of "petticoat tyranny" (342).[5]

The Bad Boy book was not the only genre comprising turn-of-the-century boyology. There are also the instructional handbooks of "the American pseudo-science of boy analysis that flourished in the early twentieth century," such as William Bryan Forbush's *The Boy Problem* (1901), and YMCA leader Henry William Gibson's 1916 book *Boyology or Boy Anaylsis* (Kidd 1). These texts served as "a handbook for 'boy workers,'" those adults who, though they might not be trained academics, psychologists, or doctors, nevertheless wanted to help ensure that the next generation of (white, middle-class) American boys would grow up to be appropriately masculine (Kidd 1). This genre was so voluminous that by 1916, Gibson was able to include a bibliography of 103 different "books or pamphlets 'about boys or subject analogous to boy life'" at the back of his own book on the subject (Kidd 1).

While Bad Boy books and boyology manuals waned in popularity by the 1920s, effeminate boys continued to be portrayed negatively in US culture, although they were stigmatized through slightly different means. Freudian ideas crept into discourses of childhood development during the 1920s, so that "[i]f a boy's behavior was feminine or a young girl's behavior was masculine it was [seen as] a sure sign that something had gone wrong in the child's psychosexual development, and it was feared that homosexuality might be the result" (Kimmel, *Manhood* 133–134). Furthermore, office jobs that required cooperation rather than rugged individualism—and which took place in offices that increasingly included women—meant that US men came to see "work itself" as "increasingly feminized" (Kimmel, *Manhood* 131).

And if men in the 1920s had complained about encountering women in the workplace, in the 1930s many men found that they did not have a workplace at all. During the Great Depression, widespread unemployment meant that many American men could no longer feel like successful men by way of acting as primary breadwinners for their families. US writers thinking about masculinity in the thirties—such as Dale Carnegie in his *How to Win Friends and Influence People* (1936)—tended to "shift attention away from external trappings of success to more internal forces, one's personality" (Kimmel, *Manhood* 133). Thus, in the 1930s, masculinity was "redefined away from achievement in the public sphere and reconceived as the exterior manifestation of a certain inner sense of oneself. Masculinity could be observed in specific traits and attitudes, specific behaviors and perspectives. If men expressed these attitudes, traits, and behaviors, they could be certain that they were 'real' men, regardless of their performance in the workplace. If a man failed to express these attitudes, traits, and behaviors, he was in danger of becoming a homosexual" (Kimmel, *Manhood* 136). Thus, by 1940, the year that McCullers publishes *The Heart Is a Lonely Hunter*, it was accepted that the question of whether a man is masculine or not has to do not with "his performance in the workplace" but in his "attitudes, traits, and behaviors." And when it comes to the attitudes, traits, and behaviors of US boys, masculine behavior clearly meant being physically active, rowdy, rambunctious, and repulsed by anything feminine, including fancy clothing, the fine arts, book-learning, and excessive displays of emotion. Boys who did not meet this definition of boyhood were not, in fact, real boys. At the same time, much of the American medical and social scientific establishment—as well as the mass media—was busy pathologizing the sissy, characterizing his very existence as a problem to be identified, treated with various kinds of therapy, and radically altered in the name of a cure. Meanwhile, although sissy boys appear only as supporting cast characters in her 1940s fiction, McCullers was nevertheless beginning to tell another kind of story about them.

MCCULLERS: A DIFFERENT ACCOUNTING OF EFFEMINACY

Although McCullers's central protagonists tend to be tomboyish adolescent girls, sissy boys routinely appear as important supporting characters in her fiction. While McCullers did write several adult male characters who are either effeminate and/or homosexual—John Singer in *The Heart Is a Lonely Hunter*, both Captain Penderton and Anacleto in *Reflections in a Golden Eye* (1941), and Cousin Lymon in *The Ballad of the Sad Café*—I will focus my analysis on her prepubescent sissy boy characters. I want to examine McCullers's effeminate boy characters in order to better understand how her fiction conforms to, and where and how it deviates from, the cultural discourses of boyhood that were dominant and in widespread circulation before she began publishing in 1940. The readings that follow will focus on two characters: George "Bubber" Kelly from *The Heart Is a Lonely Hunter* and John Henry West from *The Member of the Wedding*.

Bubber Kelly is the younger brother of Mick Kelly, the adolescent tomboy at the center of *The Heart Is a Lonely Hunter*. At the opening of that novel, seven-year-old George is known only by his nickname. Bubber is the sibling that Mick likes best. She frequently notes his intelligence, saying that Bubber is "sharp as a briar" (102) and that it "was like that kid [Bubber] had been born knowing how to read. He was only in the second grade but he loved to read stories by himself—and he never asked anybody else to read to him" (164). Bubber is also "so thin and little" (172), that he "looks sick" (166) and is "so small that it was like he was five years old instead of seven" (178). This combination—intellect and a love of reading, paired with small physical size and physical weakness—seems to set Bubber up as the stereotypical sissy. But that is not entirely the case. Unlike the stereotypical sissy, Bubber does not spend his days in the house, tied to his mother's apron strings. When he does read, he likes "cowboy" stories, and he is not afraid to go outside and play with the other kids (164). In fact, when Bubber appears in *The Heart Is a Lonely Hunter*, he is usually doing exactly that, playing with his sister and little brother and other neighborhood kids, doing thoroughly un-sissy things like playing marbles or shooting a slingshot.

Indeed, Mick thinks that Bubber "wasn't a sissy. . . . He just loved pretty things. . . . but he's got guts underneath that" (166).

Still, the major scene in the novel that involves Bubber is marked, indelibly, by Bubber's love of pretty things, a definitively sissy trait. This scene is an encounter between Bubber and Baby Wilson, the little girl who lives across the street, whose mother is training her to be a beauty pageant queen and eventual Hollywood actress. One day, while playing in the street with Mick and his friend Spareribs, Bubber sees Baby step outside in "last year's soiree costume," an outfit consisting of "a little pink-gauze skirt that stuck out short and stiff, a pink body waist, pink dancing shoes, and even a little pink pocketbook" (164). All in all, the outfit makes Baby look "like a fairy or something in the picture show" (164), and with "her yellow hair she was all pink and white and gold—and so small and clean that almost hurt to watch her" (164–65) as she "prissed across the street in a cute way" (165). This behavior is familiar to Mick, Bubber, and the other neighborhood kids because "last summer Baby had come out in that pink soiree costume and danced in the middle of the street. At first the kids would flock around and watch her, but soon they got tired of it" (165).

Bubber, however, never tires of seeing Baby dance while wearing her soiree costume. It is possible to read Bubber's interest in Baby as a kind of nascent heterosexual desire, but this is unlikely; Bubber is only seven years old, and as his comments in the scene reveal, Bubber's interest in Baby has more to do with his wanting to be like her than desiring her sexually. "Come over here," he says to her. "Lemme look at your little pink pocketbook" (165). He then says, "I sure do wish I had a costume. . . . a real cool costume. A real pretty one made out of all different colors. Like a butterfly. That's what I want for Christmas. That and a bicycle. . . . I'd dance around in my costume if I had one. I'd wear it every day to school" (165–66). These comments prompt Bubber's friend Spareribs to call him a "Sissy" (166), but in spite of this public shaming, Bubber continues to long for Baby's soiree costume, asking her to please "Lemme see your little pink pocketbook and touch your pink costume" (167).

Baby passes by "without letting Bubber play with her," and the scene quickly turns from playful to tragic (167). All afternoon, Bubber has been playing with Spareribs's father's rifle, pointing it at things and people as he pretends to shoot them. He does this same playful, pretend-shooting routine with Baby as he watches her prance about in her costume, but somehow his finger accidentally finds its way to the rifle's trigger. Baby is shot in the head, and nearly killed. Bubber, horrified by what he has done, runs and hides. Mick, angry at Bubber and wanting to teach him a lesson, lies and tells him that Baby has been killed and that the police are looking for Bubber and that they will take him away to the infamous Sing Sing prison, where they have "little electric chairs" waiting for him (169).

Terrified, Bubber attempts to run away. He is missing for several hours and—because he thinks he is a murderer who is going to be executed—he fights his father when the family finds him and tries to take him home, and he screams and cries all night long once he is finally home. Even though Baby is not actually killed, and Bubber is not tried for murder, Mick and Bubber's family is forced to pay for Baby's expensive medical care and recovery, and this makes their family's already-precarious financial situation even worse. Most of the siblings have to get part-time jobs in order to help bring in income, the family ends up having to sell their home, and even finding the money to eat becomes difficult, as Mick and her siblings sometimes go "downright hungry for two or three days" (239) because the family "had to pay through the nose for Baby Wilson's private [hospital] room and private nurse" (238).

The trauma of shooting Baby—and the financial hardship it imposes on the whole family—changes Bubber, almost instantly: "After he shot Baby the kid was not ever like little Bubber again. He always kept his mouth shut and he didn't fool around with anybody. Most of the time he just sat in the back yard or in the coal house by himself . . . After that night nobody called him Bubber any more. . . . The family called him by his real name—George. . . . he was a different kid—George—going around by himself always like a person much older and with nobody, not even her [Mick], knowing what was really in his mind" (180). This transformation—from carefree, playful Bubber to serious, somber

George—clearly serves as a cautionary tale. McCullers sympathizes with freaks and outcasts and oddballs throughout all of her fiction, and so I do not think that she herself is condemning Bubber's effeminate infatuation with Baby's soiree costume or his desire to have such a costume of his own. But I do think that Bubber's shooting of Baby—and the trauma it causes in both the short and long terms—is meant to be read metaphorically. Bubber lives in a culture where boys are not expected, encouraged, or even allowed to wear pink costumes and dance about like a butterfly. When boys express such desires, they are met with sanction from friends and parents alike. These sanctions run the gamut from verbal teasing to physical violence to—as Grant's work demonstrates—institutionalization. Thus, when Bubber desires Baby's costume and expresses those desires openly, McCullers metaphorizes the violent responses such an expression of desire would provoke in the real world. The violent incident of Baby's shooting (and its negative aftereffects) is a dramatized version of the very real violence that effeminate boys often encounter when they express themselves.

After the shooting, Bubber morphs, almost instantly, into George, and George's new personality—"Since he shot Baby he wouldn't buddy with a single person" (245)—causes Mick, who had once been very close to him, a great deal of pain. George seems more withdrawn, isolated, and sad than Bubber ever did. This change in his personality, this tightening and diminishing and closing off, illustrates the cost of the disciplining that effeminate boys receive in order to make them conform to masculine norms. Because make no mistake about it: George is not interested in, or attracted to, effeminacy in the way that Bubber was. In fact, "George hated Baby. He would hold his nose and stop up his ears when she passed by the house" (310). And so from the point of view of the dominant culture that he lives in, George has been effectively socialized; he is no longer the effeminate Bubber. This change is represented by the stark change in his naming. But McCullers, ever sympathetic to those whose gender performance falls outside of established norms, shows George to readers through the perspective of Mick. And from Mick's point of view, the change from Bubber to George is a loss, a diminishing.

Like Bubber, John Henry West, in *The Member of the Wedding*, is also a young sissy. Just six years old, John Henry is delicate and attracted to "beautiful" things, such as butterflies and baby dolls (266). But whereas McCullers presents Bubber's personality as a hybrid blending of sissy and "real" boy characteristics, John Henry is a pure sissy: he wears eyeglasses and fancy suits, loves cross-dressing, and dreams of an ideal world where "people ought to be half boy and half girl" (338).[6]

John Henry is open and unashamed about his love of all things girly. Frankie Adams—John Henry's cousin, and the novel's twelve year-old protagonist—is baffled and repulsed by John Henry's effeminacy; this is because Frankie is older than John Henry and beginning to experience the heightened gender policing of adolescence in a way that he has not yet encountered. Frankie also finds John Henry's effeminacy upsetting for another reason: Frankie is herself queer, in terms of both gender presentation (she is a tomboy, with her hair cut so short it looks boyish) and sexuality (she yearns to join both her brother and his fiancé in a triangular relationship and ends the novel in the throes of "the wonder of her love" for female classmate Mary Littlejohn),[7] and her queerness has already begun to be viewed negatively by both peers and adult authority figures (389).

This is why descriptions of a sense of anxious incomprehension—Frankie's conviction that important things are happening within and around her combined with her frustration and panic about not fully understanding these things—abound in *The Member of the Wedding*. The very first page of the novel announces that "Frankie had become an unjoined person who hung around in doorways, and she was afraid" (257). References to this fear, which Frankie can never precisely name or identify, recur repeatedly: "Frankie was afraid. She did not know what caused this fear, but she was afraid" (261). As she tries to figure out her own feelings,. Frankie realizes that a change has come over her because "[u]ntil the April of that year, and all the years of her life before, she had been like other people," but now "[t]hings began to change and Frankie did not understand this change" (274). Incomprehensible as it is to her, Frankie knows that this change has something to do with her behavior, and the ways in which it conforms, or fails to conform, to social norms: "She would go home and put the coal scuttle on her head, like a crazy person's hat, and walk around the kitchen table. She would do anything that suddenly occurred to her—but whatever she did was always wrong, and not at all what she wanted. Then, having done these wrong and silly things, she would stand, sickened and empty, in the kitchen door and say: 'I just wish I could tear down this whole town'" (276). Frankie thus resists John Henry's queerness out of a sense of self-loathing. She fears and dreads John Henry's queer gender performance because she fears and dreads her own emerging queerness, which manifests itself in the way that "whatever she did was always wrong." This is why Frankie, when she visits the State Fair, is afraid of the performers inside the House of the Freaks. She imagines their lives to be lonely and worries that they might recognize her as a freak-to-be.

In sharp contrast to Frankie, John Henry loves the freak show and stands "all afternoon" watching The Pin Head, whom he declares to be "the cutest little girl [he] ever saw" (272). This aggravates Frankie, who doesn't "think [The Pin Head] was cute" (272). And although Frankie, when asked how she would remake the world, suggests that it should be set up "so that people could instantly change back and forth from boys to girls, whichever they felt like and wanted," she nonetheless becomes offended when John Henry argues that "people ought to be half boy and half girl" (338). After John Henry says this, Frankie immediately threatens "to take him to the Fair and sell him to the Freak Pavilion" (338). This is clearly a fate Frankie herself considers worse than death, but upon hearing her threat, John Henry "would only close his eyes and smile" (338).

The Pin Head is not the only effeminate figure John Henry admires. He is also enraptured when Berenice Sadie Brown, the African American domestic employed by Frankie's family, tells Frankie and him about Lily Mae Jenkins, a man she knows who "prisses around with a pink satin blouse and one arm akimbo" because he "fell in love with a man named Juney Jones. A man, mind you," and thus promptly "changed his nature and his sex and turned into a girl" (324). After telling the children about Lily Mae's existence, Berenice assures them that they "don't need to know Lily Mae Jenkins. You can live without knowing him" (324). But John Henry refuses to let the subject be closed, later begging Berenice to tell him "How? . . . How did that boy change into a girl?" (325).

This unapologetic fascination with, identification with, and love of, sideshow freaks and other outsiders—especially adults with non-normative gender performance—is mystifying to Frankie, who claims that it is "impossible to understand his [John Henry's] point of view" (373). John Henry looks approvingly at the performers in the House of the Freaks and Lily Mae Jenkins because in them he sees a greater range of gendered and embodied possibilities than those offered by the adults in his and Frankie's day-to-day life. Frankie looks at the same people, but she is a twelve-year-old, middle-class white girl in the US South who is tomboyish and already beginning to internalize the tremendous pressure that she is receiving, from parents, caretakers, and peers to gender-conform to the narrow role of passive, demure, and heterosexual southern white womanhood. Thus, she sees only deviance when she looks at the freaks or hears about Lily Mae Jenkins, and deviance is the thing she herself is anxious to purge from her own being. This is also why Frankie's opinions of John Henry's cross-dressing are always so negative. Frankie equates him with the House of the Freaks itself when she says that he looks like "a little old woman dwarf" when he is "wearing the pink hat with the plume, and the high heeled shoes" (360). Later, when she sees John Henry wearing her "jonquil dress" she feels "a hollow sorriness" because he looks "so babyish and pitiful in the costume" (361, 369).

At the end of *The Member of the Wedding*, John Henry contracts meningitis and suffers tremendously for ten days—"screaming . . . stuck and blind"—before finally dying (391). He becomes merely a "presence" to Frankie, something "solemn, hovering, and ghost-gray" and that she feels "seldom now" (391). Considered together, the characters of Bubber Kelly and John Henry West form a pattern in McCullers's 1940s fiction. Both boys are sissies, and both come to bad ends. Bubber, who displays a mix of both effeminate and hegemonically masculine traits, dies a metaphorical, psychic death. John Henry, the more purely sissy of the two, dies a very painful and quite literal death. It would seem as though McCullers is punishing her sissies, meeting increasingly effeminate behavior with increasingly punitive and painful outcomes.

This might be true if one only paid attention to the states that Bubber and John Henry are in at the conclusions of their respective novels. But these characters are more than their endings: I read McCullers as being deeply sympathetic to both boys. I see her decision to have them come to bad ends as an act of realism. McCullers herself—like Frankie—was frequently mocked for her own gender nonconformity in childhood. As her biographer explains, McCullers's often-boyish style of dress alienated her from her female peers: "some of the girls gathered in little clumps of femininity and threw rocks at her when she walked nearby, snickering loud asides and tossing within hearing distance such descriptive labels as 'weird,' 'freakish-looking,' and 'queer'" (Carr 29–30). McCullers knew firsthand how badly gender-deviant children were often treated and how they were punished simply for being themselves and doing what felt comfortable and natural to them. Bubber's traumatic transformation into the sullen George and John Henry's painful death should not be read as acts of vengeance that McCullers inflicts on her characters to punish them for their effeminacy. Rather, they should be seen as metaphorical treatments of the whole range of negative reactions that effeminate young boys receive as they mature towards adolescence and are socialized to be both heterosexual and hegemonically masculine. As Eve Kosofsky Sedgwick notes in her essay "How to Bring Your Kids Up Gay: The War on Effeminate Boys," "The presiding asymmetry of value assignment between hetero and homo goes unchallenged everywhere. . . . the scope of institutions whose programmatic undertaking is to prevent the development of gay people is unimaginably large . . . in the United States, at any rate, most sites of the state, the military, education, law, penal institutions, the church, medicine, and mass culture enforce it all but unquestioningly, and with little hesitation at even the recourse to invasive violence" (161).

Sedgwick is talking here about sexuality (hetero- versus homo-), but her larger essay is about gender performance (effeminacy versus more hegemonic masculinity), and the point she makes is true of both queer sexuality and queer gender performance: almost all US social institutions are set to value the heteronormative and encourage its reproduction, while devaluing the queer and squelching its every appearance and actively preventing its reproduction. Sedgwick's essay was originally written for the MLA conference in 1989, and while I am wary of assuming that more contemporary moments necessarily represent a more progressive/liberatory moment for queers, it is safe to say that while Sedgwick's observation was true for her in 1989, it was also true (if not more intensely so) of America during the decades of McCullers's childhood and during the 1940s, the decade in which she published both *The Heart Is a Lonely Hunter* and *The Member of the Wedding*.

In other words, I read McCullers's treatment of both Bubber and John Henry as her effort to make the same point—in the 1940s—that Sedgwick made in 1989, and throughout much of the rest of her work. McCullers has both sissy boys come to bad ends in order to dramatize the sometimes violent and often traumatizing ways in which effeminate boys are socialized—by peers, by parents, by other adult authority figures, and by a wide range of US social institutions—into normative gender performance and heterosexuality. This socializing pressure is more intense the more effeminate a boy is; this is why Bubber Kelly dies a psychic death while John Henry dies a literal one. Frankie ends *The Member of the Wedding* in love with a female classmate, a turn of events that can be read as McCullers leaving queer readers with some hope for the future. But if Frankie's queer sexuality can survive—as long as it remains more or less hidden—John Henry's effeminacy, which cannot be hidden, cannot survive.

McCullers's fiction from the 1940s both witnesses this fact and mourns it. Both Bubber's transformation into the sullen George and John Henry's painful death are portrayed as real and serious losses. When Bubber and John Henry vanish from their respective worlds, those worlds are smaller, more homogenous, less vivid, and altogether poorer for their absences. When Bubber becomes George, Mick Kelly loses her main companion and playmate, a turn of events that leaves her further and further isolated from the world at large. And Bubber himself, once a brave, vibrant, smart, curious kid who played daily with the other kids in the neighborhood, becomes sullen, solitary, and withdrawn. Similarly, John Henry's passing leaves a void that is never quite filled because, despite Frankie's suspicion of his love of all things gender transgressive, John Henry, while he lived, was an important support system for Frankie. John Henry frequently listens to Frankie, offering sympathy and support for the pain she experiences during her "summer of fear" (271). For example, he attempts to console Frankie once she admits to him that the older neighborhood girls, who have snubbed Frankie because of her inappropriate gender performance, have spread "it all over town that [she] smell[s] bad" (265). "I don't think you smell so bad," John Henry tells Frankie, "[y]ou smell sweet" (265). When this fails to console Frankie, John Henry continues, saying, "I can smell you the minute you walk in the house without even looking to see if it is you. Like a hundred flowers. . . . Like a thousand flowers" (265). John Henry also attempts to comfort Frankie after her brother and his bride fail to take Frankie along with them on their honeymoon: "Frankie, don't cry," he tells her, "[w]e will go home and put up the tepee and have a good time" (380).

Take also, the example of the biscuit man John Henry makes early on in *The Member of the Wedding*. This is a very small scene in the novel, a scene that might perhaps seem unimportant. However, it is illustrative of just what exactly is lost in John Henry's painful passing. In the scene, Berenice—who is preparing dinner for Frankie's family—has given both Frankie and John Henry some biscuit dough. To amuse themselves (and likely to keep them occupied and out of Berenice's way for a few minutes), they are to make biscuit men with the dough: "John Henry did not play with the dough; he worked on the biscuit man as though it were a very serious business . . . When Berenice gave him some raisins, he did not stick them all around as any other human child would do; he used only two for the eyes; but immediately he realized they were too large—so he divided one raisin carefully and put in eyes, two specks for the nose, and a little grinning raisin mouth. When he had finished, he wiped his hands on the seat of his shorts, and there was a little biscuit man with separate fingers, a hat on, and even a walking stick . . . it was a perfect little biscuit man, and, as a matter of fact, it reminded Frankie of John Henry himself" (263).

The task of making this biscuit man is not a particularly important one. It is, after all, a way for Berenice to occupy the children for a little while so that she can tend to her other duties in the kitchen. But it is a task that John Henry takes very seriously, one he studies over "like a tiny watchmaker" (263). And because of the care and attention he gives this task, he ends up creating something both strange and beautiful, a dandified "perfect little biscuit man." This strange and beautiful creation takes a very mundane scene—two young children, bored and hanging around a kitchen—and turns it into an event, into a spectacle: something of interest and beauty.

This is a small, strange example, but it is one that McCullers chose to highlight for a reason. She could have written something like, "they made biscuit men as they talked" if all she wanted to do was inform readers of what Frankie and John Henry were doing. But she did not do that. She includes the making of John Henry's strange but beautiful biscuit man—a biscuit man who "reminds Frankie of John Henry himself"—in order to show readers something important about John Henry. McCullers wants to make it clear that John Henry is different from other boys, but that his differentness is vitalizing, that it creates beauty and interest, even in "a sad and ugly" kitchen which has "a crazy look, like that of a room in the crazy-house" (259). The difference between John Henry's biscuit man and the kitchen is the difference between the two end points of the effeminate paradox: a crazy house (the kitchen) is a place that locks up those whose difference is deemed monstrous or threatening, but John Henry's work on the biscuit man models a means of being different that is fascinating and enriching. Rather than being bad or wrong, John Henry's biscuit man–making—and indeed, John Henry period—enacts a kind of "vitalizing difference." In her portrayals of sissy boys like Bubber and John Henry, McCullers flips the script by emphasizing effeminacy's capacity to fascinate and enliven. Her sissies are sympathetic, not scorned.

CAPOTE AND "THE FAIRY *HUCKELBERRY FINN*": REWRITING THE BAD BOY NOVEL

Published in 1948, just two years after *The Member of the Wedding*, Truman Capote's first novel, *Other Voices, Other Rooms*, is arguably the most sissified work of American literary fiction. In fact, George Davis, the fiction editor at *Mademoiselle*, called the book "the fairy *Huckleberry Finn*" (Clarke, *Capote* 158). While obviously intended as a homophobic and femme-phobic dismissal, Davis's comment is also apt: *Other Voices, Other Rooms* can indeed be read as a queer rewriting of the Bad Boy novel, the genre whose most canonized representative is *The Adventures of Huckleberry Finn*.

Before one even gets to the text itself, there is the kerfuffle caused by Capote's author photo. As Gary Richards explains, "When *Other Voices, Other Rooms* appeared, one suspected it was a text preoccupied with transgressive performances of gender even before reading the first pages" because the back of the dust-jacket carried "Harold Halma's soon-to-be-famous—or perhaps even infamous—photograph of the young Capote" (31). In the photograph, "[l]anguidly sprawled on an ornately carved Victorian setee, Capote turns a provocative, pouting face to the camera. His left hand holds a cigarette, while his right hand lies draped across his crotch, almost in a parody of Edouard Manet's *Olympia*. . . . almost all elements of Halma's photograph work to establish utter passivity: the resting hands, the inclined body, the head raised only with the support of the setee. . . . [the photograph is] a brazen performance of one of the most frequently recurring gay types: the passive, effeminate, foppish gay man" (Richards 32). The story of gender nonconformity told so brazenly by Capote's author photo—which Capote himself urged his editor to use (Richards 31)—sets the mood, tone, and subject matter of the novel to come.

Other Voices, Other Rooms is a coming of age story centered on thirteen-year-old Joel Harrison Knox. At the opening of the novel, Joel is in the midst of a transition: while he has been living in New Orleans with his deceased mother's relations, he has recently been summoned—by a mysterious letter—to the home of his father. Joel has never met his father before, and the man lives on an estate called Skully's Landing, which is a good ways outside of Noon City, Louisiana, an extremely small, rural, and isolated town.

The novel opens in the midst of Joel's journey to his new home, and from the first moment that Joel appears on the page, Capote goes out of his way to emphasize Joel's effeminacy. Joel, mid-voyage to his new home, has spent the night in Paradise City, Louisiana, and is now looking for a ride to Noon City and to Skully's Landing beyond that. Readers' first look at Joel is from the point of view of Sam Radclif, "a big balding six-footer with a rough, manly face" who drives a truck that routinely passes through Noon City (4). As Radclif looks at Joel, he realizes that he is "not caring much for the looks of him [Joel]" (4). Radclif has "his notions of what a 'real' boy should look like, and this kid somehow offended them. He [Joel] was too pretty, too delicate and fair-skinned; each of his features was shaped with a sensitive accuracy, and a girlish tenderness softened his eyes, which were brown and very large" (4). Joel's voice is also "uncommonly soft," and another man tells Radclif that Joel is "[s]mart as a whip. Knows words you and me never heard of" (5).

Too pretty, too delicate, too fair-skinned, too soft-voiced, and with an apparent love of book-learning: Capote portrays Joel as the living, breathing textbook example of a sissy, which Grant defines as "a pale-faced neurasthenic aristocrat, with curly locks and immaculate dress" (832). Joel, who in this first scene is wearing "long, wrinkled white linen breeches, a limp blue shirt, the collar of which was open at the throat, and rather scuffed tan shoes," fits Grant's description perfectly: the fact that his pants are wrinkled and his shoes are scuffed just serves to underscore how ill-adapted he is to rough and tumble Paradise Chapel (5). Joel is also carrying a "huge tin suitcase" that is "colorful with faded souvenir stickers from remote parts of the globe," which serves to emphasize Joel's foreignness, the sense that he is too rich and too delicate and too foreign to really belong in rural Louisiana (6). Radclif's comment to Joel that "if I was your Pa I'd take down your britches and muss you up a bit" helps to reinforce the sense that Joel is an ill-fitting outsider, both in Paradise Chapel and to hegemonic masculinity itself (9). It also signals that there is something so non-normative about Joel's gender performance that it evokes near-violent phobic reactions from more heteronormatively masculine men such as Radclif. As the novel continues, this initial impression of Joel-as-sissy is confirmed, not challenged. As Richards explains, "Joel's activities and mannerisms are no less effeminate than his appearance, and he repeatedly behaves as a stereotypical girl. He carries a change purse rather than a wallet, neatly organizes his possessions, devours Hollywood movie magazines, whimpers, blushes violently, and cries out of homesickness" (38). Other characters notice these effeminate traits, and Idabel Thompkins, the extremely masculine girl who becomes Joel's neighbor at Skully's Landing, even mocks Joel for them, telling him to "[g]o on home and cut out paper-dolls, sissy-britches" (109).

Late nineteenth- and early twentieth-century boy workers felt that it was crucial to intervene in the lives of boys when they were young and could still be put on the path toward a "correct" masculinity. Similarly, *Other Voices, Other Rooms* also suggests that Joel, at age 13, is rapidly coming to a crossroads. As a coming of age story, the novel's central preoccupation is with what kind of man Joel will mature into. And because Capote goes to such great lengths to foreground and emphasize Joel's effeminacy, *Other Voices, Other Rooms* becomes an effeminate coming-of-age story: will Joel ditch his sissy ways and grow up to be the kind of man that will not offend the hyper-masculine Sam Radclifs of the world? Or will his effeminacy be allowed to continue unchecked? And if so, what kind of a man does an extremely effeminate boy become?

If Joel is a boy in need of normatively masculine role models, he certainly finds no such men at the Landing. After arriving, Joel soon discovers that his father is paralyzed and bedridden, unable to speak more than a few words and forced to drop a tennis ball down the stairs when he needs assistance or companionship. Joel, who had imagined many different ways that his father might be, never imagined this: "If only he'd never seen Mr. Sansom! Then he could have gone on picturing him as looking this and that wonderful way, as talking in a kind strong voice, as being really his father. Certainly this Mr. Sansom was not his father. This Mr. Sansom was nobody but a pair of crazy eyes" (171).

With Joel convinced that his biological father is a disappointing nonentity, the only remaining adult male role model for Joel at Skully's Landing is Cousin Randolph. And Cousin Randolph is perhaps not so much of a man at all. As Richards rightly says, "Capote establishes Randolph's effeminacy to excess" (35). Randolph, "[l]ike the foppish Capote of Halma's photograph," is "soft and curvaceous rather than hard and linear" (Richards 35). He wears "breezy kimonos and sandals, androgynous items with few connotations of masculinity" and "[e]ven when the clothing is removed or inadvertently opened, it reveals an insistently feminized body. . . . Like his face, Randolph's torso has virtually no hair, stock cultural designation of virility, and readers thus confront a body conspicuously lacking male secondary characteristics" (Richards 35). Randolph is also a cross-dresser: from time to time he dresses up as an aristocratic eighteenth-century woman, complete with towering wig and full make-up. Randolph does not openly discuss his cross-dressing, but one day Joel stands on the lawn below and looks up into Randolph's room, where he sees "a queer lady. . . . holding aside the curtains of the left corner window, and smiling and nodding at him, as if in greeting or approval" (67). This "queer lady" is Randolph in full drag, but not understanding this, Joel becomes convinced that there is a strange woman living in the house that only he sees and no one else talks about.

While Randolph's cross-dressing is not discussed, Randolph is quite open with Joel about his (Randolph's) homosexuality. Declaring that "love, having no geography, knows no boundaries," Randolph tells Joel that "any love is natural and beautiful that lies within a person's nature" (147). Randolph then recounts the story of his love for Pepe Alvarez, a hypermasculine Latino boxer whom Randolph loved despite—or perhaps because of?—the fact that Pepe frequently called Randolph "horrible hurting names," willfully destroyed Randolph's paintings, and once broke Randolph's nose (149). And while Joel still does not realize that the "queer lady" he has seen is Randolph in drag, Randolph reveals that for a Mardi Gras ball costume one year he dressed up as "a Countess" with "silver hair and satin slippers, a green mask," his body "wrapped in silk pistachio and pink" (150). This transformation first "horrifies" Randolph and then "pleases [him] to rapture," because he finds himself-as-Countess to be "very beautiful" (150). Later, at the ball itself, Pepe—who does not recognize Randolph and thinks that he is a biological woman—asks Randolph to dance: "[A]nd I, oh sly Cinderella," Randolph tells Joel as he recounts the story, "[I] smile beneath my mask, thinking: Ah, if I were really me! Toad into prince, tin into gold" (150). The romantic and gendered patterns of Randolph's life are thus made clear to Joel: Randolph is effeminate and gay, and he lusts for non-white men like Pepe, whose non-whiteness Randolph figures as a hypermasculinity. And hypermasculine men, of course, have no interest in effeminate men, and so Randolph's greatest romantic successes have come via his ability to dress in drag and pass as a biological woman.

Once Randolph appears, Joel likes him immediately, feeling "very much at ease with Randolph, who, at each conversational lag, introduced topics which might interest and flatter a boy of thirteen" such as "Are Headhunters Still Active? and other controversial subjects" (75). But later, when Randolph compliments Joel and asks him to "[t]ry and be happy here, try a little to like me, will you?," it gives Joel "an uneasy feeling" (86). And when Randolph takes Joel's hand, the "lady's ring" that Randolph wears, "a smoky rainbow opal clasped by sharp silver prongs" hurts Joel as it "pressed painfully between Joel's knuckles" (85). The pain described here is physical, but it comes from a woman's ring that Randolph is wearing; Capote implies that Randolph's effeminacy causes Joel psychic pain and discomfort.

Over time, this discomfort grows, and Joel struggles to distance himself from both the general weirdness of Skully's Landing and its inhabitants, as well as the specific threatening weirdness of Randolph's effeminacy. One means of metaphorical "escape" that Joel tries is the embrace of heterosexuality. While out playing in the woods, Joel and Idabel end up getting naked and bathing in a creek. While this seems like what would—in a typical coming-of-age novel—be the start of a scene where a young boy becomes initiated into the world of heterosexual desire, things do not turn out that way. While Joel feels embarrassed about getting naked in front of Idabel, she assures him that "what you've got in your britches is no news to me, and no concern of mine" (132); she also scolds him, saying that she does not think "like I'm a girl" and that Joel must "remember that, or we can't never be friends" (132). Despite Idabel's attempts to shut down any heterosexual romance, Joel still tries to play the role of heterosexual boy and,"with breathtaking delicacy" he "kissed her [Idabel's] cheek" (134). But rather than bringing about a scene of redemptive heterosexual love, the action provokes Idabel's rage. She pulls Joel's hair painfully, and the two end up in a physical altercation, one that she easily wins.

Having failed to initiate—much less complete—a heterosexual physical encounter, Joel later tries, and fails, to fulfill the role of the active, fearless, devil-may-care real boy. During another encounter in the woods, Joel and Idabel come across an "old forsaken mill" where "a heavy but rotting beam" spans the length of a creek (178). Idabel and Joel decide to try and cross the beam. Idabel, knowing how timid Joel usually is, says that she'd "better go first" since the beam is "pretty old and liable to bust" (179). But this sparks something in Joel: he "pushed in front of her" because "after all, no matter what Idabel said, he was a boy and she was a girl and he was damned if she were going to get the upper hand again" (179). Scared to cross the rotting beam but more scared of being out-manned by a girl, Joel attempts to cross. But part of the way over, he sees a huge snake, "a cotton-mouth thick as his leg, long as a whip" (179). The sight of this snake paralyzes Joel with fear; "all over" he "began to sting, as though already bitten," and Idabel is forced to come to his rescue (180). Although Joel has an actual sword in his hand—a Civil War–era relic given to him by Zoo, the African American domestic worker at Skully's Landing—Joel is unable to play the role of the heroic, brave real boy. He is frozen in place and it is Idabel who moves Joel "safely behind her" and uses Joel's sword to slap the snake off of the beam and down into the water below (180).

Around the same time that Joel fails so spectacularly at being a real boy, his relationship with Randolph is becoming more fraught.

Although Joel initially felt comfortable with Randolph, the more time Joel spends with him, the more he feels that Randolph says things "in such a funny way," a way that Joel cannot comprehend (139). Joel tells Randolph about his misgivings at the start of the scene where Randolph eventually confesses his homosexuality to Joel. The context thus implies that Randolph speaks "in a funny way" because Randolph is "funny," that is, because he is effeminate and gay. Randolph, for his part, is not offended in the slightest by Joel's comment. "[A]ll difficult music must be heard more than once," he tells Joel. "And if what I tell you now sounds senseless, it will in retrospect seem far too clear" (139). What Randolph goes on to tell Joel is that Randolph is gay and that he cross-dressed in order to seduce Pepe. And so while the meaning of Randolph's words is not clear at the time to Joel, they are clear enough to readers. Randolph's speech has the "difficult music" of homosexuality and effeminacy, and while Joel cannot understand that difficult music now, Randolph prophesizes that he (Joel) will someday. In his coded way, Randolph is suggesting here that one day Joel will be like him, that is, will be effeminate and gay.

Presented, then, with two masculine role models who fail to be hegemonically masculine—Randolph is gay and hyper-effeminate, while Joel's biological father is paralyzed and helpless—Joel finally attempts to escape them both by running away from Skully's Landing. He and Idabel—who has had a falling out with her own family—take off together one night, planning to never return. But this literal escape attempt fails just as badly as Joel's two previous metaphorical escapes (into heterosexuality and physically active/brave "real" boy-dom) did before it. The pair make it into Noon City, where a carnival is going on, but Joel remains isolated and lonely: "[N]ot a soul spoke to him, he was no part of them, they did not know him" (189). The person who does speak to Joel and Idabel is not a townsperson, but Miss Wisteria, one of the performers in the freak show that is part of the traveling carnival. A "midget" who "claimed to be twenty-five years old," Miss Wisteria initially delights Joel, who cannot quite believe that she is an adult, since she looks so much like "a darling little girl" (191).

Despite her size, Miss Wisteria is indeed an adult, and has adult sexual desires. Having "never . . . found a sweet little person" to take as a mate, Miss Wisteria fixates on young boys, who are her size, and cries "sometimes to think that little boys must grow tall" (195). When she and Joel take a ride together on the carnival's Ferris wheel, Joel finds out that Miss Wisteria's affection for young boys is not merely platonic. When their compartment is stopped at the top of the Ferris wheel, Miss Wisteria "placed her hand on his [Joel's] thigh, and then, as though she had no control over them whatsoever, her fingers crept up inside his legs," an act that leaves Joel feeling "disturbed" (195). In fact, Capote essentially cuts away from the narrative at this point. Instead of showing readers what exactly Miss Wisteria is doing to Joel, Capote has Joel's thoughts spin off into a rambling, poetic monologue about loneliness and love. This narrative turning away, combined with Joel's stated feeling of "disturbed" leaves little doubt that Joel finds this sexual encounter with Miss Wisteria to be traumatic. Earlier, when Joel attempted to initiate heterosexual sexual contact with Idabel, that encounter ended in failure. Now, with Miss Wisteria, Joel's second sexual encounter with someone of the opposite gender takes a turn to the exploitative and traumatic.

Miss Wisteria's molestation is clearly a defining event for Joel, one that propels his eventual turn away from both heterosexuality and hegemonically masculine gender performance. While at the top of the Ferris wheel, Joel looks down, sees a man, and imagines that the man is Randolph, come to drag Joel back to the Landing. Joel fears that he will "never rid himself" of Randolph and worries that "[v]ine from the Landing's garden had stretched these miles to entwine his wrists" (197). After exiting the Ferris wheel, Joel—looking for Idabel and trying to flee Miss Wisteria—ends up walking into an abandoned house which local kids believe to be haunted. Miss Wisteria follows Joel into the house, calling out, "Little boy, little boy," in a "whimper of despair" (199). She is looking for Joel in the hopes that their sexual encounter can continue. But Joel decides that it "did not matter now if Randolph found him, he would welcome it" (199) because Miss Wisteria's cries make Joel realize that "he dared not show himself, for what she wanted he could not give" (200). What Miss Wisteria wants, of course, is more sexual contact with Joel. And what Joel has realized is that he cannot give that to her, because he cannot be heterosexual. And because he cannot be heterosexual, it does not matter if Randolph finds him. In fact, Joel has stopped running from Randolph and all that he represents.

The third and final part of *Other Voices, Other Rooms* focuses almost exclusively on Joel and Randolph, and the former's acceptance of the fact that he will grow up to be like the latter. Caught in a rainstorm at the carnival, Joel contracts a serious case of the flu, and Randolph nurses him through a long convalescence. As Joel slides in and out of fever-ridden consciousness, "[a]n unrecognized voice quarreled with him, teased, taunted, revealed secrets he'd scarcely made known to himself" (206). These secrets are Joel's homosexuality and effeminacy. Randolph is there at Joel's bedside, kissing him and calling him "my darling" as he wakes up (207). And as Joel comes back to full consciousness, the long weeks and months of his recovery reveal that he has become more like Randolph on a physical level. As he lies in bed, Joel studies his face with a mirror, "a disappointing exercise on the whole, for nothing he saw concretely affirmed his suspicions of emerging manhood" (207). Instead of a young man's face, Joel sees in the mirror "an alarming face" that is "too shrewd for a child" and "too beautiful for a boy" (207). So rather than shedding his effeminacy, Joel's body seems to be embracing it, his adult features becoming "beautiful" rather than handsome. Additionally, Joel seems to welcome this change. In fact, "all that displeased him" about his new, more adult face "was the brown straightness of his hair. He wished it were curly gold like Randolph's" (207). Curly blond hair on boys is, of course, one of the signature signs of the sissy.

Joel also seems to have embraced his effeminacy on a mental or linguistic level as well. Whereas Joel once thought Randolph talked "funny," and failed to understand him, Joel now feels that the "mist which for him overhung so much of Randolph's conversation, even that had lifted, as least it was no longer troubling, for it seemed as though he [Joel] understood him [Randolph] absolutely" (208). Randolph's earlier prophecy has come true: the "difficult music" of Randolph's effeminate and gay speech is no longer confusing or off-putting to Joel, precisely because Joel is moving toward accepting his own homosexuality and effeminacy. Joel still sees Randolph as being "[f]aceted as a fly's eye, being neither man nor woman, and one whose every identity cancelled the other, a grab-bag of disguises" and asks himself, "[W]ho, what was Randolph?" (211). Earlier in the novel, Joel may not have had an answer to that question. But now thinks that Randolph is "an outline in which with crayon you color in the character, the ideal hero: whatever his role, it is pitched by you into existence. Indeed, try to conceive of him alone, unseen, unheard, and he becomes invisible, he is not to be imagined. But [those] such as Randolph justify fantasy, and if a genii should appear, certainly Joel would have asked that these sealed days [of his recovery, with Randolph at his bedside] continue through a century of calendars" (211).

In this passage Joel is working out, for himself, why Randolph is valuable and important even though—or, perhaps, because—he lies outside of so-called "normal" systems of sex and gender. In Joel's eyes Randolph is neither male nor female, but this is okay, because Randolph provides a spectacle. Or, more accurately, Randolph is a spectacle. This is why Joel cannot imagine Randolph existing "alone, unseen, unheard." In Joel's eyes, Randolph always demands an audience, in fact, needs an audience to exist. Randolph is a one-man—and sometimes, one-woman—show, one in which onlookers can project their fantasies of possibilities beyond narrow, normative definitions of proper sexual behavior and so-called normative gender roles. Randolph is thus one who can "justify fantasy." Joel, raised in a culture that proclaims real boys and the active, heterosexual men they grow up to become as both normal and worthy of praise, rejects that conception of heroism and sees the hyper-effeminate, sexually passive Randolph as "the ideal hero," as someone neither male nor female but heroic because of his capacity to perform either role or both roles.

The novel ends with Joel fully embracing Randolph as his role model, as the shape of Joel's future Or, more specifically, the novel ends with Joel embracing The Countess, Randolph's drag alter-ego, as the shape of his future. This is because toward the end of the novel, watching Randolph struggle to walk through the woods, Joel realizes "how helpless Randolph was: more paralyzed than Mr. Sansom, more childlike than Miss Wisteria" (227). In contrast, Joel recognizes that "I am me" and that, unlike Randolph, "he knew that he was strong" (228).

And so while Joel seemingly rejects Randolph the man as helpless, he embraces Randolph's feminine persona, The Countess, whom he sees as a powerful figure. The novel closes with a scene of Joel wandering around the garden at Skully's Landing, thinking that "something had happened; or was about to" (231). Joel then stands and looks up into the Landing's windows. There he sees that "someone was watching him. . . . And it was Randolph's window" (231). This person watching from Randolph's window is, of course, Randolph in drag as The Countess. Her "face trembled like a white beautiful moth, smiled," and she "beckoned to him [Joel], shining and silver, and he knew he must go" (231). The novel closes with Joel heeding this call and walking up to Randolph's room, where he will greet Randolph as The Countess for the first time. As Joel goes, he does so "unafraid, not hesitating, he paused only at the garden's edge where, as though he'd forgotten something, he stopped and looked back at the bloomless, descending blue, at the boy he'd left behind" (231). While Joel may have rejected Randall as weak, he is unable to resist the siren's song of The Countess. The novel closes with Joel heading toward her, an act that Joel himself understands to mean that Joel has left his boyhood behind. Leaving boyhood behind is, of course, a standard trope of adolescent boy coming-of-age stories. But, typically, boyhood is left behind for adult heterosexual masculinity. Here, in sharp contrast, boyhood is left behind for homosexuality and hyper-effeminacy, for a kind of drag that—if Randolph's description of his Countess costume fooling Pepe are to be believed—is indistinguishable from biological womanhood.

Thus, while the protagonists of Bad Boy novels flee from femininity and resist it at all cost, *Other Voices, Other Rooms*—"the fairy *Huckleberry Finn*"—inverts that script and documents a boy's at-first-reluctant and then finally willing and enthusiastic journey from boyhood to femininity (and homosexuality). Capote makes it clear that Joel is "unafraid, not hesitating" as he makes this choice. Contrary to popular discourses of American boyhood, effeminacy is not, for Joel, a failed state, a punishment, or a curse. In fact, the more feminine the better: Joel rejects Randolph as helpless, but The Countess is enchanting to him. And as Randolph's own story about the uses of his drag persona make clear, The Countess has power, specifically the power to captivate and seduce hyper-masculine men like Pepe Alvarez. *Other Voices, Other Rooms* thus rewrites the status of effeminacy and emphasizes fascinating effeminacy by framing effeminacy as a source of power, a means of accessing agency.

SYMPATHETIC SISSIES & THE LIMITS OF FASCINATION

While use of fascinating effeminacy opens up desperately needed psychic space by redefining effeminacy as a position of worth (McCullers) and/or power (Capote), it also clearly has problematic elements. Capote's account of effeminacy, for example, always equates effeminacy with male homosexuality. As Richards rightly notes, "Capote holds male same-sex desire and gender transitivity to be mutually and exclusively indicative of one another and crucial to structuring an inescapable gay identity. Gay men are effeminate; effeminate men are gay" (31). This means that Capote's work does nothing to challenge this long-standing associative linkage.

Capote's version of effeminacy also verges very close to simply being the feminine role within sexist systems of heteronormativity. That is, The Countess gives Randolph power because it is only when he is in drag as The Countess that Randolph can attract and hold the attention of hypermasculine men such as Pepe Alvarez. The power Randolph is able to access in drag is the limited and temporally fleeting power allowed to women under even the most sexist, heteronormative regimes: the ability to gain self-worth and exercise power by using one's physical looks to attract a more physically dominant mate. Furthermore, by having Joel reject Randolph but embrace The Countess, Capote's version of fascinating effeminacy threatens to leave intact a strict, and heterosexist, male-female binary—the very same binary that results in the strict censure of effeminate boys in the first place. This is because Capote's version of effeminate power is The Countess, the image of a man in drag of such quality that he may convincingly pass as a woman. This veers close to Capote simply suggesting that effeminate gay men are women or that gay men should at least become women if they ever want to access power for themselves.

In his reading of *Other Voices, Other Rooms*, Richards criticizes Capote for suggesting that "gay identity is contingent upon an inversion of gender in which performances of femininity take precedence over those of masculinity" (61); Richards also compares *Other Voices, Other Rooms* unfavorably to William Goyen's 1950 novel *The House of Breath*, which he (Richards) suggests provides space for both feminine and masculine gay men. As my comments above make clear, I think that Richards is right to fault Capote on this point: Capote's novel does fail to imagine a world in which both effeminate straight men and masculine gay men are possible. That said, I think Richards is a bit harsh to Capote. He uses Capote's novel as foil for, a negative counterexample to, Goyen's novel. And in comparison, Capote's novel does suffer.

But given the incredible degree to which effeminacy had been figured as the threatening grotesque in US culture prior to 1948, I do still think there is something valuable and important in Capote's emphasis of effeminacy as the fascinating grotesque in *Other Voices, Other Rooms*. It is true that the economy of sex/gender roles articulated in *Other Voices, Other Rooms* is not completely free or equitable; in the novel, gay men must be effeminate, and straight men must be hypermasculine. But Capote was publishing at a time when effeminacy was seen, almost universally in mainstream US culture, as threat: pathetic at best, monstrous at worse. And while Capote's novel does not provide a great range of gender presentations to men wishing to assume a gay identity, it does—counter to much US cultural discourse at the time—re-frame effeminacy as something positive, as a means by which gay men can become both powerful and fascinating. So while it does suggest that all gay men must be effeminate, it also suggests that effeminacy might in fact be something desirable. In that sense, it opens up more imaginative possibilities for queer identity than Richards gives it credit for, although the specific type of queerness it opens new space for is queerness of gender presentation (effeminacy's meaning is rewritten), not queerness of sexuality (gay men are still assumed to always and only be effeminate).

While his version of fascinating effeminacy may be a mixed bag, Capote is at least willing to explore what happens when effeminate boys mature into adulthood. *Other Voices, Other Rooms* gestures to the fact that Joel may one day soon be sexually active. In contrast, McCullers's major sissy characters are boys, and they remain boys, either because they vanish from the scene or die, at least in her fiction from the 1940s. It is not until her last novel, *Clock Without Hands* (1961), that McCullers can write an effeminate teenage boy who, by the close of the novel, has evaded both psychic diminishment and physical death and seems poised to mature into an effeminate gay man. This character is Jester Clane, whom an observer describes by saying, "There was something hidden about the boy and his softness, his brightness seemed somehow dangerous—it was as though he resembled a silk-sheathed knife" (23). It takes McCullers twenty-one years to move from the small but sympathetic portrait of Bubber Kelly and his diminishment in *The Heart Is a Lonely Hunter*, to Jester Clane being "a silk-sheathed knife," an image that provocatively blends effeminacy (silk) and power (the knife). Prior to Jester, McCullers had been sympathetic to sissy boys but had also consistently portrayed them as helpless victims, unable to mount any kind of resistance to a world that actively worked for their erasure.

In emphasizing the limits of McCullers's use of sympathetic sissies, my reading of her work both somewhat agrees with and somewhat diverges from that of Sarah Gleeson-White, author of the most recent single-author, book-length study of McCullers's fiction. In *Strange Bodies: Gender and Identity in the Novels of Carson McCullers* (2003), Gleeson-White argues that McCullers's recurring use of freak/oddball/outcast characters is not—as many previous critics have argued—a symbolic representation of a universal "alienating (and sexually indifferent) human condition," but should instead be read as McCullers's serious engagement with "issues of subjectivity in the material realms of gender and sexuality" (3). I agree with this and also agree with Gleeson-White's assertion that McCullers's texts employ "Mikhail Bakhtin's concept of the grotesque, which is at once both affirming and revolutionary" (1).

But my reading of McCullers diverges from Gleeson-White on the issue of how optimistic McCullers does or does not remain about the queer potential of her grotesque characters. Gleeson-White does not specifically address McCullers's sissy boy supporting characters, but in a chapter that focuses on Mick from *The Heart Is a Lonely Hunter* and Frankie from *The Member of the Wedding*, Gleeson-White says previous critics are wrong to have read those characters' "plight at the end of their respective stories as a victory of socialization" (33). That is, Gleeson-White argues that we should not read those two novels not as stories about the ways in which queer or proto-queer adolescents are "forced to surrender to the confines of conformity, to a restricted identity, as they take up the appropriate socially assigned roles of womanliness" (33). Gleeson-White contends that a careful reading of the endings of both novels reveals that "creative adolescent subjectivity"—the kind of subjectivity that imagines possibilities outside of a rigid male/masculine, female/feminine binary—survives into adulthood (35). Mick and Frankie both live to adulthood, and in Gleeson-White's reading, the queer possibilities of their identity are not wholly crushed or exterminated; Mick and Frankie represent the Bakhtinian grotesque and thus "point to the possibility of transformation or lines of flight" (37).

Gleeson-White is absolutely correct to suggest that McCullers's fiction is about the specificities of gender and identity, and to reclaim it from readings that characterize it as being about some vague, de-sexualized and de-gendered notion of "alienation." But I worry that Gleeson-White's reading is overly optimistic. In a rush to claim McCullers's fiction as a body of texts that might serve as a road map for a wholesale, queer-affirmative transformation of the heteronormative status quo, she overlooks and under-emphasizes the degree to which McCullers's fiction is, very often, about recognizing—and mourning—the shunning, shaming, and silencing of queer youth.

Gleeson-White's reading also puts a great deal of emphasis on the future and on the imagined adulthood of McCullers's queer adolescent protagonists. McCullers's fiction, Gleeson-White seems to say, can be read as radical/transformational (in a queer affirmative sense) if we can arrive at a reading of it that proves that Frankie and Mick's queerness survives into adulthood. An odd side effect of this approach is that it prioritizes queerness in adulthood. In Gleeson-White's reading, queerness only seems to count or matter or last if it survives into adulthood. This is why she highlights Frankie's crush on a female classmate (as proof that McCullers preserves Frankie's queerness into adulthood) and why she downplays John Henry's death, mentioning it only in passing. But why is queerness illegitimate or unreal when it occurs in children? McCullers's use of fascinating effeminacy suggests that queer gender performance is both real and powerful when it occurs in children. As McCullers depicts them, Bubber and John Henry's lives are not queer seeds lying dormant, waiting to flower when the boys reach adulthood. It is not that Bubber and John Henry *will be* queer; it is that they are queer already. They are queer now, their queerness is valuable, and the silencing/erasure of their queer gender performances is already a loss for their respective communities; a loss in the present, not just a loss for the future. In evaluating McCullers's work, both Frankie's survival/crush on a female classmate and John Henry's painful death need to be taken into account. Gleeson-White may well be right that some of McCullers's queer adolescent protagonists survive—with their queerness intact—to adulthood. But her work also contains many cautionary tales, many examples of how queer children and adolescents do not survive. Surely, as critics, we can both point to the hints of queer adulthood/future that McCullers provides readers, while also acknowledging that her work both dramatizes and mourns and rages against the destruction of what Segrest calls "vitalizing" queer difference in the present (which, in McCullers, almost always means in childhood/adolescence).

Against a huge tide of both rhetoric and representation that depicted the sissy as lack/failure/horror/pathetic-ness/monstrosity, McCullers and Capote found their own ways to assert a counter-narrative, to suggest an alternative mode of thinking about the sissy, one which insisted that he was valuable, worthy of both praise and preservation. In their individual acts of sympathy for the sissy, they provided a starting point for later authors interested in non-traditional accounts of what exactly effeminacy might mean. In doing so, they paved the way for other, later modes of fascinating effeminacy—such as James Baldwin's Truth-Telling Queens and Tony Kushner's Healing Queens—in which sissies are seen as an empowered, empowering, and vitally necessary part of their communities.

TWO

THE STRAIGHT-ACTING GAY MAN VERSUS THE TRUTH-TELLING QUEEN

GORE VIDAL, JAMES BALDWIN, AND GAY MEN'S DEBATES ABOUT EFFEMINACY

Eight years separate the publication of Gore Vidal's *The City and the Pillar* (1948) and James Baldwin's *Giovanni's Room* (1956), but the novels have a great deal in common. Both tell the story of a white American man who serves in the Army, travels widely, and comes to realize that he is sexually attracted to men. In both novels, the protagonist experiences a deep and lasting attraction to another man, and in both cases this attraction ends disastrously. In the original 1948 edition of *The City and the Pillar*, Jim Willard murders Bob Ford, the man he has loved since high school, when Bob rejects his sexual advances; in the revised edition of 1965, Jim rapes Bob instead of murdering him.[1] And David, the protagonist of *Giovanni's Room*, denies his love for the Italian bartender Giovanni, an act that sends Giovanni into a downward spiral that ends with Giovanni's execution for murder. Another similarity these texts share—one that is crucial to understanding why these stories of same-sex love end horrifically—is that both Vidal and Baldwin choose to center their novels around what was, at mid-twentieth century, a new social type: the masculine gay man.

Historian George Chauncey argues that "the hetero-homosexual binarism, the sexual regime now hegemonic in American culture"—wherein the gender of one's sexual partner is presumed to constitute proof of an inner quality called sexuality, which is either heterosexual, homosexual, or bisexual—"is a stunningly recent creation" that came into existence only in the middle decades of the twentieth century (13). Prior to it, there was an older regime—dating to at least the 1890s in New York City, especially among the working class—in which a man's gender performance, not the gender of his sexual partner(s), determined whether he was understood to be normal or abnormal.[2]

Under this older classification regime, men could have sex with men and remain ostensibly normal in the eyes of wider society so long as they conformed to masculine codes of dress, styling, and bodily comportment, and were careful to only take the ostensibly "active" (penetrative) role in sex with other men. Men who took the ostensibly "passive" (penetrated) role in sex with other men were known as fairies. According to Chauncey, masculine-appearing men could have certain kinds of sexual contact with fairies and not be seen as abnormal or unmanly. Gender performance was what mattered in terms of "defining the deviant," not sexual object choice (Chauncey 22).

What Chauncey calls "[t]he ascendancy of *gay*"—first as a code word for homosexual, and later as the name for an identity—"reflected, then, a reorganization of sexual categories and the transition from an early twentieth century culture divided into 'queers' and 'men' on the basis of gender status to a late-twentieth-century culture divided into 'homosexuals' and 'heterosexuals' on the basis of sexual object choice" (22, emphasis Chauncey's). Furthermore, Chauncey points out that the transition from one system of classification to the next was hardly instantaneous, smooth or final: "[T]he transition from one sexual regime to the next was an uneven process, marked by significant class and ethnic differences. Multiple systems of sexual classification coexisted throughout the period in New York's divergent neighborhood cultures" (13–14).[3]

So while the gay man—who can have any kind of sexual contact with other men and retain a masculine gender performance—may seem more familiar to contemporary readers than the fairies Chauncey describes, it is important to remember that he was a new social type at mid-century. Prior to "the ascendancy of *gay*" in the 1930s–1950s, male-male sexual relations generally required one partner to have a feminine gender performance. "The ascendancy of *gay*" changed this. When a fairy and a man had sexual contact, both partners were biologically male, but only one (the man) was seen as having a masculine gender performance; in a sexual encounter between two gay men, both partners maintained a masculine gender presentation. This change resulted in "a masculinization" of the culture shared by men who desired men: "Jeans, T-shirts, leather jackets, and boots became more common in the 1940s, part of the 'new virile look' of young homosexuals. Increasing numbers of conventionally masculine men identified themselves as gay, in part, because doing so no longer seemed to require the renunciation of their masculine identities. Many gay men still considered themselves 'sissies,' but it was no longer as necessary for them to do so, and growing numbers adopted a self-consciously masculine style" (Chauncey 358). Vidal and Baldwin's protagonists are both representatives of this new type, the masculine gay man, and the debates staged within both *The City and the Pillar* and *Giovanni's Room* serve as a crisp reminder that while postwar US culture has long conflated effeminacy and male homosexuality (so that the two are seen to be co-extant, one serving as proof of the other and vice versa), US gay men themselves have long debated the relationship between, and relative values of, homosexuality and effeminacy.

As I will demonstrate in close readings below, both Vidal and Baldwin consistently emphasize their respective protagonists' masculinity and make it clear that their protagonists are repulsed by effeminate men. Jim Willard, a tennis jock who prides himself on routinely being mistaken for straight, sees effeminate gay men as "strange womanish creatures" (66).[4] David is an army veteran who sleeps with both women and men but finds that effeminate gay men "made me uneasy; perhaps in the same way that the sight of monkeys eating their own excrement turns some people's stomachs. They might not mind so much if monkeys did not—so grotesquely—resemble human beings" (27). To borrow a term from contemporary gay male discourse, we can say that both Jim and David are "straight-acting" gay men: gay men who appear and act masculine, who take pride in being different from heteronormative straight men only in the matter of their sexual object choice.

This term, "straight-acting," is my own application of an admittedly anachronistic term to Vidal and Baldwin's novels. It does not appear in either *The City and the Pillar* or *Giovanni's Room*, and I am not aware of either Vidal or Baldwin ever having used it in an interview. The precise origin of the term is difficult to date, but it does appear frequently in contemporary US gay male subculture, particularly in gay male personal ads, and has since at least the mid-1990s. As Dan Savage, an openly gay syndicated sex advice columnist and editor of Seattle's *The Stranger*, explained in 2005: "[I]n the personals in *The Village Voice, The Chicago Reader* and *The [San Francisco] Weekly*, almost every other boy seeking a boy winds up his ad with 'No fats, no femmes' or the truly appalling 'straight-acting, straight appearing.'" The main page of the website StraightActing.com, which was created in 2000, defines the term this way: "Just as people have preferences for the type of guys they like, for example, 'TALL men,' many of us have a preference for 'straight acting' men— Men [sic] that have very few effeminate traits but still like to get down with other men" (StraightActing.com).

In his study of the discourse of StraightActing.com, Jay Clarkson defines "a straight-acting gay identity" as being one "positioned in opposition to cultural stereotypes of gay men that conflate femininity with homosexuality" (192). This is notably not the same thing as contesting effeminacy's status as threat. The straight-acting gay man agrees that effeminacy is threat, and for that very reason he strives to distance himself from any association with effeminacy.

Far from being a mere subcultural curiosity, the straight-acting gay man is, for some scholars of sexuality, central to their understanding of contemporary male homosexuality. Eve Kosofsky Sedgwick points out that for many scholars of sexuality "what is presumed to define modern homosexuality 'as we understand it'" is the "straight-acting and -appearing gay male," a figure marked by his stark "gender intransitivity" (*Epistemology* 46). Debate has, of course, raged over the political implications of straight-acting gay identity. Is claiming to be, wanting to be, or wanting to be with a straight-acting gay man an ironic subversion of heteronormative norms or simply a reinscription of them?[5]

When read alongside one another, *The City and the Pillar* and *Giovanni's Room* illustrate how central effeminacy and issues of its meaning and value have been to gay male literary fiction in the United States, even in its early stages. Both novels focus on straight-acting gay male protagonists, but Vidal and Baldwin's authorial attitudes towards their protagonists—and their protagonist's views of effeminacy—vary greatly. *The City and the Pillar* relentlessly portrays effeminacy as threat and suggests that it is better for a gay man to be a murderer than a queen; *Giovanni's Room*, on the other hand, actually critiques the straight-acting gay man, suggesting that David's obsessive investment in maintaining an "immaculate" masculinity (untainted by femininity) is a primary source of the ruination that he inflicts on himself and on others (30). Structurally, Baldwin places this authorial critique of David firmly in the mouths of effeminate gay male characters that David himself has scorned, thereby employing fascinating effeminacy and suggesting—contrary to what David himself actually believes—that it is effeminate gay men, not straight-acting ones like David, who are truly rebellious and courageous. Published during a period when "gay" was a relatively new way of organizing and describing male same-sex desire, these novels both weigh in on the issue of what gay men's proper relationship to effeminacy should be; Vidal lauds the Straight-Acting Gay Man by suggesting that gay men should view effeminacy as threat and rejecting it in order to gain "normality," while Baldwin and his Truth-Telling Queens critique this stance as a type of immature madness, suggesting that effeminate gay men are the only gay men brave enough to live openly in both a homophobic wider world and a femme-phobic gay male subculture.

THE CITY AND THE PILLAR: THE STRAIGHT-ACTING GAY MAN VERSUS "STRANGE, WOMANISH CREATURES"

Although literary historians agree that *The City and the Pillar* is by no means the first American novel to focus on a portrayal of male-male desire,[6] they still afford it a special place in their histories of gay male publishing. The critical consensus is this: *The City and the Pillar* was not the first American novel about male-male desire, but a number of factors—its sexual explicitness, its sexually mature (and sexually active) protagonist, its author's celebrity status and literary reputation, and its sales figures—made it both remarkable and difficult for the mainstream reading public to ignore.[7]

Literary historians have also greatly emphasized the way in which the novel seeks to normalize homosexuality, to detach it from the associations with mental illness, sexual perversion, moral deficiency, and criminality that had stigmatized it in America since at least the 1930s.[8] Stephen Adams says that "Vidal committed the heresy of choosing a clean-cut all-American boy as his protagonist" and that, consequently, "the public were shocked by the projection of the sheer ordinariness of homosexuality" (17). James Levin concurs, saying that "[a] great achievement [of *The City and the Pillar*] was the first candid presentation of some scenes of the gay world . . . Earlier writers treated the public gay world as bizarre and exotic. Vidal minimizes the grotesque and emphasizes the ordinary . . . [Vidal presents a] more middle class, less frivolous public gay world [that] is far more likely to be one into which respectable men may venture" (76–77). Editorial material in *The Columbia Anthology of Gay Literature* also highlights the novel's normalizing impulse: "*The City and the Pillar* asserts that gay men are not women in disguise nor, indeed, even very special . . . Vidal's book carried the normalizing of homosexuality into respectable fiction and would in turn be the model for much of the normalizing fiction to follow" (Fone 690).

Vidal himself agrees with this literary historical consensus, saying repeatedly that the novel's intent was to normalize male homosexuality. In a 1974 interview he said, "Up until then [the novel's publication], homosexuality in literature was always exotic. I wanted to deal with an absolutely ordinary, all-American, lower-middle class young man and his world. To show the dead-on 'normality' of the homosexual experience" (Clarke, "The Art of Fiction" 39). Vidal also expressed this same idea in more sensationalistic terms in his Introduction to the revised 1965 edition: "Until [the novel's publication], American novels of 'inversion' dealt with transvestites or lonely bookish boys who married unhappily and pined for Marines. I broke that mold. My two lovers in this novel were athletes so drawn to the entirely masculine that, in the case of one, Jim Willard, the feminine was simply irrelevant to his passion to unite with his other half, Bob Ford" (xiii).

In the face of this critical and authorial consensus that *The City and the Pillar* was a landmark in normalizing male homosexuality, I want to pause for a moment, return to the book's two endings, and ask: What exactly is "normal" about being a murderer? Or a rapist? How does a book that presents a gay man as someone capable of either murdering or raping the man he loves come to be enshrined as a classic credited with doing the much-needed work of normalizing male homosexuality for mainstream, heterosexual readers?

The answer concerns the specific way in which Vidal seeks to normalize male homosexuality in the novel. As the emphasis he places on a clear opposition between "athletes so drawn to the entirely masculine" and "transvestites or lonely bookish boys" makes clear, *The City in the Pillar* attempts to normalize male homosexuality by detaching it from any association with effeminacy. Some critics have also copied Vidal's definitional move and assumed that normalizing male homosexuality must mean detaching it from effeminacy; remember, for example, that *The Columbia Anthology of Gay Literature* counts *The City and the Pillar* as a normalizing text precisely because it "asserts that gay men are not women in disguise" (Fone 690). And Levin's argument that Vidal's depiction of gay male subculture "minimizes the grotesque and emphasizes the ordinary . . . [presenting a] more middle class, less frivolous public gay world [that] is far more likely to be one into which respectable men may venture" also has a distinctly gendered subtext to it: the grotesque is often conflated with the feminine, and "respectable" middle-class men are not supposed to be "frivolous," another term often associated with the feminine (76–77).

Even a cursory reading of the novel provides ample evidence that Vidal deliberately constructed Jim Willard to be completely devoid of any hint of effeminacy. Jim is, after all, a high school jock, "popular because he was the school's tennis champion and all athletes were admired" (12). Even when Jim briefly assumes the feminized role of kept boy for closeted Hollywood film star Ronald Shaw, Vidal is careful to preserve Jim's masculinity. He does this by having Shaw tell Jim that "I also didn't think you could be made. You don't seem the type" to be seduced by another man, which makes Jim feel "pleased" (70). And after Shaw introduces Jim to L.A.'s underground gay male subculture, Jim maintains a psychic distance between himself and other gay men, whom he finds effeminate: "[Jim] made no connection between what he and Bob had done [the sex they have in high school] and what his new acquaintances did. Too many of them behaved like women. Often after he had been among them, he would study himself in the mirror to see if there was any trace of the woman in his face or manner; and he was always pleased that there was not. Finally, he decided that he was unique" (66). The worldview implied in this passage repeats itself throughout Jim's consciousness and throughout the novel: Jim values masculinity in himself and finds it attractive in other men.

For Jim, effeminacy is grotesque; it both captivates and repels: "[A]s Jim got more and more involved in [L.A.'s gay] world, he found himself fascinated by the stories they [effeminate gay men] told of their affairs with one another. He could not imagine himself doing the things they said they did. Yet he wanted to know about them, if only out of a morbid desire to discover how what had been so natural and complete for him could be so perfectly corrupted by these strange womanish creatures" (66). Effeminacy is, for Jim, a sign of weakness, an aberration, something unnatural. Jim, like most men in the United States, sees effeminacy as threat.

It thus comes as little surprise that Jim is attracted to the writer Paul Sullivan, whose masculinity sets him apart from the other gay men who attend Shaw's private parties. These effeminate gay men turn Jim off because "[s]exually they were obvious, unlike Sullivan who appeared perfectly normal" (81). Sullivan's apparent normality—that is to say his ability to not be effeminate—is a turn-on for Jim. As is the fact that Sullivan was "married once and divorced, an impressive achievement which explained why he was not like most of the sensitive young men who visited Shaw. Obscurely, Jim was glad" (81). And, indeed, Jim soon leaves Shaw for Sullivan.

Jim's hatred of effeminacy continues throughout the novel. Jim deems the vast majority of gay men he meets too effeminate and thinks of them disparagingly as "the league of dressmakers and decorators" (104). Later, in New York, Jim is introduced to Nicholas J. "Rolly" Rolloson, an effeminate gay man who is "heir to a notorious American fortune" and who has "two passions, modern art and the military" (157). When the two first meet, Rolly is wearing "a scarlet blazer with a crest" and despite being male has "breasts [that] jiggled beneath a pale yellow silk shirt" (158). Jim finds Rolly's handshake "predictably damp" (158) and in a later appearance Rolly wears "a light grey suit pulled in tightly at the waist, a mauve shirt gorgeously monogrammed, and a sea green crepe de chine ascot at his rosy throat" while "smelling of violets" and "wearing make-up" (175). These signs of femininity repulse Jim when they appear on a male body: "Rolly rather revolted Jim" (161).

As Jim spends more and more time in urban gay subcultures across America, he comes to realize that "for every one [man] who lived openly with men, there were ten who married, had children, lived a discreet, ordinary life, only occasionally straying into bars or Turkish baths, particularly at five o'clock, that hour between office and home when the need for relief is particularly urgent" (164). Unsurprisingly, it is these closeted, straight-acting men, not the Rollys of the world, that Jim is attracted to: "these masculine, rather tense men appealed to Jim, who disliked the other sort he met through Shaw . . . the bold homosexuals . . . he was repelled by the queens" (164). Indeed, Jim "most liked the innocents who would say the next morning, 'Gee, I was sure drunk last night!' and pretend not to remember what had happened" (182). Even though "[f]urtive encounters with young married men seldom lead to anything" resembling a lasting relationship, Jim prefers these encounters to a life lived fully within a city's gay community (164).

This is because Jim's extreme loathing of effeminacy makes life in such a community impossible for him: "For a time, he hoped that if he saw enough of the queens, he might begin to like their society and be happy in it. But this was not possible . . . Jim dropped out of the gay world, preferring to haunt those bars where he could find young men like himself" (164). Gay, for Jim, means effeminacy. It means the Rollys of the world, the "strange womanish creatures." And for Jim, effeminacy is doubly cursed: it is a turn-off in other men and impermissible in himself. This doubled prohibition is so strong that Jim continues to heed it, even when doing so makes him an outcast in all possible worlds; he is too gay for the straight world, but the gay world is, for Jim, too effeminate to be habitable.

It is important to remember that Chauncey's scholarship suggests that many mid-century men adopted the term "gay" because it was a more masculine alternative to "fairy" or "sissy." But even this is not good enough for Jim. He also works to distinguish his own desires from those other gay men. During his original and idyllic sexual encounter with Bob in high school, Jim looks at Bob's body and "felt as if he were looking at an ideal brother, a twin, and he was content" (24).[9] Once Jim grows older and experiences gay urban subcultures, he takes this twin brother ideal even further. He comes to feel that "the idea of being in love with a man was both ludicrous and unnatural; at the most a man might find his twin, like Bob, but that was rare and something else again" (72). Jim believes that "all homosexuals talked constantly of love" between men, and such talk revolts him (83). Gay men are effeminate and, therefore, revolting to Jim; if gay men talk of love, then what Jim desires with another man must have another name: brotherhood, the search not for lover but for a "twin" (72).

Jim is by no means a one-to-one correspondence to Gore Vidal himself, but Jim's inability to make peace with a gay culture that he perceives to be overly effeminate is certainly in keeping with Vidal's claims that sexual desire is a matter of behavior, not identity: "If there is such a thing as a homosexual identity, you must then admit that there is such a thing as a heterosexual identity . . . Since I don't recognize such a thing as a heterosexual personality how can I define or detect a homosexual personality?" (qtd. in Behrendt, 50). Or as Robert J. Corber puts it, Vidal insists "on using the term homosexual as an adjective rather than a noun" (139). That is, in Vidal's view, one can participate in a homosexual act, but one cannot *be* a homosexual, because there is no such thing. Participation in specific kinds of sexual acts has, for Vidal, no bearing on personality or identity. This is why Jim can sleep with men and also reject gay culture (on the grounds that it is too effeminate).

Jim is thus the quintessential straight-acting gay man. Take, for example, Clarkson's description of the straight-acting gay men he studied: these straight-acting gay men "see their [masculine] gender identities as the only normal identities for all men, gay or straight," use "virtual space . . . as a substitute for the 'gay scene' that they see as overly feminine," and "continue to model their version of masculinity on the images of the working-class man" (204). Although Jim is many decades too early to cruise for men on the Internet, this description otherwise applies to him perfectly. Jim thinks an extremely masculine gender performance is the only way for men (both gay and straight) to be normal, and he derides the gay scene because he finds it too effeminate. Jim thinks the idea of romantic love between men is ludicrous, loathes gay culture, hates most gay men he meets, and exerts Herculean effort to convince himself that he is nothing like them; it thus seems odd to me that gay critics and literary historians have embraced *The City and the Pillar* as a landmark text in the effort to normalize homosexuality.

Without a doubt, publishing a sexually explicit novel that centers on a male protagonist who sleeps with men in 1948 was a radical move on Vidal's part and a courageous one. Prior to *The City and the Pillar*, Vidal had published two well-received war novels. His first novel, *Williwaw* (1946), "along with Norman Mailer's *The Naked and the Dead*, of 1948, was often cited at that time as the best novel of new generation of American writers" (Pease 72). Vidal knew how deeply taboo any discussion of homosexuality was at that time, not to mention portraying it in any kind of sympathetic light. But Vidal did discuss it and incurred considerable professional repercussions for having done so. Donald E. Pease says that after the publication of *The City and the Pillar*, many newspapers simply refused to review, or even advertise, anything that Vidal wrote, sending him into a "ten-year exile from literature," during which he "worked primarily in television, writing original scripts and dramatic adaptations" (79).

Furthermore, making his protagonist masculine was also a radical move in 1948, when the widely accepted understanding of homosexuality in the United States at the time absolutely equated male homosexuality with gender inversion. Corber rightly praises *The City and the Pillar* for "undermin[ing] the set of narratives available for representing gay male experience, narratives that reduced gay male identity to a form of gender inversion" (136). Given how universal this discourse about gay men was in 1948, *The City and the Pillar* was doing immensely difficult work: redefining male homosexuality in a way that revealed "that masculinity was not a monolithic entity but a contested terrain in which different modes of masculinity competed for dominance" (Corber 158).

In doing so, Corber suggests that Vidal's novel articulates a sexual politics even more radical than those of Donald Webster Corey, "the leading proponent of gay and lesbian rights in the 1950s" (135). Corey argued "the homosexuality constituted a minority identity rather than a form of psychopathology . . . by reifying the category of *homosexual* and arguing that it preexisted social relations rather than . . . [being] a product of them" (Corber 157, emphasis Corber's). Corber argues that Corey thus "sacrificed the ability to interrogate the discourses and practices that gendered sexuality," a mode of critique that *The City and the Pillar* valuably sustains (157). That is, Corey argued that male homosexuality was a fixed and narrowly defined category of identity, where Vidal's novel suggested that homosexuality was more fluid and contested, taking different forms and meanings in different men. I certainly agree with Corber on the point that *The City and the Pillar*—published at a time when it was widely assumed that male homosexuality always equaled effeminacy and vice versa—aims to de-couple questions of (homo)sexuality from questions of gender performance and that that effort is progressive, in the sense that it opens up a wider range of possibilities for what "gay man" might mean.

But to say that the novel expands possibilities for gay men—but suggesting that they can be either masculine or effeminate—is not the same thing as saying that the novel values all modes of gay male gender presentation equally. It most certainly does not. *The City and the Pillar* makes its case that Jim Willard can be both gay and masculine (and therefore normal) by associating most other gay men with threatening effeminacy. Interestingly enough, this is also the same rhetorical strategy that Vidal used to distinguish himself from fellow gay novelist Truman Capote. In a 1984 interview, Vidal said that publishers and critics engaged in "nothing but fag bashing" after the publication of *The City and the Pillar* (Ruas 90). When asked "how Truman Capote's early novels escaped that," Vidal responds by saying that the notoriously effeminate Capote: "played the part. He was entirely what you would expect a person of that sort to be . . . They don't mind hairdressers. They are not threatened by someone who is effeminate and freakish and amusing: he's good copy. I was a six-foot soldier with a much-admired war novel who had suddenly written a book of the sort that nobody else had ever done [in this country], showing the normality of a certain sort of relationship. This was unbearable to the media" (qtd. in Ruas 90). This comment expresses Vidal's admirable desire to normalize "a certain sort of relationship" but it also names that relationship normal by denigrating effeminate men—calling them "freakish"—in order to claim power and prestige for masculine gay men, a group Vidal includes himself in by reminding readers that he himself was "a six-foot soldier with a much-admired war novel."

Vidal's novel makes the same moves as his interview comment. What is progressive about *The City and the Pillar* is that it seeks to uncouple male homosexuality from an exclusive connection to effeminacy, an idea that harms because it denies the simple truth that the gender performances of gay men run the gamut from butch to nelly, with stops at all points in between. What is not progressive about *The City and the Pillar* is that it does nothing to challenge the idea that effeminacy must mean buffoonery at best, weakness and degeneracy at worst. Rather than challenging notions of threatening effeminacy, *The City and the Pillar* seeks to normalize both Jim Willard's homosexuality and his masculinity by portraying effeminate gay men in terms of threat, as "strange womanish creatures" who are not quite fully human. The normalcy to which Jim clings (the normalcy that Vidal repeatedly trumpets in interviews and which gay literary historians have championed), like the normalcy of the contemporary straight-acting men, "constitutes selective homophobia because it comes at the expense of those homosexuals who do not conform to heteronormative expectations of gender performance" (Clarkson 205). Jim Willard's brand of normalcy is about squeezing himself into dominant culture's perception of normal, not challenging and redefining the idea of normality altogether.

In addition to the attainment and maintenance of a "pure" masculine gender performance, Jim's notion of normality includes an implicit attachment to whiteness. There are no major characters of color in *The City and the Pillar*, and the novel could almost be said to be completely whitewashed: in all of his travels, Jim never has any substantive interaction with non-white people, and even when he travels to Mexico, he interacts only with his white traveling companions (one of whom, Maria, has gone to Mexico in the first place because she has inherited a plantation there). Perhaps the one exception to this whitewashing is the setting of Jim's first homosexual encounter, the encounter with Bob that becomes so central to Jim's sense of self. Vidal sets this scene in an abandoned cabin that "had been the home of a onetime slave, recently dead" and that "stood deserted now" (14). This cabin, on the bank of the Potomac River, is a place where "more than once Bob had brought girls" (14) and which now housed "tramps" who passed through the area, "as well as lovers" (23). By setting Jim and Bob's love scene in the former home of a former slave in a book that is otherwise devoid of people of color, Vidal implicitly links blackness with both illicit sexuality (the cabin is a place where boys, including Bob, take girls to have premarital sex, and it is also the place where Jim and Bob have gay sex) and deviant, non-heteronormative lifestyles (the cabin provides temporary housing for vagabonds who choose to live outside of middle-class respectability). Both Jim and Bob can visit the cabin from time to time, but their whiteness allows the cabin (and its illicit charms) to be a place they visit, not a place they live; the cabin was once the home of a black man, but Jim and Bob have the (white) privilege to invade and abandon it as they please.

Vidal never critiques either Jim's attachment to whiteness or his attachment to heteronormative masculinity. Yes, Jim's quest to reunite with Bob ends in tragedy, but Vidal has been explicit that it is Jim's inability to let go of the past that is the source of the bad ending(s) that Bob and Jim come to. In a 1960 interview, Vidal emphasizes the Biblical allusion—to Lot's wife, who gazes back on Sodom and Gomorrah and is turned into a pillar of salt—in the novel's title and says that the novel is "not 'about' homosexuality. The actual theme is . . . if one continues always to look back, to relate everything to a first affair, one is emotionally, even humanly destroyed. The pillar of salt" (Walter 7).

Indeed, there is very little evidence—in the novel itself or in interviews with Vidal—to suggest that Vidal wants Jim's straight-acting gay masculinity to be open to critique. Quite the contrary, in fact. Jim's over-abundant masculinity is presented by Vidal—and has been received by critics—as precisely the thing that makes him both normal and/or valuable. For instance, in Corber's reading of the novel, "the gay macho style" that Jim embodies "represents the use of an oppositional form of masculinity that first emerged in the fifties as a means of staging a desire that does not conform to the domesticated values of the white suburban middle class" (146). Corber situates his reading of *The City and the Pillar* within the context of the United States' mid-twentieth-century shift from an industrial to a post-industrial/consumer economy. He says that "in the 1950s a model of masculinity that stressed domesticity and cooperation gradually became hegemonic" in the United States and that "[m]en were no longer encouraged to show initiative or to exert their independence from the domestic sphere. Rather, they were expected to define themselves through their identities as consumers—an expectation hitherto confined to women—and to take an active role in child-rearing" (5–6). Corber argues convincingly that Jim resists assuming this type of masculinity by refusing to get a corporate job, marry, and/or devote himself to the creation and rearing of a nuclear family.

Corber is right that Jim certainly lives an adult life that contradicts or contests Cold War notions of conformity, marriage, and the nuclear family. In this sense, he is outside the US mainstream. But I question Corber's assertion that "Jim does not identify fully with either masculinity or femininity" (153). As the close reading above has hopefully shown, Jim is deeply fearful and resentful of anyone and anything he deems to be feminine. As evidence that Jim does not hate women, Corber cites a passage from the original 1948 edition of the novel in which Jim thinks that "his homosexuality was not the result of negation, of hatred and fear of women; it came, rather, from a most affirmative love" (271). But if we consider the full context of this citation, it becomes clear that

Jim does indeed fear women. The scene occurs during an argument that Paul Sullivan and Jim are having. Paul accuses Jim of being "afraid of women" and "afraid of their bodies":

> Jim was taken aback. Sullivan was attacking him and he realized that what he said was true: he *was* afraid, their bodies *did* frighten him. But there was one thing Sullivan didn't know about and that was Bob; because of Bob everything Sullivan said was false; his homosexuality was not the result of negation, of hatred or fear of women; it came, rather, from a most affirmative love. He thought of Bob and this gave him the assurance to combat Sullivan.
>
> "Maybe you're right, but I don't think so. I don't like women, that's true, and I guess I don't really care for the way they're built, but I don't dislike them as people." (271, emphasis Vidal's)

It's clear that Vidal is using this scene to refute the homophobic canard that male homosexuality stems from woman-hating. But while Jim realizes that his homosexuality doesn't stem from woman-hating, he also does admit that he is frightened of women. He says that he likes them as people (a notably ungendered category), but their gendered bodies do make him uneasy. So while Jim purports to not having a problem with women "as people," he remains decidedly anxious about female bodies.[10]

To support his claim that Jim does not "identify fully" with masculinity, Corber convincingly demonstrates how Jim does not identify with (or even like) the kind of masculinity that became hegemonic in the 1950s. Corber says that this type of mainstream Cold War masculinity is best typified by what sociologists called "the organization man," the corporate worker who "depended less on personal ambition and individual initiative than on respect for authority, loyalty to one's superiors, and an ability to get along with others—all qualities traditionally associated with femininity" (6). And it is certainly true that Jim loathes organization men; Corber's deft reading of Jim's strained relationship with his father (who is absolutely an organization man) demonstrates this. But as Corber's own definition of the organization man points out, many US men in the Cold War era resisted the rise of the mode of masculinity represented by the organization man precisely because the organization man and the mode of masculinity he represented were understood to be feminine, or at least disastrously feminized. Thus, the mode of masculinity that Jim rejects in *The City in the Pillar* is a mode of masculinity that he finds to be suspiciously feminized. Jim adopts an outsider or marginalized masculinity—and is attracted to men who embody this same type of masculinity—precisely because he sees it as a genuine, truly masculine alternative to the feminized mode of masculinity represented by the organization man. Jim's rejection of organizational man masculinity is actually yet another instance of Jim rejecting something that he perceives to be feminine. Contrary to Corber's claim, Jim loves all that he sees as truly masculine.

There is much to honor about *The City and the Pillar*—its relatively early publication date, its sexual explicitness, its efforts to detach homosexuality from mental illness and criminality—and it is, of course, unrealistically utopian to expect the novel (or any novel) to be unproblematically progressive on all issues of race, gender, and sexuality. But that does not mean that we should ignore the ways in which a novel is problematic. We should strive to see *The City and the Pillar* for what it is, for both its triumphs and its tragedies. Its triumph is that at a time when mainstream US culture was deeply hostile to both homosexuality and effeminacy, it worked hard to redefine homosexuality in more positive light. The tragedy of the novel is that it undertook this redefinition by further denigrating effeminacy. In doing so, Vidal's novel anticipates a long tradition of the conscious rejection of effeminacy in gay male subcultures. The gay macho leather clone style of the 1970s is an example of this tradition, which, according to sociologist Peter Hennen's observations of contemporary gay male bear and leather subcultures, continues into the present day.

GIOVANNI'S ROOM: TRUTH FROM THE MOUTHS OF FLAMING PRINCESSES

Like Jim Willard, David, the protagonist of *Giovanni's Room*, is a straight-acting gay man. David is raised by a manly father who nicknames him "Butch" (90), fears any sign of effeminacy in his son, and wants him to "grow up to be a man. And when I say a man . . . I don't mean a Sunday school teacher" (15). The emphasis David's father places on active, aggressive, heteronormative masculinity instills in David a sense that heteronormative masculinity is precious and that its maintenance is paramount. This helps explain David's feelings about his first sexual experience, which occurs with a boy named Joey, when David and Joey are both teenagers. David initially enjoys the sex he has with Joey but wakes the next morning to find that his own body "suddenly seemed gross and crushing" and that the desire he feels to have sex with Joey again "seemed monstrous" (9). Most importantly, what David feels on that first same-sex morning after is fear for his masculinity, which for David, is fear for his very self: "But, above all, I was suddenly afraid. It was borne in on me: *But Joey is a boy* . . . [his] body seemed the black opening of a cavern in which I would be tortured till madness came, in which I would lose my manhood" (9, emphasis Baldwin's). This pattern—attraction to other men, sex with them, shame, fear, and denial of same-sex attraction until it eventually reoccurs—repeats itself throughout David's adult life.

But unlike Jim Willard, David can actually consummate sexual relations with women. Finding himself in Paris after the end of World War II and his discharge from the Army, David is on the verge of marrying Hella, an American woman. David even "told [Hella] that I had loved her once and I made myself believe it" (5). But when Hella leaves on a long trip to Spain—in order to give David time to decide if he wants to marry her—David finds himself alone under "under a foreign sky, with no one to watch, no penalties attached" and drifts back towards Paris's gay subculture (5). In *The City and the Pillar*, Jim Willard distanced himself, mentally, from L.A.'s gay subculture even as he participated in it, and David makes the same move in Paris: "Most of the people I knew in Paris were, as Parisians sometimes put it, of *le milieu* [the city's gay subculture] and, while this milieu was certainly anxious enough to claim me, I was intent on proving, to them and to myself, that I was not of their company. I did this by being in their company a great deal and manifesting towards all of them a tolerance which placed me, I believed, above suspicion" (22–23, emphasis Baldwin's). David attempts to have it both ways: he wants to play the role of the cosmopolitan straight man who is worldly enough not to mind gay men and gay bars but who certainly isn't gay himself.

His struggle to keep his mental distance from the gay subculture in which he is increasingly participating has everything to do with David's fear and loathing of men who have sex with men. Describing a Parisian gay bar, David says that its clientele is made up of three types: "the usual, knife-blade lean, tight-trousered boys" who work as male prostitutes, the "paunchy, bespeckled gentlemen with avid, sometimes despairing eyes" who solicit them, and "les *folles,*" extremely effeminate gay men who "always dressed in the most improbable combinations . . . always called each other 'she' . . . [and] looked like a peacock garden and sounded like a barnyard" (27). In David's eyes effeminate men are either criminal (the prostitutes), pathetic (the men soliciting the prostitutes), or sub-human (the animalistic *les folles*, whose name means either lunatic or buffoon). From the point of view of middle-class, white, presumably heterosexual manhood—which is to say from David's point of view—none of these roles are acceptable.

David thus finds himself in the same straight-acting dilemma that Jim Willard does in *The City and the Pillar*: David is sexually attracted to men, which draws him toward gay culture, but to his mind all available forms of identity based around same-sex desire involve what he sees as a renunciation of his manhood. Taking any kind of identity based around same-sex desire will involve David going back to that "black opening of a cavern" that he sensed the morning after his first same-sex experience, the cavern "in which I would be tortured till madness came, in which I would lose my manhood" (9). Unable to see any positive possibility in effeminacy, David sees it only as failed masculinity. David wants to sleep with men, but he wants to do so while retaining the privilege that comes along with being a middle-class, gender-normative, white man.

The fact that Baldwin was African American, while David and all the other characters in *Giovanni's Room* are white, has been both a stumbling block for critics and a point of origin for their readings of the novel. Summarizing older critical response to the novel, Marlon Ross explains that "[w]hile the novel has gained a central place in (white) gay culture and is often a focus of (white) gay studies, in the context of African American literary and cultural studies, historically it has been alternatingly dismissed or ignored altogether, stumblingly acknowledged or viciously attacked" (16). Luckily, a number of more recent readings (Ross's most certainly among them) have engaged the operation of both race and sexuality in the novel in fascinating ways.[11]

Trudier Harris demonstrates that blackness actually functions as a very present absence in "Baldwin's so-called raceless novel" (18).[12] Harris's argument is that David, "without specific references to black people, or any encounters with them, uses the terminology of the cultural myths attached to them to define what he envisions as being outside, filthy, and dirty if he were to give in to his homosexual proclivities" (24); this is why David's imagination figures homosexuality as a "black opening of a cavern." Harris argues that David behaves, throughout the novel, like a plantation master, using the bodies of women and darker men (Giovanni is Italian and noticeably darker than David) for his pleasure in private, while not treating them as fully human in public. Robert Reid-Pharr's reading of *Giovanni's Room* agrees that "the question of blackness, precisely because of its very apparent absence, screams out at the turn of every page" (125) and notes that David constantly tries "to claim both Giovanni's labor power and his sex . . . [Giovanni is] at once both the brutalized black male slave and the sexualized black female slave" (129). Harris and Reid-Pharr's readings of the novel help to illuminate then, the ways in which David's clinging attachment to a pure masculinity unsullied by even the hint of femininity is always already interconnected with his clinging attachment to a pure whiteness that seeks to use darker bodies without ceding its own privilege.

Despite his obsession with purity (of masculinity, of whiteness), David has to make adjustments when he runs low on money in Paris. Down on his luck financially, David calls on Jacques, "an aging, Belgian-born, American businessman" known locally for "his big apartment, his well-meant promises, his whiskey, his marijuana, [and] his orgies" (23). David is revolted by Jacques, who is effeminate, but he also knows that Jacques is attracted to him. In desperate need of money, David is willing to play on this attraction, flirting slightly with Jacques in exchange for Jacques loaning him money and buying him dinner and drinks.

It is in Jacques's company that David enters a gay bar and meets Giovanni, a beautiful Italian bartender. David is unable to resist his attraction to Giovanni, and the two of them hit it off immediately, staying out all night, going to an after-hours club, and then going home to the shabby room that Giovanni rents, where they have sex for the first time. In the days and weeks that follow, David and Giovanni become a couple and live together openly. But being in his first long-term relationship with another man does nothing to assuage David's dread of effeminacy. In fact, being with Giovanni aggravates it. Throughout the time that they are together, masculine identity, and threats to it, remain at the forefront of David's mind.

It is important to note that Giovanni's masculinity is precisely what David finds attractive about him; David likes Giovanni because Giovanni is straight-acting. Except for the one exception of sleeping with David, Giovanni appears to be a working-class heterosexual patriarch. For example, Giovanni is bisexual: he tells David that he himself was once "very interested in women" (79) and "was never like this before [David] came" (138). In fact, back in Italy, Giovanni had a girlfriend and fathered a son with her; the boy was stillborn, and Giovanni only came north to Paris after his death. Giovanni is also a misogynist who hates "these absurd women running around today, full of ideas and nonsense, and thinking themselves equal to men—*quelle rigolade!*—they need to be beaten half to death so that they can find out who rules the world" (80, emphasis Baldwin's). When David asks him if the women he knew liked to get beaten, Giovanni says that he doesn't "know if they liked it. But a beating never made them go away" (80). This causes David and Giovanni to laugh together, two men enjoying the male privilege afforded them by having collectively denigrated women.

Giovanni also hates effeminacy. He works in a gay bar but generally holds its patrons in contempt. Giovanni finds his boss, Guillaume, to be "a disgusting old fairy" (107). The two men have slept together, once, but Giovanni tells David that this happened only because Giovanni was desperate to get a job and that he found sleeping with Guillaume to be loathsome: "I was weak with hunger and had had trouble not to vomit" (107). Talking about Guillaume and most of the patrons of his gay bar, Giovanni says, "Guillaume's disgusting. They all are" (109) and later calls them a "disgusting band of fairies" (140).

David's attraction to Giovanni's (misogynist and femme-phobic) heteronormative masculinity clashes with David's desire to preserve his own. The paradox of how to both be a man and be with one sexually consumes David's thoughts. For a brief time, David tries to resolve this conflict by embracing a traditionally feminine role: "I invented in myself a kind of pleasure in playing the housewife after Giovanni had gone to work" (88). But this pleasure does not last, and he soon declares: "I am not a housewife—men never can be housewives" (88). David thus remains tormented.

Indeed, this conflict continues to preoccupy David's thoughts and even intrudes on an otherwise happy day. One afternoon when David and Giovanni are walking together, they buy some cherries and begin playfully spitting cherry pits at one another as they walk down the steet. This spontaneous sillyness makes David realize that he "really loved Giovanni, who had never seemed more beautiful than he was that afternoon" (83). But this happiness does not last: as Giovanni and David flirt with one another, a man passes them on the street. This man is attractive, and David finds himself cruising the man. Giovanni sees this and is not angered by it in the slightest. But it makes David feel "sorrow and shame and panic and great bitterness. At the same time—it was part of my turmoil and also outside it—I felt the muscles in my neck tighten with the effort I was making not to turn my head and watch that boy diminish down the bright avenue. The beast which Giovanni had awakened in me would never go to sleep again; but one day I would not be with Giovanni anymore. And would I then, like all the others, find myself turning and following all kinds of boys down God knows what dark avenues, into what dark places? With this fearful intimation there opened in me a hatred for Giovanni which was as powerful as my love and which was nourished by the same roots" (84).

For Giovanni, David looking at another man is simply proof that David is alive and young. For David, being caught cruising another man means that someone else has seen, and known, his attraction to men. It means that Giovanni knows that he is not the only man David has ever, or will ever, be attracted to. It means that Giovanni knows that David is gay, that he is attracted to men generally, not just Giovanni specifically. And this is unbearable to David, because it means that in Giovanni's eyes he is marked as fully and wholly gay. And for David, to be that is to also be wholly and unredeemably effeminate, which is also (in David's eyes) wholly and unreedembaly abnormal.

Worse yet, David begins to notice that it is not just Giovanni who sees him as gay (and therefore, in David's mind, effeminate). One day while David is walking by himself in Paris, he passes a sailor on the street. David "was staring at [the sailor], though I did not know it" because the sailor "seemed—somehow—younger than I had ever been, and blonder and more beautiful, and he wore his masculinity as unequivocally as he wore his skin" (92). David's moment of rapture ends abruptly, however, as the sailor "gave me a look contemptuously lewd and knowing: just such a look as he might have given, but a few hours ago, to the desperately well-dressed nymphomaniac or trollop who was trying to make him believe she was a lady" (92). Thus, David's pleasure in cruising this young sailor turns quickly into horror. The horror comes from the fact that the sailor has recognized that David is cruising him; the sailor has understood that David is gay, and the sailor—who is the heteronormatively masculine ideal that David both wants to be and wants to be with sexually—reacts to this understanding with contempt and revulsion. Although David had identified with the sailor's masculinity—"He made me think of home . . . I knew how he drank and how he was with his friends and how pain and women baffled him"—the sailor's contemptuous look shatters David's identification, disallowing it (92). David had felt great pleasure in identifying with the sailor, whose masculinity David sees as unassailably normal, but the sailor's look says no; it tells David that they are not alike, that David is an abnormal sex criminal, like a "nymphomaniac" or a "trollop" pretending to be a lady.

Horrified to have been marked as abnormal by one he sees as so wholly normal, David immediately wonders what provoked the sailor's reaction. More specifically, David wonders what exactly the sailor saw that marked him (David) as gay: "I wondered what [the sailor] had seen in me to elicit such instantaneous contempt. I was too old to suppose that it had anything to do with my walk, or the way I held my hands, or my voice—which, anyway, he had not heard. It was something else and I would never see it. I would never dare to see it. It would be like looking at the naked sun . . . I knew that what the sailor had seen in my unguarded eyes was envy and desire: I had seen it often in Jacques' eyes and my reaction and the sailor's had been the same. But if I were still able to feel affection and if he had seen it in my eyes, it would not have helped, for affection, for the boys I was doomed to look at, was vastly more frightening than lust" (92–93).

The sailor's look makes David realize that he has fallen from the grace of heteronormative masculine privilege; it announces to him that he is no longer a "normal" man. Once David was the contemptuous straight boy who sneered at the lust of gay men, but now David is the older gay man being sneered at by a younger straight boy. The sailor's contemptuous look makes no distinction between gay men like Jacques and gay men like David. The sailor's look makes David realize that he can avoid the "black opening of a cavern . . . in which I would lose my manhood" or he can be with Giovanni (9). He cannot do both.

Soon after this encounter with the sailor, David learns that Hella is returning to Paris. Seeing a relationship with Hella as a means of reclaiming heteronormative masculinity, David decides that his relationship with Giovanni "would be something that had happened to me once" (94), even though when he daydreams "the face that glowed insistently before me was not her face but his" (95). David chooses the appearance of heteronormative masculinity over the reality of his love for Giovanni: "I hoped to burn out, through Hella, my image of Giovanni and the reality of his touch" (122). In doing so, he reveals a profound need for the sense of safety that the privilege of white middle-class masculinity provides, the privilege of normality. This need is made explicit when David, unable to sleep, roams around Paris and agonizes about whether he should be with Hella or with Giovanni. As he roams, David looks at middle-class French houses where "the French nation was clearing away the dishes, putting little Jean-Pierre and Marie to bed, scowling over the eternal problems of the sou, the shop, the church, the unsteady State. Those walls, those shuttered windows held them in and protected them *against the darkness* and the long moan of this night. Ten years hence, little Jean-Pierre or Marie might find themselves out here beside the river *and wonder, like me, how they had fallen out of the web of safety.* What a long way, I thought, I've come—to be destroyed . . . I wanted children. *I wanted to be inside again*, with the light and the safety, *with my manhood unquestioned*, watching *my woman* put *my children* to bed" (104, emphasis mine).

David does love Giovanni, but being with Giovanni means being expelled from "the web of safety" afforded by white middle-class heteronormative masculinity; it means being out amongst "the darkness." It means becoming effeminate, which David can see only as threat and failure. Ultimately, David is unable to turn his back on the safety net: he breaks up with Giovanni and makes plans to marry Hella, a move that will put him a step closer to the vision of wife-and-child-owning white patriarchy he longs for.

During his breakup with Giovanni, David's words reveal his obsessive concern with appearing both masculine and normal (which, to David, are the same thing). "What kind of life can we have in this room?" he asks Giovanni. "What kind of life can two men have together, anyway?" (142). David then accuses Giovanni of wanting to feminize him: "All this love you talk about—isn't it just that you want to be made to feel strong? You want to go out and be the big laborer and bring home the money, and you want me to stay here and wash the dishes and cook the food and clean this miserable closet of a room and kiss you when you come through that door and lie with you at night and be your little *girl*"(142, emphasis Baldwin's). The italics Baldwin uses to place extra emphasis on "girl" indicate the venom with which David says the word; they make it clear that for David, there is no position more unbearable than being feminine. Giovanni responds by saying that he is "not trying to make you [David] a little girl. If I wanted a little girl, I would be *with* a little girl," but David cannot hear that (142, emphasis Baldwin's). "But I'm a man," David says, "a man! What do you think can happen between us?" (142). Although Giovanni can imagine an answer to that question, David cannot.

In abandoning Giovanni, David confirms Giovanni's major complaint about him, that he (David) has never "loved anyone" because he "want[s] to be *clean*" (141, emphasis Baldwin's). Giovanni tells David, "You think you came here covered with soap and you think you will go out covered with soap—and you do not want to *stink*, not even for five minutes, in the meantime" (141, emphasis Baldwin's). In this speech, Giovanni is talking about sex and saying that David has to leave him because the sex they have pollutes him and sullies his virtue. Giovanni's reading of David is correct in its spirit, but off in its particulars: David isn't concerned with sexual purity, he's obsessed with the purity of his gender performance and the way others perceive it. David leaves Giovanni not because they have sex together, but because living openly with Giovanni imperils what Jacques, in an earlier moment, calls "that *immaculate* manhood which is [David's] pride and joy" (30, emphasis Baldwin's).

David's abandonment of Giovanni sets Giovanni onto a long but steady downward spiral that ends when Guillaume, the gay bar owner, is found strangled to death with the sash of his own effeminate dressing gown. Giovanni is arrested, charged with the murder, quickly convicted, and sentenced to execution. This news causes David great pain: in his depression he grows distant from Hella and returns to gay bars. Eventually, Hella finds him in one and breaks up with him. David has thus damaged both of his potential partners: Hella's hopes for marriage are dashed, and the heartbroken Giovanni awaits execution. Structurally, the book actually begins where it ends: David's narration begins on the night before Giovanni's morning execution, and most of the book is narrated with David looking back on his actions, judging them with the benefit of hindsight.

This backwards-looking structure is one of the major differences between *Giovanni's Room* and *The City and the Pillar*. Vidal's Jim Willard does almost no reflecting on his own actions, while Baldwin structures *Giovanni's Room* so that David narrates the book from a position where he realizes that his attachments to heteronormative masculinity and whiteness have played a large part in the bad ends that he, and those he loves, have come to. David's understanding—his realization that his attachment to normative modes of masculinity has made a monster out of him—comes too late to save Giovanni, but it does come. The same cannot be said of Jim Willard.

In stark contrast to *The City and the Pillar*, effeminate men in *Giovanni's Room* are representative of a type of fascinating effeminacy I called the Truth-Telling Queen because they routinely speak with a voice that shatters the straight-acting self-deceptions to which David clings so desperately. An example of this is the conversation that Jacques and David have after it becomes clear that David and Giovanni are attracted to one another. In this conversation, Jacques complains to David that Giovanni "is very fond of you . . . But this doesn't make you happy or proud, as it should. It makes you frightened and ashamed" (56). This is terrible, Jacques says, because David refuses to believe that love between men is possible: "'Love him,' said Jacques, with vehemence, 'love him and let him love you. Do you think anything else under heaven really matters? And how long, at the best, can it last? Since you are both men and still have everywhere to go? Only five minutes, I assure you, only five minutes, and most of that, *helas!*, in the dark. And if you think of them as dirty, then they *will* be dirty—they will be dirty because you will be giving nothing, you will be despising your flesh and his. But you can make your time together anything but dirty; you can give each other something which will make both of you better—forever—if you will not be ashamed, if you will only not play it safe'" (57, emphasis Baldwin's).

This speech, delivered by an aging, effeminate queen that David loathes, is the antithesis of Jim Willard's dismissal of the idea of the love between men in *The City and the Pillar*. Jacques's speech argues not only that love between men exists, but that it is transformative, "something which will make both of you better—forever." The only thing blocking a man's access to this ennobling, transformational force is his own shame: the sense—socialized into men growing up in homophobic cultures—that same-sex desire is dirty and shameful. In *Giovanni's Room*, Baldwin characterizes love as a sacred power and to deny love or name it as dirty is to hideously distort the self. Tragically, Jacques says that he himself has done just that. His own promiscuity is "shameful," he tells David, not because he believes gay sex is bad, but because sex without love is bad and his many encounters have been "like putting an electric plug in a dead socket. Touch, but no contact. All touch, but no contact and no light" (56). A lifetime of such hollow encounters, which Jacques himself has thought of as dirty, has made Jacques "trapped in [his] own dirty body, forever and forever and forever" (57).

In *Giovanni's Room*, love between men is redemptive force. And anything that would name it otherwise—including straight-acting gay identities that dismiss love between men as being either shameful or overly feminine—is part and parcel of the wider societal homophobia that works to erase love between men or name it as shameful. This view is articulated by Jacques and seconded in Giovanni's claim, during their breakup, that David wants "to *kill* [Giovanni] in the name of all your lying little moralties," a desire that makes David himself "*immoral* . . . by far, the most immoral man I have met in all my life. Look, *look* what you have done to me. Do you think you could have done this if I did not love you? Is *this* what you should do to love?" (141, emphasis Baldwin's). The "lying little moralities" that cause David to leave Giovanni are not just moralities about sexual behavior; they also include a preoccupation with preserving both heteronormative masculinity and whiteness. Thus, while *Giovanni's Room* is centered around a straight-acting gay male protagonist, the book itself implicitly condemns straight-acting gay masculinity as just another form of the "lying little moralities" by which homophobia erases or denigrates same-sex love and same-sex sex.

Here, we see the gigantic difference between *Giovanni's Room* and *The City and the Pillar* most clearly. In *The City and the Pillar*, love between men is precisely what Jim Willard loathes. He finds it ridiculous and impossible and has to name his desire for Bob Ford with another word altogether. In *Giovanni's Room*, David, like Jim Willard, also believes that love between men is impossible. But Vidal's novel repeatedly makes the case that Jim's straight-acting-ness is the source of his normality, whereas Baldwin condemns David's clinging attachments to heteronormative masculinity and whiteness, arguing that these attachments are a chief cause of David abandoning the man he loves and ending up guilt-ridden and alone. Love between men in *The City and the Pillar* is absurd and revoltingly feminine; in *Giovanni's Room*, it is the best thing men are capable of. In critiquing David's narrow views of what is possible for a man to be and do and feel, Baldwin condemns precisely that which Vidal—and his critics—have hymned.

Nor is *Giovanni's Room* the first place that Baldwin condemned American men's attachment to hypermasculinity in general, or *The City and the Pillar* in specific. In an essay called "Preservation of Innocence"—published in 1949, a year after *The City and the Pillar* and seven years before *Giovanni's Room*—Baldwin critiques America's attachment to rigid gender roles. Deciding "that men must recapture their status as men and that women must embrace their function as women" is, Baldwin argues, a "rigidity of attitude" that puts "to death any possible communion" between people (597). It is also a stupid attitude to adopt, because "having once listed the bald physical facts, no one is prepared to go further and decide, of our multiple human attributes, which are masculine and which are feminine" (597). To recognize "this complexity"—the truth that while people may have a biological sex, every person's behavior is a mix of what some might subjectively call feminine and some might subjectively call masculine—is, Baldwin says, "the signal of maturity; it marks the death of the child and the birth of the man" (597).

To Baldwin's dismay, much of the popular detective fiction of the 1940s catered to an immature love of rigid gender roles by giving America "that mindless monster, the tough guy" (597). And in tough-guy fiction, sinister homosexuals always come to "sordid and bloody end[s]" in order to protect the "immaculate manliness" of both the tough-guy hero and his male readers (599). This, Baldwin says, is horrible, but what is worse is that so many novels "concerned with homosexuality" replicate this very move, having their gay protagonists meet violent ends so that the threat their gayness poses to the innocence of American masculinity can be nullified (599). Summarizing several gay novels, Baldwin mentions *The City and the Pillar* and says that its ending, like the violent endings of other novels about homosexuals, is "compelled by a panic which is close to madness" and that such novels "are wholly unable to recreate or interpret any of the reality or complexity of human experience" (599–600). Baldwin's critique of *The City and the Pillar* here is explicitly about the novel's violent ending, but the violence Jim displays at the end of that novel is implicitly linked to Jim's rigid attachment to a very narrow definition of masculinity. It is this same rigid attachment—this obsessive preoccupation with preserving an "*immaculate* manhood" untainted by even a hint of the feminine—that Baldwin names as a pathology first in "Preservation of Innocence" and later in *Giovanni's Room*.

Achieving and maintaining this immaculate manhood is the central preoccupation of straight-acting gay masculinity. And as blackness's present absence throughout *Giovanni's Room* reminds us, immaculate masculinity is always already tied up in conceptions of immaculate whiteness. Yes, David dreads being seen as feminine. But what he fears most is being marked as abnormal in *any* way. And normality, of course, is awarded to people in many different ways: in terms of race, gender performance, sexual behavior, social class, etc. It is thus useful here to remember Dwight A. McBride's admonition that Baldwin's work "reminds us that whenever we are speaking of race, we are always already speaking about gender, sexuality, and class" ("Straight Black Studies" 58). Baldwin's critique of straight-acting gay masculinity in *Giovanni's Room* is thus multifaceted, one that reveals that gender presentation is not the only case in which straight-acting gay masculinity favors the dominant culture's definition of what is normative. Aside from a fetish for the supposed authenticity of (white) working-class masculinity, straight-acting gay masculinity prizes masculinity over femininity and whiteness over non-whiteness. Masculinity and whiteness are normative states, prized by the straight-acting gay man because his ostensible normality in these categories will presumably offset or excuse the ostensible abnormality of his sexuality. This is because, as Ross reminds us, "even the most deeply taboo and widely outlawed desire can be cushioned by the privileged invisibility of whiteness" (25). This is the strategy Vidal pursues in creating his white, straight-acting protagonist Jim Willard. Baldwin also writes a white straight-acting gay man, but unlike Vidal, Baldwin uses Truth-Telling Queens to critique his protagonist, revealing the allegiance with dominant culture definitions of normality that underlie straight-acting gay male identity.

Furthermore, Baldwin understood that straight-acting gay masculinity's obsession with normality took the form of a preoccupation with purity (of gender performance and of race). And as an African American born and reared under American segregation, Baldwin knew all too well that purity's constant companion is a phobic reaction to that which is perceived as impure. Just as the myth of white purity requires the myth of the black male beast (and his consequent disciplining/containment/exorcism through the violence of lynching), Baldwin knew that the myth of masculine purity requires its own abjected inverse: the faggot, the queer, the sissy. Thus, *Giovanni's Room* reveals "that the creation of the authentically (hypo)masculine national subject necessitates the production of the inauthentic, sterile, effeminate, non(re)productive homosexual subject" (Henderson 302). This abjected homosexual subject then requires the violence of homosexual panic in order to be disciplined/contained/exorcised by ostensibly normal men.

Baldwin understood not only that ostensibly normal men achieve and maintain normality through the rejection of the abnormal (sometimes via social shaming, other times via physical violence), but that all men—both straight and gay—who seek the privilege of normality seek to do so in the same way. Being a gay man doesn't exempt one from also being a man and having learned, through years of male socialization, how male privilege is achieved and maintained. And so while Vidal presents Jim Willard as fully human and worthy of respect precisely because his masculinity is pure and untainted, Baldwin uses David, and the terrible mess he makes of his life, to criticize both the desire for purity that underlies straight-acting gay male identity and the violence that always accompanies that desire.

More specifically—and importantly—this critique literally comes out of the mouth of Truth-Telling Queens in *Giovanni's Room*; David the protagonist may hate effeminate men, but Baldwin the author utilizes the fascinating grotesque to present effeminate men as prophetic, truly brave sexual outlaws. Jacques, as discussed above, is the one with the courage to tell David to love Giovanni. But Jacques is hardly the only effeminate man in the novel to whom Baldwin grants great powers of perception and truth-telling. First, it is Guillaume, the gay bar owner, who warns Giovanni about David, saying that David is "just an American boy, after all, doing things in France which [he] would not dare to do at home, and that [he] would leave [Giovanni] very soon," a prediction that sadly turns out to be true (108).

Another effeminate man possessed of prophetic vision is an unnamed queen that David encounters in the gay bar the night that he meets Giovanni. The description of this nameless queen is worth quoting at length, for it reveals that while David the protagonist sees effeminacy as threat, Baldwin the author views it as fascinating:

> It looked like a mummy or a zombie . . . it walked on its toes, the flat hips moved with a dead, horrifying lasciviousness . . . It glittered in the dim light; the thin, black hair was violent with oil, combed forward, hanging in the bangs; the eyelids gleamed with mascara, the mouth raged with lipstick. The face was white and thoroughly bloodless with some kind of foundation cream; it stank of powder and a gardenia-like perfume. The shirt, open coquettishly to the navel, revealed a hairless chest and a silver crucifix; the shirt was covered with round, paper-thin wafers, red and green and orange and yellow and blue, which stormed in the light and made one feel that the mummy might, at any moment, disappear in flame. A red sash was around the waist, the clinging pants were a surprisingly somber grey. He wore buckles on his shoes . . . His hands, I noticed, with an unbelieving shock, were very large and strong . . . he did not seem real" (39).

David, because of his loathing of effeminacy, initially refuses to acknowledge this man as human. Indeed, for much of the initial description, the queen is an "it" rather than a he, a mummy or a zombie, not a person. And clearly, the feminine details of his styling—the open shirt, the mascara, the foundation, the gardenia perfume—are revolting to David. These feminine details mix with the masculine size of the queen's hands to make the queen seem unreal to David, hence the recourse to the language of monstrosity.

David's encounter with this unnamed queen illustrates yet another moment of David hating effeminacy, but Baldwin also uses the scene to illustrate just how disastrously wrong that hatred is. After all, David fears effeminacy because he equates it with weakness. But look at the descriptive language that Baldwin uses to describe the very signs of effeminacy that so revolt David: the queen's hair is "violent with oil," his mouth "raged with lipstick," and the decorative wafers on his shirt "stormed in the light," threatening to burst into flame. This is not the language of weakness: it is the language of action, the language of promise and power. Baldwin describes the feminine details of the queen's styling in the same, not the opposite, manner in which he describes the queen's "very large and strong" hands. David's reaction to the queen comes straight out of effeminacy as threat, but the language Baldwin describes the queen with veers into fascinating effeminacy because it ascribes power and agency to effeminacy in a way that Vidal's descriptions of effeminate men in *The City and the Pillar* never do.

And the fascinating power this queen holds is not limited to matters of styling. Just like Jacques and Guillaume, this queen has the ability to read David, to know David better than he knows himself. Unbidden, the queen engages David in conversation, telling him that Giovanni is "*very* dangerous" for a "boy like [David]" (40, emphasis Baldwin's). Shocked by both the queen's appearance and his conversational boldness, David tells him to "Go to hell" (40). In response, the queen offers a prophetic warning: "'Oh, no,' he said, 'I go not to hell,' and he clutched his crucifix with one large hand. 'But you, my dear friend—I fear that you shall burn in a very hot fire . . . You will be very unhappy. Remember that I told you so.' And he straightened, as though he were a princess and moved, flaming, away through the crowd" (40). Again, this scene occurs very early in the novel, before David and Giovanni have even kissed, but the whole novel is itself narrated from a retrospective position, a vantage point where even David himself can see that the flaming princess's words turned out to be true.

The flaming princess is one queen of many in *Giovanni's Room* who is loathed by David, but nevertheless presented by Baldwin as being one of the few people with both the insight to see the truth and the courage to tell it. Baldwin's narrator is a straight-acting gay man, but he comes to ruin surrounded by a cadre of queens and les folles and flaming princesses who were absolutely right about him and about the high price he would have to pay to keep his manhood "immaculate." The retrospective structure of *Giovanni's Room* thus serves to prove that David was wrong and that the straight-acting gay man's rejection of effeminacy is an act of mutilating self-denial, one that causes him to see threat where he should see—and appreciate—the fascinating power of those men strong enough to be honest about who and what they are, even in the face of a massively homophobic and heteronormative culture.

In locating truth in the mouth of queens, Baldwin builds on the base provided by McCullers's Sympathetic Sissies (specifying the particular way in which effeminate men are beneficial to their communities). He also anticipates the Healing Queens of Tony Kushner (discussed in Chapter Four) as well as the caustic truth-telling practices called "reading" and "shade" by the black and Latino/a gay men and trans women documented in *Paris Is Burning*. While most mainstream US media and conventional wisdom assumes that male homosexuality is always co-extant with effeminacy, Baldwin and Vidal's novels remind readers that gay men have never considered the question of effeminacy's relationship to homosexuality to be either simple or concluded.

THREE

"I [HEART] BOYS WHO SPARKLE"

STRAIGHT FEMALE FANDOM AND FASCINATING EFFEMINACY

Famed for his high voice, boyish attitude, theatrical costumes and gilded candelabras, the pianist and television personality Liberace (1919–1987) has come to be virtually synonymous with effeminacy in US popular culture. And while Liberace made millions and commanded a devoted audience over the course of a career that lasted from the mid-1940s until his death, he was also a deeply divisive figure, a man who inspired both passionate hatred and intense adoration.

Typically, these reactions split along gendered lines. "Men look at Liberace and what they see makes them uneasy," wrote *Inside Story* magazine in 1954. "They find his dimples too perky, his hair too wavy, and his personality too soft. The phrase 'feminine appeal' is often used to describe him. . . . Many men, after seeing Liberace, have said that their feeling is more like masculine contempt" (qtd. in Pyron 176). But on the other hand, many straight women professed deep and abiding love for Liberace and denied the persistent gay rumors that dogged him his entire career. For example, in 1954, a journalist writing for *Collier's* magazine asked a woman to explain why she loved Liberace. She answered by saying that "[w]hen he [Liberace] kisses your hand, you know he isn't going to chew off your arm" (qtd. in Pyron 172). Another female Liberace fan expressed a similar sentiment, telling the same reporter that when she looked at Liberace she saw "a little pleasant relief from what I have to look at every day: Loudmouths! Chest-beaters!" (qtd. in Pyron 172). And a third woman told the Collier's reporter that "Liberace is the sympathetic type. He looks at you and you feel beautiful. For that alone, I believe in him" (qtd. in Pyron 172).

These responses make it clear that the very things that made Liberace so loathsome to many men—his emotional sensitivity, his deference and attention to women's feelings, his interest in the fine arts, his love of material luxury, and most of all his lack of sexual aggression—are also the very things that made Liberace attractive to many straight women. This chapter takes the sentiment expressed by these women seriously. Despite the fact that Liberace was a gay man, his public persona was simultaneously extremely effeminate and adamantly straight. There is ample evidence to suggest that many of his female fans took his alleged heterosexuality seriously, and so this chapter examines the particular mode of fascinating effeminacy that Liberace's onstage and on-air persona offered them: effeminate gender presentation plus an emotional devotion to women, a combination that some women viewed as a more preferable alternative to other, more heteronormative modes of masculine gender presentation.

I call this type of effeminacy "sparkly," a term inspired by Stephenie Meyer's *Twilight* saga, her best-selling human-girl-meets-vampire-boy young adult novels. This chapter uses a close reading of the *Twilight* novels to define the term "sparkly effeminacy" as a particular mode of fascinating effeminacy. Then to prove that the *Twilight* saga represents only the latest incarnation of what has been a long-lasting and deeply felt trend of women loving sparkly effeminacy in US culture since World War II, the chapter moves backwards in time and examines the career of Liberace, who constitutes perhaps the clearest example of a performer deploying sparkly effeminacy to earn the adulation, lust, and money of straight female fans.

But as the brief examples above demonstrate, while many straight women have seen sparkly effeminacy as fascinating, many men have reacted phobically to it, characterizing it as threat. The final section of this chapter examines this bifurcated reaction to sparkly effeminacy and argues that it necessitates a revision of current theories of the grotesque. More specifically, I argue that critics and theorists interested in the grotesque need to pay closer attention to the role that readers and/or viewers of the grotesque play in shaping the meaning of a given grotesque text or image.

THE *TWILIGHT* NOVELS: EDWARD CULLEN AS "FANTASTIC SPARKLING CREATURE"

In the *Twilight* saga,[1] Stephenie Meyer tweaks the conventional mythology regarding vampires. Rather than burning to death or exploding when exposed to direct sunlight, Meyer's *Twilight* vampires literally sparkle. When high school student Bella Swan, the protagonist and main narrator of the books, sees Edward Cullen, the vampire boy she loves and eventually marries, standing in full light for the first time, she finds it "shocking . . . His skin . . . literally sparkled, like thousands of tiny diamonds were embedded in the surface" and with "His glistening, pale lavender [eye]lids" closed, Edward appears to be "a perfect statue, carved in some unknown stone, smooth like marble, glittering like crystal" (Meyer, *Twilight* 260). The overall effect is, Bella says, "too beautiful to be real" (*Twilight* 261), and she comes to see Edward as a "fantastic sparkling creature" (*Twilight* 292), one she loves with an intensity that borders on literal self-abnegation; later on in the series, when Bella fantasizes about having a son with Edward, she "hoped he [the son] would have Edward's face exactly, with no interference from mine" (*Breaking Dawn* 132).

The literal sparkle of Meyer's vampires has become a central feature in the series' mythology, one so popular that many pieces of *Twilight* merchandise prominently feature the phrase "I [Heart] Boys Who Sparkle." This chapter takes its title from those buttons and T-shirts, but it is concerned less with the ways in which Edward Cullen literally sparkles and more with the ways in which his effeminacy makes him metaphorically sparkle, the ways in which his effeminacy combines with more traditionally masculine characteristics to create a hybrid gender performance that Bella finds not just attractive, but irresistible.

First, some caveats. Edward Cullen is heterosexual. He is also not your typical sissy. He is not weak or shy or fearful; he is super-fast, super-strong, almost invulnerable to physical harm, immortal, ageless, and telepathic. If as sociologist CJ Pascoe argues, "Demonstrating dominance in a variety of ways is a central part of contemporary American masculinity," then Edward is most definitely a normatively masculine man (86). He watches Bella constantly, desires to know her every thought and often literally demonstrates mastery over her body by lifting, carrying, or supporting it. There are numerous examples of

Edward exerting literal, physical control over Bella's body. A few examples include when Edward "scooped [Bella] up in his arms, as easily as if [she] weighed ten pounds instead of a hundred and ten" (*Twilight* 97); when Edward "leaned forward and reached out with his long arms to pick [Bella] up, gripping the tops of [her] arms like [she] was a toddler" (*Twilight* 297); when Edward "pulled [Bella] along" (*New Moon* 462); and when Bella "let him drag [her] along" (*Eclipse* 201). These examples of Edward controlling Bella's body are obviously fictional, but they parallel some real-life behaviors between adolescent boys and girls that reinforce a sense that boys are dominant and girls are submissive. Pascoe, drawing on her observation of American high schoolers, reports that "[b]oys and girls antagonized each other in a flirtatious way. The flirtatious physical interaction escalated, becoming increasingly violent, until a girl squealed, cried, or just gave up. This sort of daily drama physically engendered meanings of power in which boys were confirmed as powerful and girls weak" (98). Edward's physical control over Bella's body reinforces this boy-powerful/girl-weak dichotomy in their relationship, as does the huge edge he has over her in terms of knowledge, skills, and life experience (Edward was born in 1901 and is thus 104 years old when he meets 17-year-old Bella).

But in spite of his dominance over Bella and the masculinity that his dominance signals, Meyer routinely describes Edward in language that implies his effeminacy. And because readers are given these descriptions of Edward's effeminate characteristics through the narrating consciousness of Bella, who is madly in love with Edward, Edward's effeminacy comes to be seen as a huge part of the reason that Bella is attracted to Edward in the first place. That is, Bella likes Edward—she [hearts] this particular boy who sparkles—in part because of his effeminacy, not in spite of it.

First, there is the matter of Edward's physical stature. Edward was turned into a vampire at the age of 17 and will thus look that age forever (*Twilight* 287). On her first sighting of him, Bella immediately notes his boyishness and the way it sets him apart from other male vampires, who are more manly; compared with them, Edward is "lanky, less bulky . . . more boyish than the others, who looked like they could be in college"

(*Twilight* 18). Edward does have a "muscular" chest (*Twilight* 170), but he is also a skilled dancer who moves "fluidly" (*Twilight* 25); even when he is locked in life-or-death combat with another vampire, Bella describes the violence as Edward "dancing" and moving "lithely" (*Eclipse* 545). And while Bella does call Edward "absurdly handsome" once (*Twilight* 27), she generally uses the more feminine adjective beautiful to describe him: Edward is "the beautiful boy" (*Twilight* 20) and "this bizarre, beautiful boy" (*Twilight* 50). And when Bella describes his whole face, she does so using language that paints Edward as both masculine and feminine: "the perfection of his face . . . his pale white features: the hard square of his jaw, the softer curve of his full lips . . . the sharp angle of his cheekbones . . . a thick fringe of black lashes . . . It was a face any male model in the world would trade his soul for" (*Eclipse* 17). It is also a hybrid face, one that mixes the masculinity of a "hard square" jaw with the "softer curve" of lips and a "fringe of black lashes." Edward's eyelids are also "glistening, pale lavender" (*Twilight* 260).

Nor are Edward's lips, lids, and lashes the only effeminate things about him. He dresses "exceptionally well . . . in clothes that hinted of designer origins" (*Twilight* 32) and speaks in a voice that is "velvet" (*Twilight* 81), "honey-sweet" (*New Moon* 187), and filled with the "gentle cadences of an earlier century" (*Twilight* 265). He writes in a "clear, elegant script" (*Twilight* 46) and emits an "exquisite scent" (*Twilight* 193). He is also concerned with manners and being polite (*Eclipse* 319). Perhaps most entrancing to Bella is Edward's love of the fine arts, the way he asks her about "books—endlessly books" (*Twilight* 229) and scorns contemporary rock music in favor of composing and playing his own classical music for the piano that is "so complex, so luxuriant" (*Twilight* 326).

Sociologist Michael Kimmel argues that contemporary white middle-class masculinity in America is defined by a "Guy Code" whose first and most important tenet is that guys must never be caught "showing emotions or admitting to weakness . . . Kindness is not an option, nor is compassion. Those sentiments are taboo" (*Guyland* 45). To express emotion, to be kind or compassionate, is to be seen as feminine in the eyes of other guys. And to be feminized is to be weak, to be a failed man. Drawing on the work of sociologist Raewyn Connell[2] and her key term "hegemonic masculinity," we can say that adherence to the Guy Code that Kimmel describes—emotional stoicism, physical dominance over women, homophobia, and a rejection of anything perceived to be feminine—constitutes hegemonic masculinity for white middle-class men in the early twenty-first century United States. While multiple masculinities exist simultaneously, hegemonic masculinity is the form valorized at a given historical moment by a given dominant culture: "Hegemonic masculinity is not a fixed character type, always and everywhere the same. It is, rather, the masculinity that occupies the hegemonic position in a given pattern of gender relations, a position always contestable" (Connell 76). Like all ideals, few men actually achieve or perform fully hegemonic masculinity, but men who can approach the ideal receive the greatest share of the patriarchal dividend.

Kimmel's Guy Code is hegemonic among middle-class white men in contemporary America; and by the terms of this Guy Code, Edward Cullen is a failed man. But failed according to whom? Bella certainly does not think of Edward as a failed man; she can't get enough of Edward's sparkly effeminacy and vastly prefers it to the masculinity practiced by Guy Code–adhering human boys her own age. For example, there is a more hegemonically masculine human boy, Mike, who crushes on Bella and whom she continually rejects. When Mike asks Bella what she did the previous day, Bella rankles, finding his "tone just a bit too proprietary" (*Twilight* 143), while when the less conventionally masculine Edward admits that he has been following Bella's every movement, including breaking into her bedroom at night to watch her sleep, she feels "a strange surge of pleasure" (*Twilight* 174).

It is worth noting here that while Edward's sparkly effeminacy is non-normative in some ways, it is found in a series of books that are deeply conservative in their eroticization of marriage, patriarchy, and masochistic self-abnegation for young women. Edward—like Liberace, whom I will discuss below—is thus an important reminder that gender nonconformity is not always linked to progressive political goals or outcomes. This convergence of non-normative gender performance and a broader project of conservative sex/gender politics becomes visible when the *Twilight* novels' treatment of sex/dating/relationships is examined in greater detail.[3]

But whatever their sex/gender politics, the *Twilight* novels do consistently portray Edward's sparkly effeminacy as a more desirable alternative to other forms of straight male gender presentation. Edward's only serious rival for Bella's affection is Jacob Black, a teenaged Native American werewolf. But Bella ultimately chooses to be with Edward, in part because Jacob is more conventionally masculine, which is a turn-off for Bella. Being a werewolf makes Jacob 6'7" tall and gives him a "man's body" (*New Moon* 373); he is "muscled up the way no normal sixteen-and-a-half-year-old ever had been" (*Eclipse* 77). Furthermore, while Edward writes classical music for Bella, Jacob's passion is auto mechanics. Watching Jacob build motorcycle engines with two of his guy friends, Bella says, "Many of the words they used were unfamiliar to me, and I figured I'd have to have a Y chromosome to really understand the excitement" (*New Moon* 139). Edward never makes her feel excluded like this.

Also, Jacob is more physically aggressive with Bella than Edward is. It is Jacob who forces a kiss on Bella, "twisting [one hand] into a fist around the roots of [her] hair" while his other hand "grabbed roughly at [her] shoulder, shaking [her], then dragging [her] to him" while his lips "tried to force a response out of [hers]" (*Eclipse* 526). In contrast, Edward is resolutely, adamantly chaste with Bella. He will kiss her, but to go any further means that he might lose control and drink Bella's blood, killing her. In fact, it is Bella who demands sex from Edward, and Edward who preserves both Bella's virtue and his own by refusing her demands and insisting on no sex before marriage. "Bella," he asks her, "would you *please* stop trying to take your clothes off?" (*Eclipse* 450, emphasis Meyer's). The two do eventually wed, have sex, and have a child together in the final novel, but Edward's superhuman self-control (and the virtue it preserves in both Bella and himself) is a theme throughout the books. "It's just that you are so soft, so fragile," Edward tells Bella. "I could reach out, meaning to touch your face, and crush your skull by mistake . . . I can never afford to lose any kind of control when I'm with you" (*Twilight* 310). And this self-control, this willingness to delay having sex, is, of course, another component of Edward's sparkly effeminacy, another of his characteristics that makes Bella swoon. It is also another thing about him that makes him a loser according to Kimmel's Guy Code, wherein a real guy would never delay sex with a girl, since the sexual conquest of women is an important way of achieving status relevant to other guys.

But again, Bella does not see Edward as a loser. In fact, his self-control and willingness to delay sex are huge factors that set Edward apart from other men and contribute powerfully to Bella's attraction to him. The link between Edward's sparkly effeminacy and the sexual safety it provides is illustrated during a scene in *Twilight* where Bella is chased, threatened, and almost raped by a group of "four men" in Port Angeles, Washington (157). Although these men "weren't too many years older than [Bella] was," Meyer calls them "men" (not boys) and describes them in terms that make their hegemonic masculinity clear. Bella first sees them standing around in a group, engaging in masculine horseplay, "joking loudly amongst themselves, laughing raucously and punching each other's arms" (*Twilight* 157). And in contrast to Edward's high-fashion wardrobe, the leader of this gang of men is dressed sloppily, "wearing a flannel shirt open over a dirty t-shirt, cut-off jeans, and sandals" when he chases Bella and traps her in an alleyway (*Twilight* 157). Before anything can happen, Bella is rescued by Edward. Sitting in the passenger's seat of Edward's expensive sports car as she is driven away to safety, Bella remarks on how safe Edward makes her feel, thinking that "it was amazing how instantaneously the choking fear [of impending rape] vanished, amazing how suddenly the feeling of security washed over me" (*Twilight* 162). The implicit message here is the same message delivered by the contrast between Jacob's aggressive kissing and Edward's sexual restraint: hegemonically masculine guys are sexually aggressive at best and rapists at worst, while sparkly effeminate boys are sweet and safe. The *Twilight* saga thus ultimately critiques the abuse of power between men and women, while leaving wholly intact a vision of the world where men are figured as the more powerful protectors of less-powerful women. Bella fears being raped, but she also needs Edward, a masterful and strong man, to come and rescue her from being raped. The idea that she could escape on her own, fend off her attackers on her own, or be rescued by another woman or group of women is not seemingly possible in the *Twilight* universe. The *Twilight* saga does not reject the idea that men (even effeminate men like Edward) are more masterful and powerful than women. To the contrary, the *Twilight* saga embraces this very conservative idea; Edward is alluring to Bella precisely because he chooses to use his mastery and power to protect women rather than abuse them.[4] In either case, male mastery and power over women is presumed as a given.

So while Edward remains a deeply problematic figure for anyone with an interest in feminist or queer politics of sex/gender, Bella loves Edward's sparkly effeminacy deeply. For evidence that many flesh-and-blood women love the same thing, look no further than the sales figures for the *Twilight* saga and the ticket sales of its filmic adaptations and for evidence that these women are of all ages (not just pre-teens) see Sarah Hepola's *Salon.com* report on middle-aged, self-proclaimed "Twi-Moms" who talk online about "how smart and old-fashioned and well-mannered" Edward is.

In the above reading of *Twilight,* I have attempted to outline the main features of what I am calling sparkly effeminacy. Boys Who Sparkle are boys (or men) who have a gender presentation that tends toward the boyish instead of the adult masculine; are heterosexual or at least presumed to be so; are not sexually aggressive, threatening, or pushy; are caring, emotionally sensitive, and attentive to women; employ many stereotypically effeminate traits in their personality and their personal styling; and are received quite differently by heterosexual women and more hegemonically masculine men. Finally, Boys Who Sparkle are also generally unreal or unavailable in some sense; women's access to them is limited to fictional representations or mediated, in the real world, by the boundaries of performance and celebrity.

In enumerating these characteristics, I hope to distinguish Boys Who Sparkle from other forms of fascinating effeminacy. For example, Boys Who Sparkle are objects of women's sexual desire in a way that the Sympathetic Sissy or Truth-Telling Queens discussed in previous chapters are not. In particular, I wish to distinguish between Boys Who Sparkle and other performers—primarily musicians, such as Little Richard, 1970s-era Mick Jagger, Prince, and the members of 1980s hair metal bands such as Poison or Mötley Crüe—whose effeminacy is linked to both physical adulthood and an unquenchable heterosexual sex drive that is distinct from the boyishness and emotionally sensitive chastity offered by Boys Who Sparkle. Boys Who Sparkle should also be seen as distinct from the gay best friend stereotype, where effeminate gay men serve as a straight woman's best friend, hairdresser, stylist, and/or decorator. Those men—take the cast of *Queer Eye For The Straight Guy* as five examples[5]—are seen as explicitly gay. As such, they are coded as asexual friend figures, not idealized love interests, and thus cannot be Boys Who Sparkle.

In the case of Edward Cullen, I hope that the above close reading proves that he is boyish, heterosexual, not sexually aggressive, attentive to women, and somewhat effeminate. He is also a fictional character, and thus he is only available imaginatively to the women who love him. As for the final characteristic of Boys Who Sparkle—my claim that they provoke very different reactions among women and more hegemonically masculine men—I want to save my discussion of the gender-polarized reaction to Edward's sparkly effeminacy for later in this chapter. For now, I want to make the case that Edward is hardly the first American boy to have sparkled. And, so, I turn to a discussion of America's most famous Boy Who Sparkled: Liberace.

"THE WOMEN LOVE HIM IN GREAT DROVES": MR. SHOWMANSHIP'S SPARKLE

Wladziu Valentino Liberace—known to his family as Wally, his friends as Lee, and the public by his last name only—was a Wisconsin-born son of immigrants (his mother was Polish, his father Italian) who combined an immense talent with the piano, his natural charm, and a love of costumes as expensive as they were sparkly into a multimillion dollar career as a touring musician and television personality. A gay man who remained officially closeted all his life, Liberace nonetheless built his onstage and on-air persona around a glittery, campy brand of effeminacy. He had ornate candelabras perched on his pianos, was chauffeured onstage in Rolls Royce limousines, and employed numerous flashy costume changes. A standard bit of on-stage patter involved him asking his audiences to excuse him while he went to "slip into something more spectacular" (qtd. in Pyron 289). This persona earned the self-proclaimed "Mr. Showmanship" millions of dollars, several television shows, and celebrity that lasted from the 1940s until his death in 1987. At the risk of overstating the obvious—since the name Liberace is now virtually synonymous with glitter, glitz, and campy, effeminate excess—Liberace's onstage persona exuded sparkly effeminacy.

Boys Who Sparkle project a boyish rather than a fully adult masculinity, and Liberace was no exception. Although Liberace's national fame began in the 1940s (when he was in his twenties) and continued through the 1980s (when he was in his sixties), a projected boyishness was always an important part of his act. As a family friend explained, Liberace spoke—even well into adulthood—in "a voice you don't often hear at football games" (qtd in Pyron 55). This was a diplomatic way of expressing the fact that Liberace had a high, nasal voice, one that was often perceived as boyish or feminine. This high-pitched voice became an asset on stage, where Liberace deliberately cultivated a boyish persona: his older brother George conducted Liberace's orchestra, and their mother always sat in the audience of his shows, while Liberace himself made a point of mentioning, and talking to, both his older brother and his mother in between-song banter. (When being sponsored by a tuna fish company, for example, Liberace would ask his viewers to send any good tuna recipes they had to his mother, so that she could prepare them for him.) In this way, Liberace's television shows became a miniature family drama, with Liberace himself playing the subordinate, youthful roles of little brother and devoted son, despite actually being the top-billed star of the show. The deliberate boyishness of Liberace's act was not lost on critics and reviewers either. As one reviewer noted: Liberace "talks to his audience with a perpetual smile on his face—the kind of smile a little boy musters to prove to his parents that he's brushed his teeth—and he speaks in the carefully controlled and subdued voice of a kindergarten teacher talking to a nervous child" (qtd. in Pyron 155). Another, more derisive critic noted Liberace's "quality—which comes out in his bounciness, his sweet smile, his nasal voice, his my-oh-my prose style—of being just a big little boy" (qtd. in Pyron 171).

Liberace's boyishness only intensified his effeminacy, and Liberace was publically very effeminate during a time when effeminacy was widely presumed to be a marker of male homosexuality. In truth, he was gay, and—if his scholarly biographer is to be believed—not particularly subtle or secretive about his desires either: "'He wasn't discrete, he was daring and rather outrageous about it,' a gay television director [said], . . . recall[ing] the entertainer's escapades in the sixties" (Pyron 221). Furthermore, celebrity gossip magazines were insinuating that Liberace was gay from at least the early 1950s; for example, "Why Liberace's Theme Song Should Be 'Mad About the Boy!'" was a 1957 *Hollywood Confidential* headline (Pyron 221).

Nevertheless, while some viewers and fans undoubtedly looked at Liberace and read his persona as gay—singer Elton John recalled Liberace as the first gay person he'd ever seen on television (Pyron 175)—the onstage and on-air persona Liberace performed was heterosexual. Liberace aggressively sued for libel to quash gay rumor–mongering in the tabloid press, and he often succeeded. For example, he won $40,000 in damages in a 1958 settlement with *Hollywood Confidential* after the magazine alleged that Liberace had sexually assaulted a male press agent (Pyron 223). In 1959, as part of another libel lawsuit against a tabloid, he testified in a British court that he was not a homosexual and had never engaged in homosexual acts (Pyron 229). This was, of course, a lie. But for purposes of my argument here, the truth or falsity of Liberace's denials is beside the point. What matters is that he repeatedly made the denial. In crafting and performing his persona, he insisted, against a mountain of evidence to the contrary, that his persona was straight. To be clear, my argument here is indeed about Liberace the onstage and on-air persona, not Lee Liberace the human being. I see Liberace the persona as something that Lee Liberace the human being (and his public relations team) crafted, performed, and sold to the public. Since this persona was, as Lee Liberace and his staff constantly insisted, both effeminate and heterosexual, I include the Liberace persona here as an example of a Boy Who Sparkles, despite the fact that in private Lee Liberace was gay.

Many straight women took Liberace at his word on the matter of his sexuality and saw him as not just a heterosexual man but as the ideal heterosexual man. This opinion was immortalized in song when the girl group The McGuire Sisters, in their song "Mr. Sandman," wished for a man "with a lonely heart like Pagliacci; and lots of wavy hair like Liberace!" (qtd. in Pyron 158). To be fair, The McGuire Sisters' lyricist probably just needed to make a rhyme, but "Mr. Sandman" was hardly the only place where women expressed desire for Liberace. Indeed, the vast majority of his fan base was female: at his 1953 Carnegie Hall concert, "three-fourths" of the crowd were women (Pyron 160). And the audience of his May 1954 show at Madison Square Garden was "estimated to be 80 percent female" (Pyron 161). A study that examined all 11,368 pieces of fan mail that Liberace received during the first week of November 1956 showed that 68 percent of the letter writers were women; when the researcher grouped all the letters (from both male and female authors), he found that 23 percent expressed "much love" to Liberace, 21 percent wrote to tell him that he was "cute," and that another 7 percent wrote to express "admiration for specific qualities like smile, wink, or dimple" (Winick 133, 137). One journalist said that most of Liberace's fan mail was from "married women between 20 and 60" (qtd. in Pyron 170), and another journalist described Liberace as a teen idol for older, married women: "He has marshaled these middle-aged mommas and exhorted an intensity of hero-worship that is akin to the earlier demonstrations of their teenage daughters for Sinatra or Johnny Ray" (qtd. in Pyron 170). Nor were middle-aged women the only women Liberace entranced. "Girls, adolescents, and young married women adored him too" and "after the summer of 1953, Liberace went nowhere without being overwhelmed by masses of adoring females" (Pyron 172). During one appearance to promote a bank opening in Miami, Liberace's presence actually inspired a riot in which several people were injured as the crowd of women pressed close in hopes of getting to see the performer (Pyron 157). *TV Guide* summed up the female fervor for Liberace when it wrote that "his appeal is strictly to women. The women love him in great droves" (qtd. in Pyron 150).

While perceived as heterosexual, Liberace's appeal was also predicated on his not being sexually aggressive or threatening. The quotes from female fans that opened this chapter certainly reflect this view. Some women saw in Liberace "the possibility of sophisticated companionship, witty discourse, male strength, and masculine attentiveness without the likelihood of rape or even sex" (Pyron 172–173). Liberace cultivated this blend of masculinity and safety by projecting "the attributes of a loyal son, a devoted brother, an endearing friend. His personality was 'nonthreatening' in the most positive, engaging ways; he charmed and delighted people" (Pyron 108). Furthermore, he "described the central relationship between men and women as that of son and mother. In this way, the ideal man, was, by definition, the ideal son. Men were stars, but their purpose was to celebrate women—mothers, rather—not to court or make love to them" (Pyron 170–71). Liberace provided some female fans with the fantasy of male companionship "devoid of overt, physical sexuality . . . he was a desirable, attractive man, but one purged of masculine loutishness" (Pyron 172). That is, in looking at Liberace, women saw a new kind of man, an entirely different possibility for what masculinity might be, and some of them liked what they saw.

Liberace and his management knew about, and deliberately played up, this specific type of appeal. For example, when Liberace's management tried to squash gay rumors by having Liberace date—and allegedly become engaged to—a woman named Joanne Rio around 1954, they publicized the relationship by putting out ghost-written newspaper articles published under Rio's name. Written by members of Liberace's staff, these articles from the point of view of "Rio" talked about what a kind and considerate partner Liberace was. "He's so considerate on dates," writes "Rio," emphasizing Liberace's (positive) difference from other, less emotionally sensitive men. "He never forgets the little things that women love. He brings me orchids. He lights my cigarettes and opens doors. He makes you feel that when you are with him, well, you are really with him" (qtd. in Pyron 210). This new—and very desirable to some—way of being an (ostensibly) heterosexual male that Liberace offered is what I have been calling sparkly effeminacy. That is, what many men called Liberace's effeminacy was not something that (some) women ignored so that they might feel attracted to him; rather, it was a central reason for their attraction. Indeed, the one time Liberace deliberately tried to not be effeminate, his career suffered for it. According to Pyron, Liberace's career only suffered one period of downturn: from roughly 1955 to roughly 1962. What Pyron calls the "lowest ebb" of Liberace's career came in 1959, after a financially disastrous period in which Liberace remade his image by masculinizing it (250). On a television show that aired from October 1958 to April 1959, fans saw a more conventionally masculine Liberace with no candelabra and no glitzy costumes. According to a review in *Variety*, the musician even deliberately worked to speak in a voice several octaves lower than normal (Pyron 201–202). Fans hated the change and by the early 1960s Liberace returned to effeminate glitz and never looked back.

Given the degree to which the name Liberace has become synonymous with effeminacy in US pop culture, it seems almost ludicrous to ask what exactly made Liberace effeminate. Nevertheless, I will provide a quick summary. Liberace's boyhood was that of the classic sissy: "As a boy, he disliked sports and the rough-and-tumble games his peers played" (Pyron 35). Liberace himself remarked on this in one of his many memoirs, saying: "you got dirty playing [sports]. I didn't like that" (qtd. in Pyron 35). Pyron puts all of this more bluntly later, when he says that "Wally Liberace was a mama's boy, a sissy, and faggy ways distinguished almost everything he did long after 1932" (55). While shying away from sports and other activities that might get him dirty, Liberace gravitated toward the fine arts. In addition to his hours of daily piano practice, he also enjoyed drama and liked cooking so much that he got a home economics course for boys instituted at his high school (Pyron 56). He was also a skilled typist at a time when typing was considered a decidedly feminine skill, and he loved drafting and painting (Pyron 56). In terms of clothing, he "loved pretty things and dressed accordingly" (Pyron 56). A devout Roman Catholic his whole life, he loved the pomp and ceremony of Catholic Mass, and once he became famous, he made pomp and ceremony (and extreme luxury and excess) a signature part of his stage routine. The fur coats with long trains that he wore; the glittering candleabra that became his symbol; the Rolls Royce limos he was driven onstage in; the lush style of home decorating that he emphasized in publicity photos and interviews; and the outrageous, often literally sparkly costumes that he wore: the great pleasure that Liberace took in wearing, using, acquiring, and owning all of these things served to link him, in viewer's minds, with consumer capitalism and shopping, a realm gendered as feminine in post-WWII American culture (Pyron 174).

Liberace thus embodied the key features of sparkly effeminacy: boyishness, heterosexuality without the risk of physical aggression, a sensitivity and devotion to women's feelings, and mannerisms that many more hegemonically masculine men would find effeminate. Also, most of his adoring fans knew him only through his television shows and live performances; like all Boys Who Sparkle, Liberace thus remained somewhat unreal and inaccessible to most of his fans. Indeed, if Liberace did not invent the Boy Who Sparkles type, he certainly perfected it and is thus the symbolic ancestor of all later Boys Who Sparkled. Edward Cullen is, in a sense, an undead, perpetually teenage Liberace with fangs, one whose sparkly costumes have become internalized and reconstituted as sparkly skin. Liberace is thus a thematic ancestor to a host of teen idols whose public personas have utilized elements of the Boy Who Sparkles trope: David Cassidy and early Michael Jackson are good examples, as are the members of Boy Bands from the 1980s (New Kids on the Block, New Edition) and the 1990s and early aughts (Backstreet Boys, *NSYNC). Finally, early Justin Beiber would be a good contemporary example of a performer whose persona includes elements of the Boy Who Sparkles trope.[6]

"STONING HIM TO DEATH WITH MARSHMALLOWS": GENDER-POLARIZED REACTION TO SPARKLY MALE EFFEMINACY

Beloved as they may be, Boys Who Sparkle also present challenge of interpretation to the women who love them. Bella insists that Edward is not a monster but an ideal lover. If she is wrong, if her interpretation of Edward's ability to control himself around her is incorrect, she will literally lose her life. Liberace did not have fangs, but if his female fans "read" him incorrectly, then their dream man was not heterosexual at all but in fact a homosexual, a figure often portrayed as shadowy, corrupt, and dangerous throughout the decades of Liberace's fame (from McCarthy's queer-baiting in the 1950s to gay men as being characterized as both the cause and carriers of HIV/AIDS in the 1980s to name just a few "high" points of homophobia in mainstream American culture).

Controversies about how to "read" these sparkly men have not been limited solely to their fans, and so I now want to turn to the last, and perhaps most important, feature of sparkly effeminacy: the fact that it inspires markedly different reactions in women and men whose sense of self is closely aligned with hegemonic masculinity. As the above discussions of Liberace and Edward Cullen have hopefully proved, many heterosexual women respond quite favorably to sparkly effeminacy, seeing it as an alluring alternative to more misogynistic and sexually aggressive forms of male heterosexuality. But what is simultaneously true is that many more hegemonically masculine men react to Boys Who Sparkle with a mix of mockery and hatred that might best be called phobic. In other words, straight women have tended to see Boys Who Sparkle as fascinating, whereas many straight men have seen Boys Who Sparkle as threatening. Using both Liberace and Edward Cullen as examples, I will survey some of this phobic male reaction before moving into a discussion of what this gender-polarized reaction means for theories of the grotesque.

In a May 1957 TV interview with Mike Wallace, American novelist, essayist, and social critic Philip Wylie describes being stuck in traffic in Miami because of Liberace. Wylie does not say what exactly Liberace was doing in Miami at the time, but whatever the reason, the sheer number of the musician's fans, and their exuberance, annoyed Wylie. Seeing "the streets blocked with morons and having to drive around these swarms of hysterical middle-aged gals," makes Wylie think of "getting a bunch of the last few male men left in the continent and stoning him [Liberace] to death with marshmallows" (Wylie, Interview).

It is little surprise that Wylie—the American Cold Warrior famous for his breathtakingly misogynistic bestseller *Generation of Vipers* (1942) and its condemnation of what he called Momism—should have dreamed of stoning Liberace to death. After all, in the collection of essays that make up the book, Wylie argued that middle-class prosperity, which enabled the purchase of time- and labor-saving household appliances, had left (white) middle-class American women with no work to do. And because "the machine has deprived her of social usefulness," and "time has stripped away her biological possibilities" (childbirth), the middle-aged American housewife has turned to consumerism and her husband, the American man, has "sealed his own soul . . . by handing her the checkbook and going to work in the service of her caprices" (*Generation* 199). By honoring the figure of "Mom," Wylie argues, America has gone astray: "The mealy look of men today is the result of momism" (*Generation* 210). That is, American men have become weakened by doting mothers, who, for Wylie, are controlling, enervating harpies mad for a tawdry consumer culture (*Generation* 214). *Generation of Vipers* drew a line in the metaphorical sand. It declared an intra-American culture war, and Liberace—who counted middle-aged women amongst his biggest supporters, and who enthusiastically participated in consumer culture (both by wearing outlandish jewelry and costumes, and by using his show as a popular advertising venue through which companies could market to his female fans)—stood firmly and clearly on the opposite side of that conflict from Wylie.

In Wylie's eyes, Liberace is a man, but he is not truly male. To make matters worse, he incites "swarms of hysterical middle-aged gals," which forces Wylie to look at and think about the existence of such women. For this offense, Wylie says that Liberace deserves to be stoned to death, an ancient manner of execution typically used by men to kill women who violated the norms of patriarchy by engaging in sex outside of the bonds of marriage. What is needed to kill Liberace, though, Wylie suggests, is not real stones. Liberace is so weak that even soft, squishy marshmallows would do the job. Wylie's comment, like most phobic discourse, is internally contradictory: on the one hand Liberace is so threatening that he must be executed by the community (of "male men"), while on the other hand Liberace is so weak and ludicrous that even a thrown marshmallow would kill him.

Nor was Wylie the only man to react so violently to Liberace. In a 1956 article in London's *Daily Mirror*, William Connor, writing under the pseudonym Cassandra, called Liberace a "deadly, winking, sniggering, snuggling, chromium-plated, scent-impregnated, luminous, quivering, giggling, fruit-flavored, mincing, ice-covered heap of mother love" and concluded that the performer was "the summit of sex—the pinnacle of masculine, feminine, and neuter. Everything that he, she, and it can ever want" (qtd. in Pyron 194). In British court, Liberace sued for libel in response to this article, saying that it insinuated that he was homosexual and therefore hurt his career. After testifying in court that he himself was not a homosexual and had never engaged in homosexual activities, Liberace won the libel case.

But that hardly stopped the rumors or the scorn that more hegemonically masculine men heaped upon him. Pyron describes how by the mid-1950s, there were a number of Liberace jokes in circulation—for example, "What is better than roses on a piano? Tulips on your organ!"—which both mocked his effeminacy and insinuated his homosexuality (158). And according to the biographer of Edward R. Murrow, the famous journalist "looked faintly nauseous" after interviewing Liberace and said that he'd found the horrors of World War II less offensive to report about (qtd. in Pyron 176).

And if Cold Warriors on the right (and the anti-Red Scare reporter Murrow) had hated Liberace in the 1950s, the Northeast-based critics of the 1960s (and beyond)—both in the avant-garde and the center-left—were not kind to him either. To the 1960s leftists, art was political, commercialism was suspect, mainstream American values were to be questioned, and difficulty/complexity in art was in vogue. From their perspective, Liberace—who insisted that art was apolitical, reveled in lavish consumerism, counted legions of fans in the American heartland, and delighted in making art that so-called regular folks could enjoy—was hopelessly out of step with the times. Despite

Liberace's massive fame and success, the *New York Times* mentioned him in its pages only four times from 1959 to 1980 (Pyron 294). Even as late as 1981, *Rolling Stone* magazine blasted Liberace for founding "a fey sort of evangelism that celebrates schmaltz, glitter, and vanity" (qtd. in Pyron 283). (Apparently the glitter and vanity so central to the band that the magazine took its name from was the acceptable kind of glitter and vanity.) And the *Village Voice*, reviewing the showman's final public performance, at Radio City Music Hall in the fall of 1986, wrote that Liberace "gives emptiness form—specifically, a crust of rhinestones and fluff" (qtd. in Pyron 283).

Edward Cullen has also inspired similar (gendered, phobic) reactions in more hegemonically masculine men. These men do not exist in the pages of the *Twilight* novels (where no one pokes fun of Edward for being effeminate), but for evidence of *Twilight* hate amongst hegemonically masculine men in the real world, simply Google the phrase "I hate Twilight" or "Twilight backlash" and marvel at the results. For example, in a July 2009 post, *Variety* magazine blogger Anne Thompson describes a "Twilight backlash" led by men at San Diego's Comic-Con International in 2009. Angry about the long lines caused by (mostly female) *Twilight* fans at Comic-Con events, some men walked around the convention with signs reading "*Twilight* has ruined Comic-Con," and "Comics Fans Agree: *Twilight* Sucks" (Thompson). It is interesting to note that San Diego's Comic-Con is the annual Mecca of comic book nerd boys, who are themselves hardly considered hegemonically masculine and who nevertheless react misogynistically when the fans of a for-girls franchise is perceived as invading their space. Blogger Annalee Newitz sums up many male criticisms of the books by saying "there is a general consensus that these movies are 'just for girls/women/mothers/daughters/sisters.' I can't tell you how many men have told me informally—or written formally in various publications—things like, 'My daughter is obsessed with Twilight [*sic*] and I don't understand,' or 'My wife and daughters are downstairs watching a Twilight [*sic*] movie. I am hiding upstairs.' . . . I think if you scratch the surface of comments like that, what you find underneath is a room full of men screaming 'booo' because they hate pop culture aimed at women. Or because they are scared of it."

An anti-*Twilight* illustration that accompanies Newitz's post is also useful in illustrating male dismissal of *Twilight*. The illustration shows a glittery pile of human excrement, and its text reads: "A sparkling piece of shit / Is still just a piece of shit" (Newitz). Obviously, this illustration is an attack on the *Twilight* saga as a whole (and, one suspects, the alleged "shittyness" of Meyer's writing), but it ties that attack quite explicitly to Edward's sparkle. In this argument, Edward's brand of sparkly effeminacy is shitty, and it transfers over to, and ruins, the whole series.

Feminist cultural critic Anita Sarkeesian—who produces the online video blog series *Feminist Frequency*—dramatizes the phobic male reaction to Edward. One of her video blogs features a man saying, "Thought it [*Twilight*] was gonna be about a bunch of badass vampires who wanted to kill people and drink their blood, but no, it was some teenage pussy who didn't want to kill people instead he just wanted to be sensitive and play piano." Sarkeesian also shows examples of what she calls "the endless 'he's so gay' comments on YouTube" about Edward, including "TWILIGHT IS GAY AND FOR HOMOS!" and "That Twilight is a crock of shite[sic], and Edward is like some pale gaylord vampire." Here, quite explicitly, we see that the centerpieces of a certain line of male criticism about Edward are some of the very things that make him a boy who sparkles: his preference for non-violence, his emotional sensitivity, and his interest in music.

Having now established that both Edward Cullen and Liberace have provoked extremely gender-bifurcated reactions (the fascinating grotesque from some straight women, the threatening grotesque from some more hegemonically masculine straight men), I want to return to theories of the grotesque and discuss what these gender-bifurcated reactions mean to our understanding of the grotesque itself and its functions.

THE GROTESQUE RE-EVALUATED: TOWARD A MORE VIEWER/READER-CENTRIC APPROACH

In the Introduction, I argued that effeminacy is routinely portrayed in terms of the grotesque. I also provided the following general definition of the grotesque: it is is an interdisciplinary style (it occurs in both visual art and textual art); it is concerned with the non-normative human body; it focuses on both the tensions and the pleasures produced by hybridity; its overall effect on readers/viewers can be both alluring and revolting, often both at the same time; and its overall relationship to the status quo has been a subject of great debate. This debate has tended to separate theorists of the grotesque into two camps: those who think the grotesque is conservative, in the sense that its use reinforces the status quo in a given culture, and those who think that it is radical, in the sense that its use can subvert or otherwise challenge the status quo.

Wolfgang Kayser takes the conservative side, arguing that the grotesque provides "the most obvious and pronounced contradictions of any kind of rationalism and systematic use of thought" (188). But in the hands of a true artist, Kayser says that the grotesque can lead to "a secret liberation" (188). It can do this because "[i]n spite of all the helplessness and horror inspired by the dark forces" represented in the grotesque, the use of the representational mode shows viewers/readers that "[t]he darkness has been sighted, the ominous powers discovered, the incomprehensible forces challenged" (188). The grotesque is, for Kayser, ultimately "AN ATTEMPT TO INVOKE AND SUBDUE THE DEMONIC ASPECTS OF THE WORLD," a point he thought important enough to express in all caps (188). Grotesque art (both visual and textual) disturbs viewers and readers by presenting types of hybridity that challenge cultural norms, but in its use the abnormal (what Kayser calls "THE DEMONIC ASPECTS OF THE WORLD") is ultimately subdued and triumphed over. In Kayser's reading, grotesque art threatens an upheaval of the status quo, but it does so only to ultimately insist on the goodness and correctness of that status quo.

For Kayser, the conservative nature of the grotesque is a net positive. For Mab Segrest, it is decidedly negative, but she nonetheless agrees with Kayser about the grotesque's political ends. In twentieth-century fiction by women from the US South, Segrest says, the grotesque sorts people into two categories: the normal and the freak. Grotesque writing then goes on to stigmatize the freak and "this scapegoating process cuts the freak off from the community" (25). This is obviously harmful to those deemed to be freakish, but Segrest argues that it is also harmful for those still defined as normal because "everyone is a freak" and "no human can cram her/himself into the narrow space that is the state of normalcy" (25). Grotesque writing thus does nothing more than re-stage real-world communal practices wherein an ostensibly normal majority singles out a few ostensibly freakish individuals and then punishes those individuals (with humiliation, isolation, violence, and/or death) so that the supposed normality of the majority is preserved.

Whereas Kayser and Segrest have conservative interpretations of the grotesque, Mikhail Bakhtin is the giant figure in the grotesque-is-radical camp. Examining the work of French writer Francois Rabelais (1494–1553), Bakhtin argues that Rabelais's grotesque imagery was adapted from the European folk traditions known as carnival. During carnival, the social order was temporarily suspended or upended: peasants were allowed to make fun of and/or briefly "rule over" the nobles and religious leaders who were normally their social superiors. For Bakhtin, one important detail of carnival is that it is truly communal and thus "does not acknowledge any distinction between actors and spectators . . . Carnival is not a spectacle seen by the people; they live in it, and everyone participates because its very idea embraces all people" (7). Rabelais's grotesque—the literary form adapted from the real-world practice of carnival—is therefore also, according to Bakhtin, communal. It is not like a modern-day freakshow where a mass of spectators look at a few individuals deemed to be freakish. In Rabelais's grotesque, everyone participates. But what exactly do they participate in?

According to Bakhtin, the "essential principle of grotesque realism" is "degradation, that is, the lowering of all that is high, spiritual, ideal, abstract; it is a transfer to the material level, to the sphere of earth and body" (21). Bakhtin does not see the degradation involved in the grotesque as a negative. Instead, "to degrade is to bury, to sow, and to kill simultaneously, in order to bring forth something more and better . . . Degradation digs a bodily grave for new birth; it has not only a destructive, negative aspect, but also a regenerating one . . . it is always conceiving" (21). That is to say, yes, people are made fun of in grotesque art. Their faults and flaws and eccentricities are mocked, but everyone is mocked in this same way. Everyone is degraded. The target of grotesque humor is not a single individual but human nature in general. Grotesque art often mocks those in power, but it does so to degrade them and to show the artificiality of the power and elevated position they hold over others. The Rabelaisian grotesque shows that even popes and kings fart and puke and masturbate. This is why Bakhtin finds the grotesque, at least as Rabelais practiced it, radical in its relationship to the prevailing status quo.

He does admit, though, that more modern forms of the grotesque (those appearing from the Romantic era forward) have changed. Specifically, Bakhtin argues that grotesque art since the Romantic era has lost the older form's communal character and has "acquired a private 'chamber' character" (37). Grotesque art since the Romantic era has become "an individual carnival, marked by a vivid sense of isolation" (37). Over time, then, grotesque art has become, for Bakhtin, less radical and more like the modern freak show, which makes a stark distinction between "normal" audience and "freak" performer. Thus, in a sense, Bakhtin both disagrees and agrees with Kayser and Segrest. He says that older forms of grotesque art are deeply radical, but that that radical potential has been blunted over time. (And, to be fair, the majority of Bakhtin's work is focused on a much earlier historical period than that of either Kayser or Segrest. Where their subject matters overlap chronologically, Bakhtin leans towards agreeing with Kayser.) Still, Bakhtin insists that all grotesque art—even its more modern forms—is radical because it "discloses the potentiality of an entirely different world, of another order, another way of life . . . [in grotesque art] the world is destroyed so that it may be regenerated and renewed" (48).

Another representative of the grotesque-is-radical school of thought is Patricia Yeager. Diametrically opposed to Segrest, Yeager argues that the grotesque—at least in the hands of the black and white women writers from the southern United States—is a radical tool for illustrating "what is known but not thought" in a given culture (25). That is, the grotesque can work as a "Semiotic Switchboard" that moves "background information into the foreground of a novel or story" (25).

For example, Yeager discusses a scene from *Uncle Tom's Cabin* in which a young black boy comically imitates an older black man, who is severely infirmed and walks with a limp, in order to amuse two white men. The white men in this example are slave-owners, and both the black man being imitated and the black boy doing the imitation are slaves. Yeager's argument is that when the able-bodied slave boy slips into his imitation of the limping older man, "this sudden grotesquing of the child's body skewers the 'background' features of slavery and shoves them into the foreground; the child's old body maps for the reader the slaveholders' predations," reminding the reader that slave-holders' wealth and luxury is quite literally the product of a system that works black bodies to disability and early death (26). In doing work like this, the grotesque "constructs a shock effect that can reveal the delirium of the familiar" (237); it throws the normative into sharp relief, and in doing so it can make the everyday rules and conventions of a given culture seem suddenly strange, which can lead to readers questioning those rules and conventions.

What I want to draw attention to here is the way in which both sides of this debate argue for a singular overall meaning or effect for the grotesque. The two camps differ about the political ramifications of the grotesque's effects on a viewer/reader, but both sides are convinced that the grotesque has a single end result on the reader or viewer. In other words, each of these theorists disagree wildly about the nature of the grotesque's effect, but each of them assumes that the grotesque's effect resides in the text (and/or image) itself, just waiting to be discovered by a reader or viewer who—regardless of race, gender, age, sexuality, religious faith, physical ability, and cultural background—will experience the effect of the grotesque in the same way.

The above exploration of both Edward Cullen and Liberace has shown that this account of the grotesque is inadequate. The gender-polarized reactions to Edward and Liberace's sparkly effeminacies prove that theorists of the grotesque need to account for the fact that grotesquerie (or the lack thereof) is often in the eye of the beholder. In other words: men reading Liberace and Edward as threatening is consistent with Kayser's conservative reading of the grotesque: for these men Boys Who Sparkle are figures of some fascination (their existence seems to require discussion, demand outrage, and sometimes even necessitate violence), but ultimately they are judged to be repulsive. Sparkly effeminacy requires attention from hegemonically masculine straight men, but it also demands condemnation; the status quo of a hegemonic American masculinity that admits no trace of the feminine must be maintained. On the other hand, women who love Boys Who Sparkle don't see them as freakish or bad and would likely object to the word *grotesque* being used to describe them at all. Nevertheless, women who love Liberace and Edward do view them as grotesque: not grotesque in the sense of monstrous, but grotesque in the sense of otherworldly, unreal. Women who love Liberace and Edward consistently stress how the objects of their affection are almost too good to be true, and both Liberace and Edward have been credited with embodying alternative forms of heterosexual maleness, forms their female fans find preferable to options available to them in the real world. In this sense, Liberace and Edward fulfill the grotesque function of gesturing to new worlds, new possibilities.

What is key here is that when confronted with the same allegedly grotesque thing—Liberace's or Edward's fascinating, sparkly effeminacy—different people have reacted very differently. This seems almost embarrassingly simple to say, but it nevertheless remains true: theorists of the grotesque have tended to overlook the possibility that different viewers/readers might view/read the same grotesque image in different ways. To be fair, some of the theorists of the grotesque discussed here have gestured toward the reader's role in shaping the ultimate meaning of grotesque imagery. Kayser does admit that "it remains true that the grotesque is experienced only in the act of reception" but then quickly backpedals, cautioning that we should remember "not to define the grotesque exclusively on the basis of its effect" (181). We should instead, he argues, focus on the unique "stylistic" elements of the grotesque and insist that while uneducated viewers/readers might name anything that displeases them "grotesque," the true grotesque itself has "certain specific forms and motifs which are predisposed to certain contents" and can thus be corrected identified and analyzed by a careful scholar (181). Yeager does not explicitly discuss viewer/reader reception as it relates to the grotesque, but she does admit that there are multiple kinds of grotesque writing. She also says that not all forms of the grotesque are radical, reminding readers that some of "its avatars can be less than politically progressive" (27). Yeager is thus careful to identify the specific writers she's talking about and the specific time period in which they wrote, and to make arguments about the specific kind of grotesque imagery they employed. This is, of course, perfectly fine. Specificity and clarity are to be admired in analysis, and all of the critics of the grotesque discussed above demonstrate plenty of both. What is noteworthy to me, however, is that once they have taken care to specify which type of grotesque they are talking about, they each go on to argue that it is universally received in the same way by all readers. That is, while all of the previously discussed critics take care to articulate the specific subjects of their respective analyses, both of those analyses focus on the grotesque as though the images and/or words that make up the grotesque have universal meaning.

To correct this oversight—and to build on the excellent work of Kayser, Segrest, Bakhtin, and Yeager—we need a new conception of the grotesque, one that is more attentive to the role viewer/readers play in creating the overall meaning of the grotesque. We need, that is, to follow Kayser's observation "that the grotesque is experienced only in the act of reception" (181). We need to take it more seriously than Kayser himself took it. We do not need to naively say that authorial intent doesn't matter with the grotesque; it absolutely does. But for a more complete understanding of any grotesque image, we need to look not just at how its creator shaped it and deployed it in their work, but also how it was and is received by a variety of viewer/readers.

It is not enough to say that Liberace's gender performance was hybrid and that hybridity makes him grotesque. Certainly, the phobic reaction of many men to Liberace can be read as evidence that Liberace was indeed perceived as threatening. But surely not all men felt "masculine contempt" when they looked at Liberace. Elton John alone is proof that some gay men looked at Liberace and saw the fascinating grotesque, an example that a life lived outside of strict heteronormativity was both possible and attractive. It is also not enough to draw simple binaries, to say that straight men hated Liberace and gay men loved him. After all, the lure of hegemonic masculinity (and the privilege that accompanies it) is hardly lost on gay men. While I have no archival evidence to support this claim, surely there were gay men in America who looked at Liberace and despaired at what they saw: confirmation of their worst nightmares, proof that to be gay was to be effeminate, to make a sparkly spectacle of oneself.

Nor will it do to insist that women's reactions to Liberace and Edward have been uniform. Surely not all women who saw Liberace perceived him to be heterosexual or felt attracted to him. And Edward Cullen has drawn a great deal of ire from some women, namely feminists concerned with the deeply conservative gender politics of the *Twilight* saga. For example, Sarkeesian condemns both homophobic male anti-*Twilight* backlash and the *Twilight* books themselves, saying, "[T]he wrong reasons [to hate *Twilight*] are that Edward is too sensitive, that he's gay, and that he's not violent enough" while the "right reasons" to hate *Twilight* are that "Edward is a creepy, manipulative, controlling, overprotective stalker." Another thing to remember when discussing this and other feminist critiques of *Twilight* is that not all feminists are women, which further complicates the project of understanding how the identity of viewer/reader may relate to the overall end-effect of grotesque imagery.

While detailed reader-response studies regarding the grotesque are sorely needed,[7] the sparkly effeminacy of Liberace and Edward Cullen also suggests that scholars need to be more attentive to the ways in which readers/viewers of the grotesque actually help to create the meaning of the grotesque. That is, we need to examine the ways in which readers/viewers of the grotesque actually collude in (or subvert) its meaning-making; we need to stop figuring viewers/readers of the grotesque as purely passive recipients of grotesque imagery whose meaning has been entirely predetermined by its creator/author.

For example, Liberace certainly did not intend to present himself as monstrous or threatening. Even at his most lavishly excessive (in terms of costuming and stagecraft), he sought to entertain people, not to alienate them. This is why a signature part of his stage routine was to allow a period of time, at the end of each performance, where fans could approach the stage and get a closer look at his jeweled rings, touch his lavish fur coats, examine his fancy automobiles, etc. Liberace felt that people needed fantasy and spectacle and said that he tried in his shows, "to help them [audience members] forget work and problems and enjoy, vicariously, a folderol of fun, good music, and fancy dress. I give them a little recess from the humdrum" (qtd. in Pyron 290). Liberace saw his own role as that of a helper, someone who provided some soothing escapism for his fans. This self-image is worlds apart from the simultaneously threateningly monster that Philip Wylie and other men more closely aligned with hegemonic masculinity saw in Liberace. Lee Liberace the human being certainly did not intend for his creation, Liberace the stage and TV persona, to be perceived as contemptible. It was some of his male viewers and critics, not Lee Liberace himself, who authored the Liberace-as-grotesque-monster trope and circulated it.

On the flip side, Lee Liberace certainly had a hand in writing and performing the Liberace-as-ideal-lover trope (for example, his management ghost-wrote and circulated those articles by "Joanne Rio" about what a kind and considerate lover he was). But even that was not a simple matter of a creator transmitting his work to an audience (of straight women) who simply received it as is. Because to believe that Liberace was straight, and that he was an ideal lover for women, likely took some doing during all those years where more hegemonically masculine men were mocking him and tabloid headlines were repeatedly insinuating his homosexuality. Female fans who loved Liberace clearly made decisions about what kinds of media to consume and what sources of information they would believe. They clearly were active in crafting their own narrative about their idol, and for them the end meaning of the Liberace persona was the outcome of a complex process of writing and reading involving many different agents: Lee Liberace and his management, the female fans themselves, gossip magazines, and the condemnations voiced by more hegemonically masculine men were all players, to greater or lesser degrees, in this process.

In Edward Cullen's case, too, we find evidence that the viewer/readers who receive the *Twilight* product are anything but purely passive recipients of a meaning constructed solely by Meyer herself. Meyer, Edward's creator, certainly did not author the Edward-is-a-fruity-failed-man narrative. That is an invention of some readers of the books and viewers of the movies. Within the world of the books, Meyer's narrative is that Bella rightly chooses sparkly Edward over the more hegemonically masculine werewolf Jacob. But this narrative hardly accounts for the love and devotion that some fans of the book have shown to Jacob; the Meyer-authored narrative of the *Twilight* books does not explain the "Team Jacob" phenomenon, wherein fans of the series root for Jacob and insist that he would be a better boyfriend/husband for Bella than Edward would. Meyer's narrative itself is resolutely pro-Edward. "Team Jacob" is a counter-narrative, one that fans have created themselves, using the component parts of Meyer's narrative as construction materials.

Perhaps most fascinating, though, is the way in which even on the page of the *Twilight* novels, it is viewers who create the effeminate grotesque and decide which part of the effeminate paradox a given grotesque image will emphasize. That is, within the fictional world of the *Twilight* novels, Bella does not just passively apprehend Edward's sparkly effeminacy and then heap praise upon it. On the contrary, it is Bella, not Edward, who creates Edward's sparkly effeminacy. After all, Bella is the primary narrator of the *Twilight* novels.[8] So when readers get a description of Edward, it is through Bella's eyes. Readers come to know Edward's physical appearance and mannerisms—his sparkly effeminacy—through the narrating consciousness of Bella. The novels never provide any first-person insight into Edward's consciousness and in his spoken dialogue, Edward certainly does not describe himself as either effeminate or especially sensitive. Instead of describing himself as any kind of an ideal mate, Edward spends much of the novels emphasizing his vampiric nature and insisting that he is a monster, one that Bella should avoid at all costs. Because of his ceaseless desire for Bella's blood, he says that "allowing myself to be alone with [Bella]" is "very dangerous" and a "mistake" because he could lose control at any second (*Twilight* 187). He also says that he doesn't "*want* to be a monster" but insists that he is one (*Twilight* 187, emphasis Meyer's). In the second novel, Edward becomes convinced that his being close to Bella is endangering her, and he abandons her for a time, saying that the separation is for her own good. Before he leaves, he insists that Mike Newton, the more hegemonically masculine human boy at Bella's high school, "would be a hell of a lot healthier for [Bella] to be with" (*New Moon* 45).

Edward believes himself to be threatening. He emphasizes his own hybridity (as a vampire he is both dead and living) and classifies it as monstrous (he is a superhumanly strong predator with an unquenchable desire to drink Bella's blood). He also suggests that Bella should purge his monstrousness from her life and return to the status quo (wherein high school girls date hegemonically masculine boys who aren't undead bloodsuckers). But Bella doesn't see Edward as threatening. Despite her discovery of Edward's vampirism (fairly early on in the first novel), she refuses to accept his interpretation of himself. She sees him as fascinating: a sweeter, safer, and more sensitive alternative to boys like Mike Newton.

This means that what fans of *Twilight* and members of "Team Edward" have fallen in love with is not Edward, but *Bella's interpretation* of Edward. Bella does see Edward as fantastic and otherworldly, but she does not focus on the same kind of hybridity he does (she doesn't care that he's a vampire, she loves that he's a Boy Who Sparkles), and she doesn't come to the same conclusions about that hybridity as he does (Edward thinks Bella should send him away, but Bella can't stand the thought of doing such a thing). Toward the end of the series, when Bella and Edward are married and have a child together (and after he has made her into a vampire), they settle down together in a small but lavishly decorated cabin in the woods. This cabin is, as Bella thinks, "a place where anyone could believe magic existed" and being there with Edward makes her realize that "Edward had always thought that he belonged to the world of horror stories. Of course, I'd known he was dead wrong. It was obvious that he belonged *here*. In a fairy tale" (*Breaking Dawn* 479, emphasis Meyer's). The runaway success of the *Twilight* saga would seem to leave little doubt as to whose interpretation of Edward wins the day, at least in the hearts and minds of fans.

The readings here—of both Liberace fans and *Twilight* fans—are enormously tentative and need to be backed up with more intensive research into, and reading of, texts produced by fans themselves, such as fan club magazines, websites, and fan fiction. A full undertaking of that work is outside the scope of this chapter, but I hope that what I have done here is make a convincing case for a revision of our understanding of the grotesque. Before we can truly conclude the "Is it conservative or is it radical?" debate we must attend to the ways in which viewers/readers of grotesque imagery actually help create the end-meaning of that imagery. This process of meaning-making is, as I have suggested, complex and involves many different agents (the author of a given grotesque image, the viewer/readers who receive that image, the critics who evaluate it, the various media which transmit it, etc.). The work ahead of future critics of the grotesque is thus difficult, but the contradictory reactions to sparkly effeminacy in American culture suggest that this work is necessary if we want to fully understand the uses that the grotesque has been put to in visual art, television, film, and literature of the twentieth century and the uses it will be put to in the early twenty-first.

FOUR

AMPLIFYING THE PARADOX

EFFEMINACY IN THE AGE OF HIV/AIDS

While the effeminate paradox greatly predates the onset of the global AIDS epidemic in the early 1980s, it has nevertheless been indelibly transformed and intensified by HIV/AIDS. In the stark shadow of HIV/AIDS, effeminate men emerged, in US literary and cultural discourse, as more grotesque than ever, in both senses of the word. In major US literary works dealing with HIV/AIDS, effeminate men have alternately been portrayed as both more threatening and more fascinating than they had been before. To begin to prove this point, I want to highlight two of the best-selling, most critically acclaimed, and publicly lauded works of US literature responding to the AIDS epidemic—Randy Shilts's non-fiction novel *And The Band Played On* (1987), and Tony Kushner's epic, two-part play *Angels in America* (1992–93)—and describe their wildly different characterizations of effeminacy.

Shilts names Gaëtan Dugas (1953–1984), an effeminate, gay, French Canadian flight attendant, as the "Patient Zero" of the AIDS epidemic, the first person to bring the disease to North America. Shilts alleges that Dugas knowingly spread HIV in the gay discos and bathhouses that he frequented in major North American cities. When told by a public health official that he needed to abstain because he could infect others via sexual intercourse, Shilts portrays Dugas as saying, "It's my right to do what I want with my own body. . . . it's their [Dugas's sexual partners] duty to protect themselves. . . . They know what's going on there. They've heard about this disease. . . . I've got it. . . . They can get it too" (200). Dugas thus emerges, in Shilts's account, not as someone who unknowingly spread HIV, but as a sadistic, willful, and modern Typhoid Mary, a vengeful slow motion murderer, a bathhouse-haunting Angel of Death. Furthermore, Shilts goes out of his way to link Dugas's murderous promiscuity to a powerful vanity that Shilts, drawing on misogynist stereotypes, characterizes as effeminate. Dugas, Shilts says, was "the major sissy of his working class neighborhood in Quebec City," a neighborhood Dugas used his job as a flight attendant to escape (22). Being a sissy boy earned Dugas a childhood full of bullying, but in North American and Western European discos and bathhouses, Dugas was considered beautiful. "Gaetan was the ugly duckling who had become the swan" (22), writes Shilts, who argues that Dugas's sense of self-worth depended, in a way that sexism typically frames as feminine, on men finding him sexually attractive. That is why he refused to give up sex even when he knew having it would mean infecting his partners with HIV.

Shilts's characterization of Dugas intensifies the degree to which effeminacy is seen as threatening. Effeminacy had been viewed as pathetic or monstrous in US culture long before Shilts introduced readers to Dugas. But AIDS intensifies this discourse by attaching infection, illness, and death to effeminacy's associative meanings. Prior to AIDS, an effeminate man in the United States might have been portrayed as a monster, but Shilts's portrayal of Dugas ups the ante: Dugas's effeminacy has been weaponized, it literally kills.

But threat is not the only end of the effeminate paradox to be amplified by HIV/AIDS. In *Angels in America*, Kushner does for fascinating effeminacy what Shilts did for threatening effeminacy. Although epic in its intention and scope, *Angels* is primarily centered on the lives of gay men in New York City who are struggling to endure both HIV/AIDS and the homophobia of Reagan-era America. In the play, Kushner repeatedly imbues his effeminate characters with special, and sometimes even superhuman, abilities. For example, the play's protagonist, Prior Walter, is an effeminate, HIV-positive gay man who literally becomes a prophet, wrestles an angel, and appears on stage at the end of the play to deliver a prophecy of hope to the audience. And Norman Arriaga, better known by his former drag name of Belize, both initiates the play's greatest act of moral courage and explicitly links that act of moral courage to his effeminacy.

This act concerns the villain of *Angels*, Roy Cohn, who Kushner based closely on the real-life closeted gay male Republican lawyer who served as Senator Joseph McCarthy's right-hand man during the Red Scare. In the play, as in real life, Cohn dies of AIDS-related complications. Immediately after his death, Belize and another gay male character named Louis steal Cohn's private stash of AZT, a drug that means the difference between life and death for their HIV-positive friends and which—at the time the play is set—is not yet available to the general public (Cohn had called in political favors to get his stash). After they steal the AZT, Belize refuses to let Louis simply take the drugs and run. Instead, he insists that Louis say the Kaddish, the Jewish prayer for the dead, for Cohn. This is a tremendous act of forgiveness—the oppressed mourning for the humanity of a man who'd oppressed them—and Belize admits that "it isn't easy, it doesn't count if it's easy, it's the hardest thing. Forgiveness" (256). In spite of the difficulty, Belize insists that Louis say the Kaddish for Cohn, because "[a] queen can forgive her vanquished foe" (256). This is a crucial scene in *Angels*, one that Kushner uses as evidence that his liberal/radical characters' personal politics are preferable to those of the Reagan-era Republicans in the play. The compassion that Belize demonstrates stems from his belief in a basic level of connection between all people, regardless of identity or politics. This is the compassion that Kushner finds so damningly lacking in the Reagan-era United States.

By explicitly linking this crucial act of moral courage to the fact that "[a] queen can forgive her vanquished foe," Belize's dialogue draws a clear line connecting effeminacy, emotional maturity, compassion, and courage. In fact, Belize's effeminacy is what allows him to access the other qualities in that list. This is how Kushner can be said to amplify fascinating effeminacy. Rather than being depraved killers (as in Shilts's portrait of Dugas), Kushner's Healing Queens are heroic. Possessed of liberal politics, great moral courage and—in the case of Prior—magical powers, the effeminate men in *Angels* serve as healers and prophets, the bandagers of wounds and the redeemers of the American dream. In this way, they are both an extension and an amplification of previous modes of fascinating effeminacy. They are James Baldwin's Truth-Telling Queens on steroids, speaking truth not just to individuals, but to the nation as a whole. No longer merely entertaining, they are vital to the utopian vision of America that Kushner articulates at the end of the play.

In what follows below, I read Shilts and Kushner's texts in greater detail and situate each of them within their specific historical context (they were, it should be noted, published at different moments in the evolving history of US cultural reactions to HIV/AIDS). Finally, this chapter closes with my discussion of Sarah Schulman's novel *Rat Bohemia* (1995), a text that is set in much the same milieu as Kushner's play—leftist/radical gays and lesbians weathering the full brunt of the AIDS epidemic in New York City's East Village in the 1980s—but that takes a very different approach to characterizing effeminacy. Rather than engaging with either side of the effeminate paradox, Schulman's novel counters them both. It rages against the femme-phobia and homophobia that effeminate men with AIDS face from their straight parents and siblings (thus rejecting effeminacy as threat as bigoted ignorance), but it also pushes back against the idea that queer people with AIDS (PWAs) need to be superhumans in order for their deaths (and their lives) to have mattered. In doing so, *Rat Bohemia* charts a new and uncharted course, one in which effeminacy is viewed as neither threat nor fascination. It critiques the way in which in the wake of HIV/AIDS both sides of the effeminate paradox end up treating effeminacy, rhetorically, the same way we treat disease: as either something sinister that must be fought off/resisted or as something ennobling, a experience that might be unpleasant but that is ultimately also positively transformative.

AND THE BAND PLAYED ON: PATIENT ZERO AS (WILLFUL) TYPHOID MARY

Shilts's account of the early years of the AIDS crisis, *And the Band Played On: Politics, People, and the AIDS Epidemic* (1987), is a sprawling book. It covers the period from 1976 to 1988, often in month-by-month detail, and it focuses on so many different people—including public health officials, AIDS victims, and city politicians—that a list of "Dramatis Personae" is provided for the reader's help at the front of the book (xiii). The title of this list is apt: while Shilts's book is nonfiction based on reporting, it is written in a novelistic style, and that style makes its various subjects feel like characters in a nineteenth-century realist novel. Shilts often writes from the point of view of his subjects, presenting their interior thoughts and feelings to his readers in the same way that a fictional work of psychological realism might. And while the list of Shilts's "Dramatis Personae" runs on for three full pages, Gaëtan Dugas undoubtedly emerges as one of Shilts's most memorable, and indeed infamous, characters.

Today, the Gaëtan-Dugas-as-Patient-Zero theory has been debunked,[1] and indeed, the very notion of needing to find (and then blame) an AIDS Patient Zero has been questioned. Nevertheless, *And the Band Played On*'s representation of Dugas remains important because of the text's mainstream success: the book was a best-seller and was made into an HBO docudrama in 1993, while Shilts himself "became a media celebrity" for having written it (Crimp, "Randy Shilts's" 118). This notoriety stemmed from the fact that *And the Band Played On* was received, in the mainstream press, as objectively and dispassionately telling "the *true* story of the epidemic's first five years" (Crimp, "Randy Shilts's" 120, emphasis Crimp's). In it, Shilts repeatedly emphasizes Dugas's effeminacy, making Shilts's depiction of Patient Zero a watershed moment in the history of US representations of effeminacy.

Having already called Dugas a "sissy," Shilts argues that the combination of Dugas's effeminacy and his working-class roots made for an unhappy childhood and fueled fantasies of escape to more cosmopolitan locales: "adopted into that rough-hewn life of the French-Canadian working class," Dugas "knew he was meant to be born into a better life, far from the brawny bullies who called him a faggot and rubbed snow in his face during those bitter Canadian winters" (22, 196). Effeminacy may have caused Dugas pain during his childhood, but adulthood allowed him escape into gay male subcultures, where the "[s]andy hair [that] fell boyishly over his forehead" and the clothes he bought "in the trendiest shops of Paris and London" gave him power and social currency (21). What had been vulnerabilities and signs of stigmatizing difference in Dugas's childhood—his boyish rather than manly looks and his interest in fashion—became transformed, in the gay male world of discos and bathhouses, into immense (sub)cultural capital. And Dugas's job as a flight attendant (itself a traditionally feminine occupation)[2] gave Dugas access to the world of North American and Western European gay discos and bathhouses, enabling Dugas to be popular not just in one city but many. According to Shilts, Dugas loved, cultivated, and craved the desiring sexual attention he found from other men in discos and bathhouses; he "loved his family and adored his older sister, but they were dark and plain looking while he had always had delicate features and light, winsome hair. He was like the prince taken up by the farmers, he thought . . . [in adulthood] he had found his own niche in the royalty of gay beauty, as the star of the homosexual jet set" (196).

All this attention and praise made Dugas, in Shilts's account, tremendously vain; Dugas is depicted as looking around crowded dance floors and boosting his own ego by laughing and saying "I am the prettiest one" (21). Shilts's argument is this: Dugas's childhood effeminacy made him the victim of bullying, and this early victimization instilled in Dugas an unquenchable need for approval. As an adult gay man, Dugas searched for this approval in sexual terms; Dugas came to see that his self-worth and personal efficacy were tied to his ability to appear sexually desirable to men. In fact, the very first image of Dugas in *And the Band Played On* highlights Dugas's vanity: when readers first meet Dugas he is posing in front of a mirror, fretting about a scar under his ear (we learn later that the scar marks the site of a surgically removed Kaposi's sarcoma [KS] lesion) and hoping that his face will be "unblemished again" soon, despite "troubling news" from his doctors (11). Thus, from the very beginning of *And The Band Played On*, Shilts highlights Dugas's vanity, a personality trait he connects to Dugas's effeminacy.

Shilts then argues that Dugas's vanity—his need to always be "the prettiest one"—leads directly to his promiscuity, which in the wake of HIV/AIDS, becomes lethal both to Dugas and the men he slept with. Shilts contends that Dugas was so addicted to the validation of being desired sexually that he continued to have anonymous sex with multiple partners in bathhouses, even after doctors and public health officials had warned him that he could infect other men by doing so.

When Dugas's hair begins to fall out from chemotherapy treatments (administered to treat KS lesions), "he simply shaved his head so no one would notice. His Yul Brenner look was quite attractive. As he traveled between San Francisco, Los Angeles, Vancouver, Toronto, and New York, he realized that if he kept to bathhouses where the lights were turned down low, nobody would ask him about those embarrassing purple spots. He was still the prettiest one" (79). And when a doctor explicitly tells Dugas that he is at risk of infecting others and must therefore stop having sex, Dugas "looked wounded, but his voice betrayed a fierce edge of bitterness. 'Of course I'm going to have sex,' he told [the doctor]. 'Nobody's proven to me that you can spread cancer'" (138). According to an unnamed friend of Dugas's, asking Dugas "to give up sex . . . would be like asking Bruce Springsteen to give up the guitar. Sex wasn't just sex to Gaëtan; sex was who Gaëtan was—it was the basis of his identity" (251). There is also the scene, cited in the opening of this chapter, in which Dugas tells a public health official that he will not abstain from sex because "I've got it [HIV/AIDS] . . . They [his future sexual partners] can get it too" (200). A later anecdote further supports the idea that Dugas was an angry, vengeful man who would put his own vanity and need for sexual release above the health of his partners. Shilts quotes an unnamed friend of Dugas who recalls that when he and Dugas had cruised discos and bathhouses together in the days before AIDS, Dugas would continue to trick even after he'd gotten a gonorrhea diagnosis from a doctor. "The doctors always said to wait a few days," after getting the gonorrhea treated with antibiotics, "but Gaëtan figured that since somebody gave it to him, he could give it right back" (252).

In Shilts's depiction, the lines between Dugas's effeminacy and his promiscuity are often blurred. Shilts notes, for example, that Jim Curran, the director of AIDS research at the Centers for Disease Control (CDC) in Atlanta, "passed up the opportunity to meet Gaëtan, the Quebecois version of Typhoid Mary. Curran had heard about the flamboyant attendant and frankly found every story about his sexual braggadocio to be offensive. Stereotypical gays irritated Curran in much the same way that he was uncomfortable watching Amos n' Andy movies" (157). Ostensibly, Curran is repulsed by Dugas's promiscuity, his Typhoid Mary–like role in spreading disease. But Dugas's effeminacy—the fact that he is a "flamboyant" flight attendant—suddenly sneaks its way into the sentence and is conflated, grammatically, with the "sexual braggadocio" that spread HIV and that offends Curran. Thus, when Shilts reports that Curran hated "Stereotypical gays," it is impossible for readers to determine whether gays are stereotypically promiscuous or stereotypically effeminate. Shilts's sentence construction makes the two terms literally impossible to separate.

In doing so, Shilts intensifies the trope of effeminacy as threat: in his account, effeminacy makes Dugas promiscuous, even after he knows that his promiscuity makes him a mass-murderer. What interests me is the way that Shilts's depiction of Dugas, his claim that Dugas was likely "the person who brought AIDS to North America," focuses so heavily on not just Dugas's sexual behavior, but on his effeminacy as well (439). It is unprotected sex with a positive partner that results in HIV transmission, not effeminacy. And yet Shilts's ongoing critique highlights Dugas's effeminacy at least as much as it highlights his promiscuity. In fact, Shilts constructs a chain of associations: Dugas's effeminacy leads to childhood bullying which leads to a need for acceptance in adulthood, which leads to vanity, which leads to promiscuity, which leads to infection, which leads to death. The novelistic style of *And the Band Played On* makes it a dramatic narrative, one with heroes and villains. And Dugas is clearly a villain, arguably the biggest villain in the book. He is threateningly grotesque because he is promiscuous, and this is why Shilts must repeatedly emphasize Dugas's effeminacy: because without effeminacy, male promiscuity is generally understood to be a good thing. This is the age-old sexist double standard: men who sleep with many partners are studs, worthy of praise and approval. Women who sleep with many partners are whores, worthy of derision and shaming. Dugas is male and promiscuous, but Shilts needs him to fill the role of a villain. Thus, Shilts emphasizes Dugas's effeminacy, making Dugas's promiscuity (and the vanity that drives it) conform to well-known, sexist narratives about the dangers of female promiscuity. *And the Band Played On* raises the stakes of threateningly grotesque effeminacy by transforming it from something scary into something lethal.

In doing so, Shilts's text both contributes to and conforms to broader trends of how both effeminacy and gay men were portrayed in US culture in the wake of HIV/AIDS. Media coverage and artistic representations of the onset of the AIDS epidemic afforded gay men in the United States. and Western Europe a strange and often deeply problematic visibility. Writing in 1995—and thus looking back on more than ten years of the AIDS epidemic—Leo Bersani says, "Nothing has made gay men more visible than AIDS. . . . AIDS has made us *fascinating* . . . Thanks largely to television and movies, the entire country has been able to take in (while of course distancing itself from) images of our wasted bodies. The normal fear of homosexuality has been promoted to a compelling terror as a secret fantasy becomes a public spectacle: the spectacle of men dying from what I called in [the essay] 'Is the Rectum a Grave?' the suicidal ecstasy of taking their sex like a woman" (*Homos* 19, emphasis Bersani's).

What Bersani refers to here—men "taking their sex like a woman"[3]—is receptive anal intercourse, the specific sex act that came to be seen as the primary means of HIV-transmission between gay men. Indeed, Cindy Patton has argued that because of its role in HIV transmission, anal sex eventually came to be seen, in the safer-sex literature of AIDS prevention education, as the only kind of sex that gay men could have with one another: an "insistence that intercourse is the real sex. . . . [meant that] safe sex discussions inevitably began with a discussion of the importance of condoms, and only then discussed the range of other possibilities for a fulfilling sex life" (*Inventing AIDS* 48).

AIDS thus forced mainstream, straight America to contemplate gay men in general and male-male anal intercourse more specifically. Bersani, drawing on the work of Simon Watney, argues that much of the phobic reaction to people with AIDS (PWAs), regardless of the means of their infection, is based in the fear and loathing triggered by the mental image of a man voluntarily allowing himself to be penetrated by another man and receiving pleasure from such an act. According to the "logics" of sexism and homophobia wherein men are active and penetrating, but never penetrated themselves, such an act is, of course, inherently feminizing and, therefore, unspeakably taboo. Again drawing on Watney's work, Bersani notes that representations of female prostitutes in nineteenth-century London—who were alleged to be willfully spreading syphilis via their unquenchable promiscuity—are very similar to late twentieth-century representations of gay men who are alleged to be willfully spreading HIV/AIDS via their insatiable promiscuity. He then goes on to say that "the similarities between representations of female prostitutes and male homosexuals should help us to specify the exact form of sexual behavior being targeted, in representations of AIDS, as the criminal, fatal, and irresistibly repeated act. This is of course anal sex . . . The realities of syphilis in the nineteenth century and of AIDS today 'legitimate' a fantasy of female sexuality as intrinsically diseased; and promiscuity in this fantasy, far from merely increasing the risk of infection, is *the sign of infection*. Women and gay men spread their legs with an unquenchable appetite for destruction" ("Is The Rectum a Grave?" 211, emphasis Bersani's). This illustrates the deep connection between homophobia and woman-hating. Sexism has long portrayed female promiscuity as diseased, and so when a mode of male promiscuity (that is gay male promiscuity) becomes, from the point of view of the dominant culture, problematic, then gay men, or at least their promiscuity, must be portrayed as feminine.

Bersani arrives at this conclusion psychoanalytically, but Steven F. Kruger, in his examination of medical and scientific discourses about AIDS, makes a similar point: "Western homophobia has consistently operated by associating gay men's bodies—as they open sexually in ways inimical to 'real' masculinity—with the imagined fragmentation and permeability of the feminine. The body of the person living with HIV or AIDS . . . [is understood to have] lost control over its internal systems of signification and of gender hierarchy, and that, in sustaining such losses, is consolidated to a misogynistically imagined female body and a homophobically imagined queer one" (45). This line of thinking is what underlies the homophobic canard that AIDS is "punishment" for gay men, that it is a specifically gay disease somehow simultaneously created by and enacting the punishment for, the dirty—and effeminate—gay sex that men are unable to stop having with one another, due to their unquenchable, effeminate promiscuity. As is hopefully already clear, this is precisely the argument that Shilts makes throughout his characterization of Dugas.[4]

While Shilts denied that the Dugas-as-Patient-Zero story was "that prominent in the book," Douglas Crimp describes how St. Martin's—the publishers of *And the Band Played On*—emphasized the Patient Zero story in their marketing of the book ("How to Have Promiscuity" 241–242). That marketing campaign was successful, and the story of Patient Zero went on to garner a great deal of media attention: in 1987, *People* magazine named Patient Zero one of its twenty-five most intriguing people, and Shilts's account of the Patient Zero story went on to be reported in the *New York Times*, the *New York Post*, the *New York Daily News*, *Time*, and *McClean's* (Crimp "How to Have Promiscuity" 242).

And the Band Played On thus contributes to what was a major trend in US mainstream media representations of AIDS after 1985: the symbolic separation and distancing of risk groups from the general population. Mainstream media outlets in the mid- to late 1980s thus faced a problem: gay sex needed to be stigmatized (so that gay men could be seen as a risk group distinct from the "normal" population), but gay sex acts couldn't be shown. Effeminacy could be shown, however, and was made to stand symbolically, as it long had before, for male homosexuality. This equation of effeminacy and male homosexuality is further aided by the fact that the sex act that is presumed to be making gay men sick is itself already perceived as outrageously effeminate. This explains why, after 1985, "[h]ealth and life insurance companies began calling for wholesale screening of applicants in 'high-risk areas' and 'high-risk occupations' (e.g., hairdressers, florists, interior designers)" (Grover 368). Hairdressing and floral arrangement are the stereotypical demimondes of effeminate gay men, and the calls to classify them as occupations that put one at "high risk" for HIV/AIDS is a good example of the way in which the panic sparked by the AIDS crisis caused a chain of associative tangles in US cultural discourse. A specific sex act (male-male receptive anal intercourse), an identity (gay male), a mode of gender performance (effeminacy), and the risk of an infectious disease-causing agent (HIV) all become associatively conflated, with effeminacy emerging as a specific and depictable sign with that a photographer, videographer, or writer (like Shilts) could use to signal the whole linked chain of meanings.

Shilts's intention in writing *And the Band Played On* was clearly anti-homophobic, and the book did tremendously valuable work in pointing out how homophobia in both the US government and the scientific community contributed to making an already terrible situation worse. But *And the Band Played On* is also a good example of how a work can be anti-homophobic at the same time that is also femme-phobic and sex-negative. The mainstream media's interest in, and interest in repeating, Shilts's Patient Zero saga demonstrates how easily Shilts's characterization of Dugas contributed to the project of distancing and othering gay men in relation to a general populace presumed to be straight. By making Dugas into a murderous villain, Shilts provides the basis for a fantasy wherein, if the murderously promiscuous effeminate gay man could simply be purged from both the gay community and the larger American community, then health and safety could return to all.[5]

But as the AIDS epidemic progressed through the end of the eighties and the beginning of the nineties, US literature sees the production of a new work—Tony Kushner's *Angels in America*—which treats both AIDS and effeminacy very differently than Shilts does. In *And the Band Played On* effeminacy represents promiscuity, death, and disease, while HIV/AIDS occasions of fantasy of the end of gay male promiscuity and perhaps the end of gay men altogether. But in *Angels*, effeminacy means moral courage and compassion, and HIV/AIDS occasions a fantasy of gay inclusion and full American citizenship.

ANGELS IN AMERICA: HEALING QUEENS REDEEM THE NATION

Angels in America's two parts—*Millennium Approaches* and *Perestroika*[6]—cover the period from October 1985 to February 1990. *Angels* thus essentially begins where *And The Band Played On* ends. Kushner also handles illness, promiscuity, and effeminacy very differently than Shilts does. Where Shilts's portrayal of Dugas implicitly links effeminacy to disease-spreading promiscuity, Kushner is careful to separate these issues in his play. There are two very effeminate characters in *Angels*. One is the play's protagonist, Prior Walter, a former drag queen who, according to Kushner's character description, "[o]ccasionally works as a club designer or a caterer, [but] otherwise lives very modestly but with great style off a small trust fund" (n.p.). The other is Norman Arriaga, "a former drag queen and former lover of Prior's" who now works as a registered nurse and who is better known by his former drag name, Belize (n.p.). Prior has HIV, and his health deteriorates over the course of the play. Belize's HIV status is not specified in the play, but he is certainly not perceptibly ill. The same goes for Prior's boyfriend, Louis Ironson, who is also somewhat effeminate: Louis never did drag, but he works in an essentially secretarial job at the Federal Court of Appeals, and Prior teases Louis about having a lisp (26). Having a range of effeminate male characters, some of whom are positive (Prior) and some whose HIV status is unknown (Louis and Belize), helps Kushner short-circuit any easy conflation or equation of HIV/AIDS and effeminacy.

Kushner also disallows any easy association between infection/disease and sexual promiscuity. Louis is surprised that Prior is the sick one since he (Louis) "fucked around a lot more than he [Prior] did" in such male-male cruising sites as "the Ramble [in Central Park], or the scrub pines on Fire Island, or the St. Mark's Baths" (202). And HIV-negative Louis is the only character audiences see having unsafe sex onstage in *Angels*: after abandoning a very sick Prior in the hospital, Louis goes to the Ramble in Central Park and bottoms for a stranger he meets there. While Louis brings a condom to the encounter and initially insists on its use, he tells the top to "[k]eep going" once the condom breaks and begs the man to "Infect me. I don't care. I don't care" (63). Thus, while Shilts's focus on Dugas's promiscuity frames AIDS as a direct consequence of gay male sexual promiscuity, Kushner's portrayal of the disease emphasizes its randomness. Rather than being some kind of natural or cosmic price that promiscuous gay men pay for their promiscuity, HIV/AIDS in *Angels* is more random, crueler, and more nonsensical. Louis has been—and is, onstage—more promiscuous and unsafe than Prior, but it is Prior who is infected, while Louis, as far as the audience knows, remains HIV-negative. Shilts focuses on the hunt for a Patient Zero to whom all subsequent infections can be traced, logically and scientifically, by the epidemiologists who are the heroes of his story. In contrast, HIV/AIDS in Kushner's play is cruel precisely because it is random and illogical: incidences of infection do not seem to correlate to quantity of unsafe behavior. In the world of *Angels* there is, as Louis says, when talking about his own prior promiscuity, "[n]o justice" or at least not the justice of an easy-to-follow line of cause and effect (202).

Effeminacy is also routinely portrayed as a source of power and strength in *Angels*. Take, for example, Act One, Scene Four of *Perestroika*, where Roy Cohn is admitted to the hospital AIDS wing where Belize works as a nurse. Cohn himself does not appear in this scene, but his doctor, Henry, arrives onstage and interrupts Belize, who is on the phone with Prior. The exchange between Belize and Henry shows how Belize uses effeminacy as a source of strength, a tool for disrupting the typical channels of power and privilege that devalue or altogether ignore gay men, especially effeminate gay men of color such as Belize.[7] When Henry approaches Belize's duty station, he asks if Belize is the duty nurse, to which Belize, who is still on the phone with Prior, brusky replies, "Yo" (154). Henry, a wealthy doctor who treats men as powerful and influential as Roy Cohn, is taken aback. When he asks Belize a second time if Belize is the duty nurse, Belize responds disrespectfully, "*Yo*, I said" (154, emphasis Kushner's). Shocked, Henry looks at Belize and asks, "Why are you dressed like that?" (154). And when Henry says, disapprovingly, "Nurses are supposed to wear white," Belize refuses to recognize his authority or be shamed by him and snaps, "Doctors are supposed to be home, in Westchester, asleep" (154). Belize then makes Henry wait as he (Belize) and Prior sing the Christmas carol "Hark, The Herald Angels Sing" to one another over the phone. Only then does Belize hang up, turn his full attention to Henry, and say, "Now may I help you doctor or are you just cruising me?" (155).

This scene—in which Belize's effeminate, campy humor both neutralizes and makes a mockery of the presumed authority of an older, white, straight, wealthy doctor—is a useful microcosm of how effeminacy is figured as fascinating in *Angels*. Belize's effeminate behavior is so deliberately outrageous and provocative, so entirely and intentionally disrespectful of existing power structures that it stuns Henry—a man who assumes that they will always function in the same way, a way that benefits him—into a kind of disbelieving passivity. He is so surprised by Belize's outrageous repartee that he cannot react. Strictly speaking, Henry's age (he is older than Belize), job status (he is a doctor; Belize is a nurse), race (he is white; Belize is not), and gender performance (he is hegemonically masculine; Belize is a queen) should all make him the superior in their exchange, but Belize's effeminacy neutralizes these advantages and leaves Henry at Belize's mercy; Henry must wait for Belize to finish his phone call, and Belize is never reprimanded for the way that he speaks to Henry. Belize is figured as fascinatingly effeminate in this scene: relative to Henry, Belize is definitely not "normal," but his non-normalcy makes him both charismatic and powerful.

This is, of course, nothing particularly new. Broadly conceived, all of the taboos that Belize's insolence and back-talking challenges can be described as middle-class conventionality (which tacitly demands/expects deference to age, vocational status, whiteness, maleness, etc.). And fascinating effeminacy has a long history of existing outside of, and confounding, middle-class conventionality. As George Chauncey's study of male same-sex desire and gender nonconformity in New York City reveals, even as far back as the 1890s, "the style of the fairy was more likely to be adopted by young men and poorer men who had relatively little at stake in the straight middle-class world," and the particular style of femininity that they aped was a female prostitute's femininity (102). Already excluded—by virtue of youth, social class, and/or racial or ethnic identity—the fairies Chauncey studies adopted the effeminate persona of the fairy and used it as both a means of cultivating power/attention and a protective defense mechanism. Humorous, quick-witted barbs have, of course, long been used by gay men as both a survival strategy and a means of exercising power. The drag ball culture documented in director Jennie Livingston's *Paris Is Burning*

(1990) is rife with examples of this, and the tradition dates at least as far back as Oscar Wilde, whose sharp tongue is almost equally as infamous as his acts of sodomy. Similarly, anyone who has ever attended a drag show and seen a drag queen pull straight boys from the audience onstage for some very public verbal (and sometimes physical) harassment has seen this same technique being wielded.

Belize engages in it by deliberately being so outré that he stuns the systems that would oppress him into a kind of paralyzed shock which prevents them from exercising power over him. But Belize doesn't just escape or evade dominant systems of power in *Angels*. He also displays tremendous moral strength, and Kushner quite explicitly links that moral strength to Belize's effeminacy. This is illustrated in the scene, already described in the opening of this chapter, where Belize forces Louis to say the Kaddish for Roy Cohn, because "[a] queen can forgive her vanquished foe."

While Belize emerges as morally heroic, Prior Walter—the play's protagonist and other major effeminate character—is literally magical. Against his wishes, Prior is chosen by the Angel of America to be her prophet. The play's cosmology is both complex and deliberately ludicrous, but essentially, the Angel wants Prior to tell the rest of humanity to stay still, to stop migrating and intermingling and progressing. Prior objects to this idea and ultimately wrestles the Angel, gains entrance into Heaven itself, and then rejects the Angel's philosophy. Nevertheless, when Prior returns from Heaven, he does return as a prophet. The prophecy that he aims to spread is his own, not the Angel's, and it says that life is a blessing, even a life with sickness and the fear of the unknown and the shadow of eventual death.

Prior delivers this prophecy to the audience in the play's epilogue. This scene takes place in February 1990, four years after the close of the preceding scene. In it, Prior and his friends—who have formed a multicultural family, united through mutual love for one another and not biological blood ties—stand in Central Park, by the Bethesda Fountain, which is, of course, capped with a statue of the angel Bethesda. Prior's powers as a prophet are emphasized throughout this short scene, not only in the sense that he delivers prophecy to the audience, but also in the sense that he now seems to have supernatural abilities of his own. First, there is the fact that he can ignore the fourth wall and speak directly to the audience, an ability no other character in the play—including its ghosts and angels—has demonstrated. Second, Prior seems to be able to command and control his reality; in the Epilogue he is able, at will, to control the volume of his friends, turning the sound of their words up and down as if they were a television show and he were holding the remote. He also has the power to compel them to speak. Looking at the statue on the fountain, Prior says, "This is the angel Bethesda. Louis will tell you her story," and then Louis steps forward, out of the muted conversation he'd been having with Belize and Hannah, and does exactly that (279). Prior then goes on to compel both Belize and Hannah to speak in similar ways.

At the very end of *Angels*, Prior delivers his prophecy to the audience: "This disease [AIDS] will be the end of many of us, but not nearly all, and the dead will be commemorated and will struggle on with the living, and we are not going away. We won't die secret deaths anymore. The world only spins forward. We will be citizens. The time has come. Bye now. You are fabulous creatures, each and every one. And I bless you: *More Life*. The Great Work Begins" (280, emphasis Kushner's). This closing message reveals that Prior's magical powers are not limited to puppet-like control of his close friends. As his words indicate, Prior is setting wholesale societal change in motion. It may not happen instantly, but Prior prophesizes that PWAs—and in this play, PWAs are all gay men—will be commemorated and that they will no longer die "secret deaths." Instead, they will become full citizens of America.

Thus, we can see that Kushner's treatment of effeminacy in the midst of the AIDS epidemic is diametrically opposed to Shilts's. Instead of being monstrous mass murderers (like Patient Zero), Kushner's effeminate men are portrayed as honest, courageous, and communitarian, while straight-acting closet cases like Roy Cohn and Joe Pitt (the butch, married, Mormon, Republican lawyer that Louis sleeps with after he leaves Prior) are the villains of the play. Indeed, Roy and Joe are both notably absent from the epilogue's idyllic vision of a diverse, tolerant America where gays and PWAs will one day achieve full citizenship.

Roy dies well before the epilogue, and Joe disappears before the epilogue, when his estranged wife Harper tells him to "[g]et lost" and "[g]o exploring" (273). Closeted Reaganite gays (Joe and Roy) are banned from the epilogue's urbane Eden, but the play's effeminate characters are the ones who bring it into existence. Prior is the prophet who foretells of its coming, and Belize's compassion forms its moral center. In *Angels*, fascinating effeminacy is no longer just entertaining, it is quite literally the force that will redeem the nation and renew its commitment to the founding principle of equality for all.

Kushner takes up homosexuality, effeminacy, and AIDS as his subject matter, but he routinely resists connecting any of these categories with easy equal signs. Gay men aren't always effeminate in *Angels*—Prior describes Joe Pitt, the gay, Mormon lawyer as "[m]ega butch. He made me feel beyond nelly"—and PWAs aren't just their disease (224). They may die, but prior to that, they live. And they don't die alone. With the exception of closet-cases like Roy Cohn, they live and die in a community of gay men who provide them with friendship, love, and support. (Although it is worth noting that while *Angels* has many gay male PWA characters, none of them have sex onstage or are implied to be having sex offstage.)

That said, effeminate men in *Angels* are never quite fully real, rounded characters either. Belize, in particular, is problematic in this way. Generally speaking, Belize's function in *Angels* is to dispense advice and care to other lighter-skinned characters. He cares for Prior when Prior is hospitalized and abandoned by Louis. He dispenses advice in the long political arguments he has with Louis, arguments in which Belize calls Louis out on the racism inherent in Louis's ostensibly liberal politics. He also leads Louis to—and forces him to go through with—the act of forgiving Roy Cohn. And it is Belize who reminds Prior, before Prior has accepted this truth and wrestled the Angel to defend it, that "the world doesn't spin backwards" (181). But who is Belize? Who is he outside of his care-giving relation to other, more major (and whiter) characters in the play?

Kushner gives his audiences a few small moments of insight into Belize. He tells Roy that his idea of heaven is a place where "everyone

[is] in Balenciaga gowns with red corsages, and [there are] big dance palaces full of music and lights and racial impurity and gender confusion," where "all the deities are creole, mulatto, brown as the mouths of rivers" and "[r]ace, taste, and history [are] finally overcome" (209–210). And when Louis accuses Belize of being attracted to Prior (and jealous of Louis), Belize shuts him down, saying, "I love Prior but I was never in love with him. I have a man, uptown, and I have since *long* before I first laid my eyes on the sorry-ass sight of you [Louis]" (228, emphasis Kushner's). These details do give a sense that Belize has a life beyond, and outside of, his role as caretaker/advice giver to the play's other characters, but they are two small details in the midst of a vast, sprawling, two-part play. Kushner alludes to Belize having a romantic partner—and thus a life outside of his care-giver role—but we never see that partner on stage. We don't even know his name. Similarly, Kushner provides a laugh for audiences when he has Belize declare, "I am trapped in a world of white people. That's *my* problem," but the humor of the one-liner doesn't change the problematic fact that Belize is the only person of color in *Angels*, and that his role is to give support and advice to other (more major, whiter) characters, while getting very little back from them in return (225, emphasis Kushner's).

Kushner does grant Belize one moment of vulnerability. When Prior recounts his story of the Angel's visitation to Belize, he (Belize) fears that the story is a sign that Prior is beginning to succumb to AIDS-related dementia. Dreading that turn of events, Belize angrily tells Prior, "You better fucking not flip out. This is not dementia. And this is not real. This is just you, Prior, afraid of what's coming, afraid of time . . . There's no angel, you hear me? For me? I can handle anything but not this happening to you" (181). But this is Belize's one and only moment of vulnerability in the play, the only time he seems to be confronted with a situation that he can't instantly turn to his advantage with a bitchy, witty quip. The rest of the time, Belize is a superhuman Healing Queen, always ready with a quick comeback for his enemies and life-changing advice for those he loves.

Late in *Perestroika*, Roy Cohn, who is very sick and mentally disoriented, becomes suddenly frightened and asks Belize who he is. Belize answers Roy by saying, "Your negation" (210). This answer is telling—and, in light of the role Belize plays in *Angels*—absolutely true. Roy Cohn is the great Satan of *Angels in America*. Everything that Roy believes in—acting on same-sex desire while rejecting and demonizing gay identity; selfish individualism as a virtue; the pursuit of power for power's sake, regardless of moral concerns; circumvention of the rule of law; the destruction of the liberal welfare state—Kushner exposes as destructive, inhumane, and counter-productive. Conversely, everything that Belize believes in—campy humor; mutual care enacted through an openly gay community; an anti-racist, anti-sexist, anti-homophobic liberal politics; a tough but necessary forgiveness of one's enemies; a belief in the necessity and virtue of human progress—Kushner holds up as constructive, nurturing, and necessary. Roy is a superhuman force that represents Kushner's definition of evil in the play, and Belize truly is his "negation," his polar opposite: a superhuman force representing everything that Kushner believes to be good. And Prior—given the core of his prophecy by Belize—is, by the play's epilogue, a literally magical figure, an enlightened effeminate prophet who has been to heaven, wrestled an angel, and returned with a message that promises to fundamentally transform America, ending homophobia and transmuting gay male PWAs from pariahs into full citizens.

But must effeminate men be superhuman to be sympathetic? Will nothing short of magical powers and the ability to transform a nation make effeminate gay men worthy of citizenship? These questions point to the limits and problems of Kushner's use of effeminacy as the fascinating grotesque, and they are questions that are central to Schulman's *Rat Bohemia*, a novel that rejects both sides of the effeminate paradox as problematic.

RAT BOHEMIA: RESISTING THREAT AND FASCINATION ALIKE

As David, a thirty-four-year-old effeminate, gay, white man and one of the three narrators of *Rat Bohemia*, contemplates his own impending death from AIDS, he wonders what it takes to make a gay death count or to make a gay life worth remembering: "I read in Herve Guilbert's book that [Michel] Foucault died, not knowing exactly what had hit him. His lover found his handcuffs and whips and couches full of leftover manuscripts on trifles such as the history of socialism. [Actor, director, and playwright] Charles Ludlam was the most profound loss. America doesn't even know what she's missing. . . . But what do we do with all the mediocrities who never created anything worth remembering and never would have even if they had lived to be eighty-five? It drives me crazy how quickly the great ones get canonized. *Blah-blah-blah is such a terrible loss.* Does that mean that the death of one mediocre slob is not as terrible? Do fags have to be geniuses to justify living?" (71, emphasis Schulman's).

In this excerpt Schulman uses David's interior monologue to question, and undermine, notions of fascinating effeminacy. In *Angels*, Kushner's effeminate men are worthy of sympathy from the audience and citizenship from the nation by virtue of being fascinatingly grotesque. Reading *Angels* in the light of David's question—"Do fags have to be geniuses to justify living?"—readers can imagine David indignantly asking why gays and gay male PWAs aren't simply granted full citizenship in the United States on the basis of their humanity. Readers can imagine David asking why effeminate gay men must fascinate the mainstream in order to be afforded full visibility and citizenship. David's larger point—and Schulman's, throughout *Rat Bohemia*—is that if one must be exceptional to be considered worthy of either citizenship or remembrance, then one isn't really considered fully human.

One of the major underlying messages in *Angels* is that the increased visibility of gay men and gay male PWAs within US culture will lead to greater, and eventually full, citizenship for them. This is precisely the message of Prior's closing monologue/prophecy, and it also explains why Kushner frames effeminacy as empowering: the queens in *Angels* are powerful because they compel attention, they demand to be seen and heard. Although *Rat Bohemia*, like *Angels*, has deeply anti-homophobic intentions, Schulman's novel is skeptical about whether the visibility conferred by HIV/AIDS (and the visibility conferred by fascinating effeminacy) will truly be liberating for gay men and gay male PWAs.

This skepticism aligns Schulman's views with those of Cindy Patton, a scholar and activist who has published extensively on the history of the AIDS epidemic and its portrayal in Western media. In *Fatal Advice* (1996), Patton argues that "the AIDS epidemic became a vehicle through which to renegotiate the meaning of being a good American" (7). Patton contends that AIDS provided a way for America to discursively close the doors opened by feminism, gay/lesbian rights, and the sexual revolution throughout the sixties and seventies. While getting to blame a fatal disease on the supposed excesses of the sexual revolution, AIDS also allowed mainstream media to construct "a new paradigm for citizenship: the compassionate, tolerant individual who, while never viewing him- or herself as susceptible to contracting HIV, could nevertheless recognize that 'some of my best friends have HIV'" (*Fatal Advice* 8). By framing gay men (and prostitutes and IV drug users) as at-risk Others, this new citizenship paradigm allows members of groups thought to be mainstream and, therefore, not at risk of HIV/AIDS, to feel simultaneously compassionate towards PWAs and safely distant from them.[8] Or as Patton describes it, "the national pedagogy [around HIV/AIDS must be understood as] as a paradox: the gap between this new citizen and the dangerous bodies from which they were distinguished widened, even as average Americans were apparently increasingly concerned about the plight of people living with AIDS. . . . . The sick within the national borders could be recognized as objects of America's compassion, but they could no longer fit into the ideal of citizenship" (*Fatal Advice* 9–10).

Thus, in Patton's analysis, the visibility that HIV/AIDS afforded to gay men is one that cannot lead to full citizenship for gays and/or gay PWAs. Her argument is the direct opposite of Kushner's in *Angels*; she claims that HIV/AIDS gives gay men and gay PWAs greater visibility in US culture but only in a way that constructs them as objects of compassion for their opposite: "normal" (read: white, straight, gender normative, non-drug using, presumed to be not at risk of HIV infection) citizens. Patton's work is thus an academic counterargument to *Angels in America*, one that challenges Kushner's neat equation of greater visibility and eventual full citizenship.

Rat Bohemia, like Patton's scholarship, challenges many of the arguments that Kushner makes in *Angels*. Whereas the ending of *Angels* suggests that the horrors of HIV/AIDS will have some upside in that they will lead to America being transformed into a more compassionate, inclusive society, *Rat Bohemia* resists transformative discourse of any kind. Schulman was a founding member of the radical AIDS Coalition to Unleash Power (ACT UP), and she lived in New York's East Village, where she was deeply connected to its lesbian and gay community during the early years of the AIDS epidemic. This is the milieu in which *Rat Bohemia* is set, and the novel refuses to make larger, grander metaphorical meaning out of either AIDS or effeminacy. On the subject of whether AIDS is transformative in some positive way, the novel is quite explicit: "AIDS is not a transforming experience. I know that we tend to romanticize things like death based on some religious model of conversion and redemption. We expect that once people stare down their mortality in the mirror they will understand something profound about death and life . . . But that's not what happens . . . So many want to believe that there is some spiritual message at the core of this disaster—something we can all learn. That makes it more palatable, doesn't it? That makes it more redemptive . . . But facts are facts. There is nothing to be learned by staring death in the face every day of your life. AIDS is just fucking sad. It's a burden. There's nothing redeeming about it" (52).

Just as this passage rejects the idea that AIDS is redemptive, *Rat Bohemia* also rejects both sides of the effeminate paradox as damaging. I will discuss this point at greater length below, but for now I want to give an overview of the novel.

The speaker in the passage above is Rita Mae Weems, the novel's main protagonist and one of its three narrators. A native New Yorker, Rita was, as a teenager, thrown out of her father's home in Queens for being lesbian. Now adult, Rita remains more or less estranged from her biological family. She considers her true family to be the other gay and lesbian residents of the East Village with whom she shares an interest in radical-left politics, arts, and a suspicion of dominant American culture and values. This is the subculture from which the novel takes half of its title: Bohemia.

The other half of the title is both a literal reference to Rita's job and a metaphorical nod to PWAs. Rita works for the city and is involved with its rat extermination efforts; she obsessively collects knowledge of rats: how their anatomy works, how they reproduce, and how various traps and poisons either succeed or fail at killing them. The city is in the midst of a tremendous rat infestation, and Rita has literal vermin on her mind, but at the same time, the wider nation is ignoring the suffering of Rita and her friends (many of whom are gay male PWAs) and treating them as though they are vermin. But even more painful than homophobic or negligent politicians is the pain inflicted by family: familial homophobia is the central theme of *Rat Bohemia*, a novel that meditates at length on the wounds—often psychic, sometimes physical—that straight parents inflict on their lesbian and gay children.

Although Rita is *Rat Bohemia*'s main protagonist and narrates two of its four major sections, two other characters also narrate sections of the novel. Both are friends of Rita's: David and "Killer," a lesbian who is so far outside mainstream, bourgeois life that she cannot hold down a regular job. All three of these characters have been, to greater or lesser degrees, abandoned by their straight parents and siblings. Schulman's argument, throughout the novel, is that the pain of this familial abandonment, estrangement, and/or marginalization—the inability or unwillingness of straight parents and siblings to love their lesbian and gay children/siblings and to support them as AIDS ravages their community—takes an already horrible situation (the AIDS epidemic) and makes it truly unbearable. For example, David, who gets rapidly sicker over the course of the novel and dies before its close, says of his parents, "It's not AIDS that makes them hate us. They hated us before because they could not control us. They could not make us be just like them. Now they're glad we're dying. They're uncomfortable about how they feel but really they're relieved. There's nothing on Earth that could kill us more efficiently than parental indifference" (87). This is the reality of David's relationship with his parents: he is in contact with them and allowed to come to their home (and in this he is more privileged than many lesbians and gays, like Killer, who is entirely estranged from her family), but they never ask him about who he's dating and any mention of AIDS is met with parental silence and indifference.

In contrast to this reality, David yearns for a future where "my mother and father would come with me to visit Gino [one of David's friends, who is hospitalized and dying of AIDS] and would ask him how he felt. They would ask me questions about myself too. They would come to a gay play and read a gay book and call me up in the morning when there was something vile on the television because *they have a gay child*. And no one is going to hurt their gay child as long as they still have air in their lungs. Because they love their gay son and all parents must love their gay children. From their first faggy moment until they are taken off of life supports, all parents must love their gay children" (94, emphasis Schulman's).

As David's reference to a gay son's "first faggy moment" implies, the source of David's alienation from his family is not just his homosexuality. His effeminacy is also a contributing factor. As Rita says, David is "a Liza Minnelli fag" (153). And in the section he narrates, David explains that from earliest childhood he "was a constant source of tension" for his parents and siblings because he "was not the way they had intended for me to be" (66). Instead of being what his parents had intended, David turned out to be effeminate: "As a child I was always being gender-corrected. I was one of those little boys with a high squeaky voice who waved his hands in the air and got too excited. It made my parents deeply uncomfortable. They tried every way they could think of to convey their disapproval of my basic self, starting at the age of four. There was always an invisible Dave, one that had never existed and could never exist, that they expected to find, miraculously each morning at the breakfast table. And when, instead, all they got was silly-willy me, with limp wrists and a will of steel, little courageous sissy-wissy me, they were deeply angry" (64). Here, we can see that Schulman's conception of effeminacy is quite distinct from either Shilts's or Kushner's. For Schulman, effeminacy is neither threatening nor fascinating.

David's effeminacy is part of his "basic self," something that has been with him since earliest childhood, and Schulman is quite specific that David's effeminacy is a large part of the reason he is denied the parental love, approval, and support that his straight, gender-conforming siblings receive. David later says that in early childhood he became "a full time warrior" capable of resisting his parents' disapproval, but Schulman makes it clear that David's strength does not come directly from his effeminacy (66). David bravely resists parental and familial homophobia, but his strength is a reaction—a survival mechanism, a necessary adaptation—to his parents' and siblings' hatred and neglect. David's effeminacy is what unjustly triggers that hatred and neglect. The strength to defend against, or combat, that hatred and neglect—David's "will of steel" and his courageousness—are other parts of his personality. They co-exist alongside his effeminacy but do not spring directly from it.

Neither pathology nor magical source of strength, David's effeminacy is central to his identity (and has been since childhood), but in this sense it is, or at least should be, unmarked. In Schulman's treatment, David's effeminacy is important because it triggers parental and familial scorn, but that scorn is unjust precisely because David's effeminacy should be unmarked. His queeny mannerisms should mean no more (or less) to his parents and siblings than the color of his eyes or any other feature over which he has no control. In both *And the Band Played On* and *Angels in America*, effeminacy carries a symbolic meaning. Shilts and Kushner disagree profoundly about what exactly effeminacy means, but each of them has a larger symbolic meaning project outward from effeminacy itself; in their works, effeminacy itself generates some larger societal effect, making men either the threatening or fascinating. Schulman is different: in *Rat Bohemia*, effeminacy simply exists, without making meaning on its own. Where meaning is generated in regards to effeminacy, in Schulman's account, it is a negative meaning created by the homophobic reactions of parents, siblings, and the larger US culture as a whole. In this way, Schulman's work refuses to engage with the effeminate paradox. She refuses to name effeminacy as either threat or fascination. It simply is, without attached value judgments, and what emerges as truly monstrous in *Rat Bohemia* is parental and familial homophobia.

Schulman's most intense condemnation of parental homophobia occurs when Rita attends David's memorial service. At the service, Rita finds herself unable to cry, and many of her and David's other friends have the same reaction. So many of their friends have already died early deaths from AIDS, and so many of them will soon face a similar death. Rita and David's other friends are simply overloaded with grief and death. This is why Rita realizes that she has "nothing to say" (160) about David and why other people at the service quickly "started to look at their watches because they had places to be and death is not enough of an anomaly" anymore in their community (162).

The only thing that snaps Rita and the other attendees out of their traumatized numbness is David's father. His presence at David's service is jarring to Rita and the others because David's "real friends . . . knew how much his father had hurt him [David]" (162). Rita can't believe that David's father would show up at David's service, given how much David's friends hated him (David's father). But her surprise lessens when she realizes that David's father "had no understanding of what we [David's friends] knew or felt about him. He did not believe that we existed. He did not know that his son had relationships" (162). Rita is no longer shocked by death, but she is shocked by David's father getting up to speak about a son he mostly ignored and largely failed to know; for example, Rita and her friends must sit quietly and endure David's father's absurd lie that David "accepted having AIDS without complaint" (163). This is another example that what is monstrous for Schulman is not effeminacy but parental and familial homophobia.[9] As Rita thinks during David's father's speech: "We took Dave's father [not having really known his son] personally because most of us know our families would do the same. The most common link between all gay people is that at some time in our lives, often extended, our families have treated us shabbily because of our homosexuality. They punish us, but we did not do anything wrong" (163).

Rita's reaction to David's father's attendance at David's funeral is Schulman's implicit rejection of effeminacy as threat. David's father's fear and hatred of David's effeminacy is why David's father fails utterly to understand who his son was, what he believed in, or what his wishes and dreams were. That parental ignorance is precisely what makes David's father so hateful to Rita and, by extension, to Schulman. This scene resembles the bit of David's interior monologue that opened my discussion of *Rat Bohemia*—his question about whether gays have to be geniuses for their lives and death to count—because that scene is Schulman's implicit rejection of fascinating effeminacy.

What is remarkable about effeminacy in Schulman's novel is that it has no meaning in and of itself. Yes, it is "a gay guy, a real queen," (163) who, by reading the Kaddish, finally gives Rita some emotional release at the funeral and reminds her that lesbians and gays "are old. We do exist. We can mourn. We do have language" (164). In doing so, this queen seems akin to Belize in *Angels*, a magical queen whose effeminacy can bring about redemption for others. But this Kaddish-reading queen is hardly the only queen in *Rat Bohemia*, and the novel reveals other effeminate gay men to be anything but saintly. David himself, for example, is extremely selfish and only ever wants to talk about himself, so much so that Rita finds herself "very, very angry at David" after his death and wishing that he'd been capable of a more mutual friendship (160). Because Schulman provides a range of complex, fully rounded effeminate characters in *Rat Bohemia*, effeminacy itself comes to be seen as a personality trait in and of itself, not a metaphorical marker of some other, higher meaning. In the same way that Schulman resists transformative discourses that paint AIDS as somehow redemptive, she also consistently refuses to assign any larger, metaphorical meaning to effeminacy.

Rat Bohemia has been much less commercially successful than either *And the Band Played On* or *Angels in America* and remains much less well known than either of them. Nevertheless, out of the three texts discussed in this chapter, Schulman's treatment of effeminacy is the most ground-breaking of all. Due to its long-standing associations with both male homosexuality and specific gay male sex acts considered to be effeminate, effeminacy was one of the many terms whose cultural definition and associative meanings were open to revision in light of HIV/AIDS. In response, Shilts and Kushner each grab one end of the effeminate paradox and run with it, giving readers Typhoid Marys and Healing Queens. In doing so, both Shilts and Kushner create new meanings for effeminacy, but each author's portrayal of a new mode of effeminacy builds on long-extant traditions of effeminate representation. It is Schulman who breaks truly new ground by refusing to participate with the effeminate paradox altogether. In doing so, she asks readers to consider that effeminate men might simply be human beings, instead of being either murderous or magical.

FIVE

"THE SISSY TRIUMPHANT"

FASCINATING EFFEMINACY GOES MAINSTREAM

The picture is of a mother and her five-year-old son. They sit facing one another, their heads at the same level. The mother holds the son's small feet in her hands and is tickling them. Both mother and son are grinning hugely. "Lucky for me," the caption reads, "I ended up with a boy whose favorite color is pink. Toenail painting is way more fun in neon" (Donaldson James). And indeed, on closer inspection, we can see that, yes, the son's toenails are indeed painted neon pink. The picture is an advertisement, one for the upscale clothing company J. Crew. It was emailed to J. Crew customers in April 2011, as part of an ad called "Saturdays with Jenna." The Jenna in question is Jenna Lyons, J. Crew's president and creative director; she is the woman pictured in the ad, and the boy with the pink toenails is her son Beckett (Donaldson James). National reactions to the ad—it was a subject of heated debate in many blogs, morning news shows, and newspaper editorials—are proof-positive that the effeminate paradox remains alive and well in the early twenty-first century.

Social conservatives were outraged by the ad. The right-wing Media Research Center called it "blatant propaganda celebrating transgendered children" (Brown). In an editorial for FoxNews.com, Dr. Keith Ablow, a psychiatrist associated with popular right-wing television and radio host Glenn Beck, recommends that Lyons "put some money aside for psychotherapy for the kid" (Ablow). From there, Ablow goes on to say that Lyons's painting her son's toenails pink is a sign of "the way that our culture is being encouraged to abandon all trappings of gender identity—homogenizing males and females when the outcome of such 'psychological sterilization' . . . is not known" (Ablow). This is alarming to Ablow because it creates a gender-confused world in which "[g]irls beat up other girls on YouTube. [And] Young men primp and preen until their abdomens are washboards and their hair is perfect" (Ablow). This "may seem like no big deal," but as Ablow explains, "it will be a very big deal if it turns out that neither gender is very comfortable anymore nurturing children above all else, and neither gender is motivated to rank creating a family above having great sex forever and neither gender is motivated to protect the nation by marching into combat against other men and risking their lives" (Ablow).

Everything old is new again; although Ablow does not use the word *sissy*, his editorial is otherwise almost an exact copy of the anti-sissy diatribes being published in the United States in the 1890s or the 1920s. In Ablow's view, Jenna Lyons is a danger to the very core of American culture because by encouraging her son to engage in effeminate behavior (toenail painting) Lyons is—unwittingly or not—hasting America toward an apocalyptic future filled with effeminate men (and butch women) who will neither make babies nor be willing or able to militarily defend America's empire. What is new, in Ablow's account, is the implication that transgression of heteronormative gender roles will lead to effeminate men and butch women "having great sex forever" (Ablow is silent on the question of whether this great sex will be homosexual, heterosexual, or a little of both) and that this "great sex forever" will distract them from the necessities of reproduction and military service.

Masculinity, in Ablow's argument, is the foundation of both reproduction and the military defense of the nation-state/empire. Furthermore, masculinity only "counts" when it occurs in male bodies (Ablow implies, without explaining why, that women who fight on YouTube could never fight in the military), and masculinity requires sacrifice; one must forego the opportunity to have "great sex forever" in order to be the soldier/husband/father/patriarch the empire requires. Similarly, Ablow implies that Lyons must make sacrifices; she must ignore the pleasure (hers, her son's, or both) of neon pink toenails. By indulging this pleasure, Lyons—in Ablow's reading—becomes a smothering, sissy-producing, monster mom for the twenty-first century, a woman so hellbent on her own feminine pleasures, and/or so indulgent of her son's, that she is willing to threaten the existence of nation/empire itself.

She thus demands the intervention of trained specialists such as Ablow.

Ablow's response clearly draws on the United States' longstanding tradition of figuring effeminacy as threat, but his was not the only response to the ad. Many cultural commentators argued that the controversy was overblown, saying that there was little evidence to link childhood play and adult sexuality and/or gender performance. For example, *Chicago Sun-Times* columnist Neil Steinberg calls the toenail painting on display in the J. Crew ad "an unobjectionable—except for the swarmy commercialism—moment between mother and son" and turns his readers' attention to a 1902 picture of a young boy wearing a dress—as was the custom at the time—and points out that the boy grew up to be "the famed macho writer" Ernest Hemingway (Steinberg). Melanie Klein, blogging for *Ms.* magazine, dismisses the outrage over the toenail-painting ad as misplaced, saying that "J. Crew's ad doesn't depict misguided and dangerous decisions made by J. Crew or parents like Jenna Lyons. The reactions and social outcry against it depict the dangerous world of gender policing within the system of patriarchy" (Klein). And comedian Jon Stewart, as then-host of the nightly news parody *The Daily Show*, lambasted the overwrought mainstream media coverage of the J. Crew ad, mocking it as "Toe-maggedon 2011" and saying that commentators were "acting like this lady gave her son an 'I love cock' tattoo" (qtd. in Sterling). And while neither Steinberg, Klein, or Stewart expressly says, "So what if a child is gay or transgendered, why is that a problem?" all of their comments clearly criticize the strict policing of gender roles that Ablow and other conservative commentators are calling for. Steinberg, Klein, and Stewart all imply that effeminacy is no cause for alarm.

These bifurcated responses to the J. Crew ad are similar to those caused by Dyson Kilodavis, a five-year-old, self-described "Princess Boy" whose parents support his love of sparkly dresses and who also made the rounds of blogs, newspaper editorials, and morning news shows (Dube). That a young boy's painted toenails (or desire to wear a dress) are national news in the United States and that that news coverage of these events ran the tonal gamut from horror/outrage to fascination/loving support proves the continued existence of the effeminate paradox in the early twenty-first century.

But in noting that the effeminate paradox is still with us, we should not assume that it has remained unchanged over the decades since 1940. For instance, Chapter One argues that the Sympathetic Sissies of Carson McCullers and Truman Capote's fiction were, at their time, relatively rare in their presentation of a counter-narrative to dominate notions of effeminacy as threat. But as the above examples of support for Jenna and Beckett Lyons attest, there are now many more voices asserting that effeminacy is either value-neutral or something positive. The causes for this change are overdetermined: clearly the rise and increased visibility of movements for both lesbian/gay and transgendered rights have helped to move a view that effeminacy is either positive or value-neutral closer to the mainstream, and the Internet itself allows people with views of all kinds to comment on, support, and/or critique information of all kinds, including the "official" dominant culture narratives of network news and newspaper editorials. Thus, while support of sissies may to some extent remain a minority view, those holding that view now have more means of voicing it than ever before.

This chapter asks: Where is the paradox now, in the early twenty-first century? In what form(s) does it still exist? How has it changed, and what are the forces driving this change? Any answers I give here are, of course, tentative. It is often most difficult to see that which is right in front of us; it is challenging to analyze the culture that we live and work and breathe in every day. Also, "discourses of effeminacy" is a huge category, one that encompasses material from film, television, novels, advertising, popular music, music videos, and much more—far more than could be fully discussed in a single chapter. I acknowledge those limitations, and, thus, this final chapter focuses on a specific claim: that while effeminacy as threat remains alive and well in US popular culture of the early twenty-first century (see Ablow's editorial for but one example of many), fascinating effeminacy has become an increasingly common, and increasingly mainstream, trope in US popular culture since 1940.

I argue this point in two stages. First, I read three texts—poet Mark Doty's *Firebird* (1999), former *Vogue* magazine editor-at-large André Leon Talley's *A.L.T.: A Memoir* (2003), and entertainment journalist Kevin Sessums's *Mississippi Sissy* (2007)—that represent a genre I call "the sissy memoir." What is interesting about this genre is that while sissy memoirs do frame effeminacy as fascinating, but they do so while always acknowledging that much of the United States still sees effeminacy as some mix of monstrous or pathetic. Sissy memoirs acknowledge all points along the continuum of effeminate representation; they represent the effeminate paradox in all of its complex, internally contradictory glory. They do so by first demonstrating that when and where effeminacy is viewed as threat that this leads to sissies being shunned, bullied, or even assaulted by peers and/or family members. Rather than ignoring the pain of this treatment, which often occurs in childhood and adolescence, sissy memoirs acknowledge it before moving on to figure effeminacy, in adulthood, as fascinating. Doty, Talley, and Sessums all attribute different special abilities to effeminacy, but their memoirs agree that once a sissy boy has passed through the considerable pain and isolation of a sissy boyhood, he finds himself gifted in some special way as an adult. Or as Doty puts it, "That's the queer boy's dynamic, simultaneously debased and elevated. . . . you can embrace your own difference. Inside the rejected boy, inside the unloved body, reigns the sissy triumphant, enraged, jeweled by an elegant crown of his own devising" (106). The sissy memoir thus depicts one extreme end of the effeminate paradox (fascinating effeminacy) as a feature of adulthood that redeems the pain experienced during childhood/adolescence because of the other extreme end of the paradox (threatening effeminacy). In insisting on the reality of both extreme ends of the effeminate paradox, sissy memoirists figure themselves as (to paraphrase Doty) Triumphant Sissies, sissies who survived the pains of a gender nonconforming childhood in a heteronormative, femme-phobic world. Surviving where so many other sissies tragically do not (because of literal death brought on by violence or the psychic death brought on by shame and silencing), the Triumphant Sissy Memorists explain not just that they weathered the storm of their childhoods but also to explain that in doing so they emerged stronger and more gifted than ever before.

Second, I argue that the formulation of effeminacy found in the sissy memoir—the idea that effeminacy makes for both a painful childhood and an especially gifted adulthood—has been popularized and mainstreamed by the It Gets Better Project. Designed to combat LGBT youth suicide by addressing the fact that many LGBT youth do not grow up in families or communities where they can see happy and successful LGBT adults, the It Gets Better Project asks LGBT adults and straight adult allies to make videos telling LGBT teens who are feeling isolated and/or being bullied that they should hang in there, weather their miserable high school years, and not commit suicide because later they will enjoy a safe, happy, fulfilling queer adulthood. These videos, which users post online, describe the narrative arc of an LGBT youth's life in the same way that the sissy memoir describes the narrative arc of a sissy boy's life: childhood and adolescence will be difficult, but with effeminate adulthood will come special privileges and joys.

The view that effeminacy constitutes the threatening grotesque—and that the proper response to such a threat is disciplining that can run the gamut from mocking and ostracization to physical violence and even murder—has by no means vanished from US cultural discourse. There is copious evidence to support that claim, including (but certainly not limited to) Ablow's editorial; C. J. Pascoe's research on the rampant homophobia in American high schools; the 2008 murder of Lawrence "Larry" King, a fifteen-year-old boy who sometimes wore skirts to school and who was murdered by a classmate (Cathcart); and the wave of gay teen suicides that prompted the founding of the It Gets Better Project ("What Is the It Gets Better Project?"). While there is not true equilibrium between the two sides of the effeminate paradox, I argue that the recent mainstreaming of effeminacy as the fascinating grotesque means that the two sides are more closely matched, in terms of discursive force, than they have been at any time since 1940.

"SON, YOU'RE A BOY": GROWING UP AS EMBODIED THREAT

Sissy memoir is a prose autobiography genre that deals, at least to some significant degree, with both the trials of a sissy boyhood and the special insight, experiences, and/or abilities that such a boyhood affords later in life. Sissy memoirs emphasize both ends of the effeminate paradox; in them, the pain and isolation that comes from peers and parents recognizing effeminacy as threat is acknowledged, but as these effeminate authors/protagonists move out of adolescence, they stress how adulthood ushers in fascinating effeminacy, as the author/protagonist's effeminacy allows him special insight denied to gender-conforming peers, helps fuel his art, and/or leads him out of or away from negative circumstances.

All three sissy memoirs discussed here contain evidence, in spades, of effeminacy as threat. For example, Doty's *Firebird* quickly establishes that his effeminacy caused him to feel isolated from other boys/men and from his own parents at an early age. An elementary school teacher tells Doty's parents that "*Mark relates so well to girls*" (56, emphasis Doty's). With some shame, Doty is forced to agree with the teacher's assessment of him: "And I do [relate well to girls], or at least better than I do with most boys, who seem already possessed of forms of knowledge opaque to me, things they grasp and I do not: baseball gloves, for instance, the inflation of rubber balls, marbles, the choosing of teams, names of models of cars. Where they got this knowledge I don't know; already I have a dawning sense that either it is too late for me to ask the questions or that questioning is not the way such understandings are gained. If you have to ask the rules of the boys' world, you can't possibly be one of the people who has the answers. To ask would betray my hopeless ignorance" (56–57).

Thus, Doty learns early on that he is different from most other boys who, like the son of one of his father's coworkers, are "All Boy, smitten to the core with astronauts, the current pursuit and obsession of All Boys" (57). In sharp contrast to his "All Boy" peers, Doty hates P.E. class—he says that the rubber ball used for kickball games "smells of inadequacy, not knowing what to do, not knowing how" (71)—and prefers to watch his female classmates play hopscotch. "I have even smuggled *Little Women* out of the school library," he writes, "because the girls have spoken so excitedly of the nobility of Jo and the tragedy of Beth, and somehow I know it's something I shouldn't be seen actually checking out" (72).

But while the distance Doty feels from his classmates is painful, it is his parents' view of his effeminacy as threat that proves to be scarring and life altering. When Doty is ten, his mother finds him dressed in drag as Judy Garland, practicing a show in which he plans to sing Garland songs and dance for his parents and their neighbors. Appalled, his mother tells him, "You can't do that for the neighbors," and then, "She says, with a hiss, with shame and with exasperation, *Son, you're a boy*," (101, emphasis Doty's). This maternal pronouncement freezes both mother and son, who are "held there in the mother's disappointment, her fear of what her son will become. His dissolute future spreads out in front of her like an oil slick: shameful, worthless, sick" (101). In this horrible moment, Doty thinks of television: "Echo of Khrushchev on a TV screen, pounding and shouting: 'We will bury you.' Or worse, *We will teach you to bury yourself for us. You're a boy*: watershed between childhood and something else. I have been ushered into the world where adults live; I have been warned, have been instructed to conceal my longing. And though I will understand, someday, that without longing there'd be nothing to carry us forward, that without longing we wouldn't be anyone at all, I can't see that now. . . . I have been initiated—whether because my mother wanted to punish or to protect me—into an adult world of limit and sorrow" (102, emphasis Doty's). Doty's larger point here is that all adults live in a world of "limit and sorrow" and must constrain and modify their desires to conform to social norms. But he is also clear that his effeminacy is the thing that "ushered" him into this heartbreaking adult world. Effeminacy is the thing about him that is so "shameful, worthless, [and] sick" that it must, according to his mother, be denied and concealed and ignored.

Later on, Doty's mother sinks into both alcoholism and depression, and when he is a teenager she quite literally tries to kill him. She calls him out of his bedroom one day, asking him to step out into the hallway. Doty does so, and there he finds her standing with his father's pistol "well out in front of her, away from her face," aimed directly at him (177). Somehow the gun does not go off. Doty lives, but he never knows if his mother did not squeeze the trigger or if she squeezed it but still had the gun's safety engaged. Either way, he feels that "once attempted, the act of obliteration isn't erasable. To raise a gun and aim is to will a death, and that act of will is ineradicable" (180). Doty also believes that his mother's desire to murder him is linked to his effeminacy and his homosexuality (which in Doty's account of his life are inseparable). Doty makes this connection explicit: just prior to describing his mother's attempt to kill him, he recounts coming home late at night (as a teenager) and hearing her "talking all night to him [Doty's father], to the wall, recounting her litany of grief, telling the beads of her sorrows . . . [her] sour voice seeping into the adobe walls like some oily pigment, this rag of a house soaking it in till its ready to combust" (175). Chief amongst this litany of sorrows is one disappointment that teenage Doty hears his mother say clearly, "Son's a homosexual" (175). As a boy Doty learned that his effeminacy was something shameful to his mother, and as an adolescent he learns that it is something she literally wants to murder him for.

Doty (born 1953) is white, and grows up middle class, bouncing from town to town across the US South and Southwest as his father changes jobs. In contrast, André Leon Talley (born 1948) is African American and spends most of his childhood in segregated Durham, North Carolina, where is raised by his maternal grandmother, Bennie Frances Davis, who worked as a custodian at Duke University. But despite these differences in race and place and social class, Talley's *A.L.T.*, like Doty's *Firebird*, describes the pain and isolation of an effeminate boyhood.

But whereas Doty learns his biggest lesson about the wrongness of effeminacy at home, Talley's grandmother creates a safe and welcoming space for him, a refuge where he is not judged or ostracized for being effeminate. I will discuss this safe space at greater length below, but for now I want to emphasize that while Talley's grandmother's home was safe and welcoming, his working-class African American neighborhood was a different story. "The truth was that I didn't have many playmates," Talley writes. "There were friends on my block, but they weren't all a day at the beach. . . . the boys on Cornell Street could be fun, but they made life hell. I was different, and while I did not go around broadcasting my interests to the other kids at school, children do have a way of preying on those who aren't exactly like them" (96). The source of Talley's childhood difference is, undoubtedly, his effeminacy.

Indeed, in describing his childhood, he enumerates practically all the signs of a sissy boyhood. He hates sports: "I never especially enjoyed or had a real aptitude for sports" (97). He loathes playing outside: "[T]hanks to my fear of snakes, I would never go alone for a walk in the woods. Even today, although I love trees, I would much rather look at them from my house or out a car window than go walking or, God forbid, bike riding in a deeply wooded area!" (109). He loves books: "I didn't have another kid in the house to trade stories with at night or after church, or more than one tired parent to look to for entertainment, so I learned early on to turn to books for much of my adventure life. . . . Books were my world, I loved everything about them" (107). He loves fashion magazines: "*Vogue*, which, since the time I turned eight or nine, had reliably provided me safe passage into the exotic world of the international jet set. While other boys may have been out practicing their fastballs or trying to break track records, I was on the couch, enrapt in the pages of the world [editor] Diana Vreeland had invented, a world of fantasy, style, and exquisite fashion" (109). And even when Talley does partake in appropriately boyish activities, the pleasures that he derives from them are inappropriately effeminate: "There were years . . . when I belonged to the Cub Scouts, but I confess that the thing I truly cared about was the uniform: that sprightly yellow kerchief, the hat. I was also crazy about the furniture in den leader Miss Katherine Shaw's living room, the first pseudo-French country furniture I'd ever sat upon" (103). It is thus little surprise when he eventually declares "I hated those exploratory field walks [of the Cub Scouts] and would rather have been at home cutting out pages from *Vogue* or *Harper's Bazaar*" (104).

And when Talley tells adults—especially male adults—about his love of fashion magazines and his aspirations to someday edit one, he learns that such interests and desires are decidedly not okay. When Talley tells an older male cousin that he wants to grow up and become a fashion editor, the cousin greets this news with "a dazed and disgusted look" (113). Talley says that the cousin's "opinion didn't matter much to me, not in my heart," but "after that incident in my bedroom, I decided to keep my dreams more firmly to myself, and I never discussed them again with any but my female friends until college" (114). What Talley learns in this exchange with his cousin is that effeminacy is something that dazes and disgusts most men.

This resistance to Talley's effeminacy—this sense that it represents threat and is, therefore, unwelcome—stems, at least in part, from the ethics of black respectability. "Historically," writes Kali Gross, "as a form of resistance to the negative stigmas and caricatures about their morality, African Americans adopted a 'politics of respectability.' Claiming responsibility through manners and morality furnished an avenue for African Americans to assert the will and agency to redefine themselves outside the prevailing racist discourses" (qtd. in McBride, "Straight Black Studies" 38). Talley's grandmother, much of his extended family, and their church community clearly subscribe to the politics of respectability. They tacitly resist Jim Crow—and the discourses supporting it, which framed black people as dirty, lazy, and immoral—by going to great lengths to always appear clean, productive, and morally righteous. But as Dwight A. McBride has pointed out, the politics of black respectability have also often necessitated the exclusion of queer sexualities and gender performances from what is considered to be authentically black: "the politics of black respectability . . . can be seen as laying the foundation for the necessary disavowal of black queers in dominant representations of the African American community, African American history, and African American studies" ("Straight Black Studies" 38). Since effeminacy is so routinely perceived as threat—especially amongst hegemonically masculine men—it necessarily falls outside the bounds of black respectability. This is the message that lies, unspoken, beneath Talley's cousin's disapproval, and it is a message that Talley himself hears loud and clear.

This is not to say, simplistically, that all black people reject Talley because of his effeminacy or that all black communities universally reject effeminacy. In fact, as I mentioned briefly earlier, Talley finds both safety and an acceptance of his effeminacy from both his grandmother and from some of his female peers. This acceptance likely stems, at least in part, from their membership in and involvement with the black Southern Baptist church. As E. Patrick Johnson writes, in the editorial material in *Sweet Tea*—his oral history project collecting the voices of southern black gay men—black churches are, and historically have been, "a contradictory space" for gay and/or effeminate black men, "one that exploits the creative talents of its gay members even as it condemns their gayness" (183). Johnson goes on to talk about how effeminacy, in particular, is welcomed, and even celebrated, in some black churches because "gay men are integral to most black church organizations" and "the flamboyant choir director, musician, or soloist" are common figures therein (184). The choir, in particular, Johnson says, is a welcoming space for effeminate boys and men; discussing his own effeminate boyhood, Johnson says that "[i]n the children's choir, we baby church sissies would flame as bright as we wanted, and it was totally acceptable" (185). Talley himself does not mention ever being in the church choir, but he and his grandmother did attend a Southern Baptist congregation each Sunday, and, thus, he likely experienced some of the same dynamics around effeminacy that Johnson and his *Sweet Tea* respondents—some of whom are roughly Talley's age—describe.

Black churches' paradoxical relationship to both effeminacy and male homosexuality may also help to explain another curious feature of *A.L.T.*, one that distinguishes it from other sissy memoirs. Whereas both Doty and Sessums link their childhood effeminacy to their later, adult homosexuality (a subject they discuss openly), Talley does not discuss his sexuality at all. Talley is quite open about having been an effeminate child and being an effeminate man, but he is noticeably silent on issues of his own sexuality. At one point, Talley recounts running into a former high school classmate who teases him about not being married yet, but he (Talley) offers no explanation as to why he is not yet married. And while he writes about going on dates with girls from his neighborhood, Talley is clear that these dates are chaste: "There were no teen gropes or fondling, no hands under her slip. Anne was too perfect for that; I would never have done anything so vulgar. But she did manage to remain my friend for life" (135). Given that Talley is sexually explicit in regard to other people—he describes a neighborhood boy demonstrating masturbation to him and other boys his age, and he acknowledges that many of the artists and designers he befriends in New York

City in the 1970s are gay—the total omission of any discussion of his own sexuality is oddly glaring.

Johnson says that "budding queens" growing up in black churches quickly learn "how to express and affirm our queerness without ever naming our sexuality" (184); that is, churchgoing black queens can be effeminate while singing in the choir (and might even be praised for it), but they cannot be openly gay. Given Talley's upbringing in a black church, and given his later-in-life devoutness (after a period of not attending church, Talley says that he began regularly attending a Baptist church in Harlem after his grandmother's death in 1989), it is possible that this black church-influenced dynamic explains the omission of Talley's own sexuality in a memoir that quite explicitly talks about his effeminacy. Whatever the reasons for Talley's silence on the subject of sexuality might be, its end effect is to create a truly sissy memoir. Whereas *Firebird* and *Mississippi Sissy* are as much about their respective authors' homosexual awakenings and eventual coming-outs, as they are their author's effeminacy, *A.L.T.* discusses effeminacy as itself and does not (explicitly) link it to male homosexuality.[1]

Another reason that Talley may be comfortable discussing his effeminacy in his memoir—and why he found safety and acceptance regarding it from his grandmother and some of his female peers—is what John Howard, in *Men Like That* (1999), calls quiet accomodationism. Howard's argument is that, in the US South, "Even as late as the mid-1960s, the gender experimentation of male youths was accommodated if not encouraged by adults, especially women" (18). *Men Like That* is specifically focused on Mississippi, and so it should come as little surprise to hear that Kevin Sessums (born 1956) recounts having also experienced quiet accomodationism during his upbringing. As Sessums's title—*Mississippi Sissy*—makes clear, he was undoubtedly an effeminate child, one possessed of "an unnerving grace, often ridiculed as girly" (41). As a youngster, Sessums fantasizes that Captain Hook, the villain of *Peter Pan*, "with his limp and his lisp, was going to come through my window and take me away to an island of boys who were, like me, lost and stagestruck and a little too lovely" (57). And when he watches the television show *What's My Line?*, he dreams of one day being on the show himself: "I would get to wear a tuxedo like Bennett Cerf. Or better yet, an evening gown like Arlene Francis" (19).

Amongst members of his family, especially women, Sessums finds his effeminacy somewhat accepted. Sessums's grandparents, for example, genially play along with him when he insists that he wants to be called Arlene (after the actress Arlene Francis) and refuses to respond when addressed by the name Kevin. And when Sessums is three-and-a-half years old, he asks his mother to sew him a skirt. One of Sessums's aunts warns his mother that making a boy a skirt is not right because "[h]e has to learn to live in this world and this world don't abide boys like that" (61). Nevertheless, Sessums's mom sews him a skirt and lets him wear it, and both she and his grandmother remark on how cute he is when he models it for them.

But this positive reception of Sessum's effeminacy does not last long, and he soon learns, painfully—just as Talley does—that there are limits to quiet accommodationism. When Sessums's father returns home and sees him wearing the skirt, he flies into a rage. When his mother says that Sessums is not hurting anyone by wearing the skirt, his father replies, "He's hurting me! He's hurting hisself with such nonsense! He's hurting this family!" (62). He then rips the skirt off of Sessums and forces him to set it on fire. As they watch the skirt burn, Sessums's father tells him, "See that? Take a good look. . . . That's what happens when boys try to be girls. That's what happens" (63).

Thus, like Talley, Sessums learns that while a select few women will tolerate or even encourage his effeminacy, in the wider world it is something that alarms others and shames Sessums himself. It is also something that sets Sessums decidedly apart from the often homosocial world of straight men, where effeminacy is only ever seen as threat. For example, Sessums says that the happiest moment of his life came when he was five and he was allowed to accompany his father into a locker room. Sessums's father was a talented basketball player and had been drafted to play in the NBA, but his mother begged his father not to move to New York, and so he remained in Mississippi and worked as a high school basketball coach. On the day that Sessums's father takes the young Sessums into that high school locker room, "the players, stripping off their uniforms—giddy and lithe—were teasing each other with that high school athlete's palaver of 'asshole' and 'dickhead' and 'faggot.' Buttocks were bared. Bodies, rank with victory, dodged the repeated snaps of tightly wound terrycloth" (9). Sessums's father looks over this scene and smiles, "a handsome crooked grin of a smile—at all the roughhousing, the random merriment" (9). The locker room also makes Sessums himself ecstatic: one of the sweaty players picks Sessums up, holds Sessums to his sweaty chest, asks him if he's okay, and then kisses the top of his head. This closeness among men, and the ease and happiness that it conjures in Sessums's father, makes the locker room a magical space for Sessums: "I can't remember ever being as happy as I was at that very moment. All attempts at happiness over the years have been failed conjuring acts to replicate those first few moments in that locker room, the one and only time I felt my father truly loved me" (9).

But the happiness does not last as both Sessums's budding homosexuality and his effeminacy end up exiling him from membership in this homosocial and homoerotic world of men. Fascinated by a player's worn and discarded jockstrap, Sessums walks over and picks it up. When his father asks him what he's "got there," Sessums holds "the jockstrap out, flourishing it with the pliancy I was developing in my wrist" (10). This causes a scene in the locker room, one where the high school basketball players begin to laugh at Sessums's interest in the jockstrap (which they interpret as homosexual) and the effeminate way in which he is displaying it. Ultimately, he is protected from their full mockery by his father; the players are unwilling to seriously mock their coach's son. But, nevertheless, the damage is done: Sessums has embarrassed his father, and his father has him removed to the coach's lounge.

While there, one of the other coaches looks at Sessums's and says, "Can you believe this sissy is Ses's [Kevin's father's]?" (11). Sessums's mixed and intense feelings—the "longing" he has to "be back inside that locker room," the pain of fatherly rejection, and the sting of the other coach's femme-phobic comment—combine and become overwhelming, making Sessum "vomit right on the man's [the femme-phobic coach's] shoes" (11). In his quick movement from membership within the homosocial/homoerotic world of men (the locker room) to humiliated exile from it, Sessums learns that his proto-homosexual desire (his interest in the worn jockstrap), effeminate body language (the limp-wristed way in which he holds the jockstrap), and inability to control his emotions (the vomiting—which Sessums's father apologizes for by saying, "He's a sensitive kid. He's sensitive") are all things that are impermissible to masculinity (11). Possessing these characteristics marks Kevin as an effeminate threat, and he is thus banned from membership in the world of men, a world his biological sex should grant him access to. Sessums quotes Flannery O'Connor's infamous observation about southerners being able to recognize freaks and then says that "[t]he first freak I ever recognized down South. . . . was my own reflection in a Mississippi mirror" (3). Sexed male, but unable to perform socially as a man, Sessums comes to understand himself as a freak.

"NO LONGER WEIGHTED": MATURING INTO FASCINATING EFFEMINACY

Freak is, of course, a term associated with the grotesque. And each of these sissy memoirists ultimately portrays their own effeminacy in terms of both the grotesque modes. That is, while effeminacy in the sissy memoir is often perceived as threatening, it can also be viewed as fascinating and empowering. While they are quite explicit about the painful nature of an effeminate childhood, Doty, Talley, and Sessums are each, in their own ways, also clear that effeminacy bestows special, positive insight and experiences.

For Doty, effeminacy is ultimately positive, even powerful, because it leads to an appreciation for the arts, which in turn enables Doty to access an ecstatic state. The young Doty discovers this when an elementary school art teacher, Miss Tynes, asks her class to get up from their desks and dance as she plays a recording of Igor Stravinsky's *Suite from the Firebird*. This is an unscripted dance; Miss Tynes tells the class the story of the phoenix's death and its rising from the ashes and then instructs her students to move in whatever way the music inspires them. The experience proves to be transformational for Doty, who is "subsumed by it [dancing to the music]. . . . I'm utterly transported, and free," so much so that "Miss Tynes is, I think, flabbergasted—or at least I imagine so now. Who is this boy who pirouettes in his Husky Boy jeans as if he hadn't a shred of shame?. . . . That is what has fallen away, like the firebird's scorched and immolated veil: my shame. How could I even know I carried it, until I had laid it down?" (80). And what about the other students, Doty's classmates, who have previously mocked and excluded him for being effeminate? What do they think when Miss Tynes has Doty dance again, to the same music, this time by himself in front of the whole class? Doty neither knows nor cares: "If the other children watch, what do they think of me at all? Do they find me a little ridiculous, heavy little sissy in glasses and a plaid short-sleeved shirt? No idea" (81). He has no idea because dancing to the music has once again transformed him, freed him. While dancing, Doty is: "power and authority. . . . now I've disappeared. . . . It is the firebird after all, no longer and hide-and-seek flitting in the trees but who he always was, beneath the scorch and the ashes, beneath the ordinary ugly body in which he has been disguised, under the shame he's worn like a cloak, under the misunderstandings and the knowledge that he can't be who they want, they they do not want who he is. . . . Unsayable moment given form, in the body of a heavy little boy no longer weighted, without limit, hardly held to earth at all" (81–82).

Prior to dancing to the *Suite from the Firebird*, effeminacy—a love of the fine arts, a joy in dancing—had been a source of shame for Doty. But in dancing to Stravinsky, what had once been shameful becomes an escape from shame, a pathway to a state of being in which it no longer matters that Doty "can't be who they want" (a hegemonically masculine boy) or that "they do not want who he is" (an effeminate boy). Effeminacy has transported him into a state of being that, while it is temporary, gives him a lasting sense that the values of his culture—the values that condemn him for being effeminate—are not the only set of values that a life can be lived by.

Later on, Doty learns the painful lesson that dance, when it is forced to conform to social norms, can be a painful, numbing experience, rather than a liberating one. Enrolled in tap dancing lessons, Doty stars as Uncle Sam in a Fourth of July–themed dance recital. And so while Mark's participation in this activity can still be read as somewhat effeminate (it is dance, and he is wearing a costume that involves "a particularly fabulous blue-sequined drum-major hat"), the transgressiveness of the routine is lessened because Doty is clearly cast as male (as Uncle Sam, he is surrounded by "five little girls in sequined outfits like bathing suits dipped in glitter"), and the routine draws on nationalistic, even militaristic themes (96). Although the girls dancing around Doty are twirling batons, Doty himself is denied one: "I am fascinated by batons, but do not have one" (96). The performance "goes without a hitch," "the adoring audience of parents cheers," and "the applause intoxicates" Doty, but it is an empty kind of intoxication; confined to the very gendered choreography of the routine, and high on diet pills that his mother has been feeding him to make him lose weight, Doty feels detached from himself, numb: "This is what becomes of the firebird, drugged and trained: everybody adores him" (96). This scene reveals that what had been so magical in his earlier *Firebird*-inspired epiphany was not dancing per se, but freedom—the freedom his teacher allowed him to be what he was (a fat kid) and to move how he wanted (effeminately) without judgment or shaming. When those freedoms are taken away, as they are in the Uncle Sam tap routine, Doty pleases his audience but fails to feel any joy himself.

Effeminacy, in Talley's *A.L.T.*, functions more like Doty's *Firebird* dance than his Uncle Sam routine. In Talley's day-to-day life growing up in Durham, effeminacy is a thing that sets him apart and isolates him, but it is also something that teaches him that another, wider world exists beyond the one he is being raised in. Talley eschews sports and Cub Scouting in favor of staying home and reading issues of Diana Vreeland's *Vogue* because in that magazine's pages he found a "sense of grandeur" and "[t]hat sense of grandeur rubbed off on me; I intuitively connected with it, and it fired my imagination. So when you see me now coming out of a party in some extravagant Galliano-Dior coat from Paris, or carrying a Fendi Russian sable muff bag big enough for a child to sit in, that's something that just comes from my childhood. That was the way I was, and that was what I loved. I had a loving, nurturing home to grow up in, but in many ways I had to make my own world. And it was a world of the imagination that I created. I only shared my world with my grandmother, and only as I approached adulthood did I find myself able to share it with certain carefully chosen friends. In high school, it was pretty much all mine" (111–112). And so, again, effeminacy isolates Talley in the short term (he can discuss his love of fashion only with his grandmother and "carefully chosen friends"), but in the long term it opens up new possibilities, new worlds for him. It literally shows him that other kinds of worlds are possible. Whereas effeminacy gives Doty an ecstasy that frees him from shame, it gives Talley a sense that it is possible to build an aesthetic life, one lived around the ideals of beauty, of grace, of fine worksmanship and things well made.

Talley, however, does not describe his journey as that of a poor, backwater hick who later flees to Manhattan to discover luxury. Today, Talley is perhaps best known, even to people unfamiliar with the world of high fashion, for the striking figure he makes: a 6′4″, heavyset, very effeminate black man known for wearing outrageously styled caftans.[2] But he is careful, in the first chapter of *A.L.T.*, to make it clear that while his life is devoted to the love and enjoyment of luxury, he does *not* define luxury as "the luxury of the clothes' presentation at runway shows, beautifully orchestrated luncheons, or designers' showrooms; [or as] the luxury of having a lifestyle that permits one either the leisure to wear such clothes or the leisure to have opinions about them" (3). Luxury, for Talley, means "the beauty of ordinary tasks done well and in a good frame of mind; of simple things suited to their purpose and well cared for" (4–5). These are lessons that Talley learned from his grandmother. "Bennie Francis Davis may have looked like a typical African-American domestic worker to many who saw her on an ordinary day," Talley writes, "[b]ut I, who could see her soul, could also see her secret: that even while she wore a hair net and work clothes to scrub toilets and floors, she wore an invisible diadem" (19). Talley describes how his grandmother kept an immaculate house and how her meticulous attention to small details—such as ironing his bed-sheets and regularly waxing the floor—made a lasting impression on him: "My grandmother never had to tell me to stand up proud, never had to explain to me or convince me that although we did not have much money, we were the equals of any people in town. I knew this just by looking around me" (17). The values of black respectability that, in some ways, made Talley's effeminacy unacceptable are, thus, paradoxically also the same values that instilled him with a love of luxury that, over time, drew him to the world of high fashion, a world where male participation therein is coded as highly effeminate.

For Sessums, the benefits of effeminacy begin to reveal themselves even when he is still a child. Although his effeminacy enrages his father, Sessums also realizes, very early on, that underneath his father's rage lies fear. And the ability to cause fear is powerful: "It comforted me to know that my father, who was afraid of nothing, was afraid of me" (11). In this moment, readers can see the grotesque nature of effeminacy, how it is always paradoxical: Sessums's father finds him threatening, but there is, for Sessums, power in that. Furthermore, he finds erotic pleasure in being shamed for being effeminate. His father, when angry, routinely mocks Sessums by calling him a girl. And one day, when his father is eager to earn his trust, he offers to never call Sessums a girl again, if Sessums will do what he wants. Sessums's father intends this as a peace offering; he thinks that his son does not want to be called a girl. But this is not the case, far fromt. "I liked him calling me a girl," Sessums writes. "It was one of my favorite things in the world. The way he had settled in to saying it could send welcome shivers down my little spine. His voice no longer sounded angry and shocked like the first time he said it. Its tone instead had ripened with his repeated ribbing until it contained the same sweet sarcasm with which he could tease my mother at times and take her breath away. . . . His calling me a girl and my eye-batting reaction to it—a mirroring of my mother's only response to such an onslaught of his dirty words—constituted the first stirrings in me of what it meant to flirt. 'You girl,' I would goad him into saying. 'You goddamned girl'" (59–60).

For Sessums, even when effeminacy triggers negative sanction (his father attempting to shame him by calling him a girl), he finds a way to reverse that negativity, finding positive pleasure in the midst of it.

Effeminacy itself is thus a source of pleasure, the thing that provokes a response from his father that sends "welcome shivers" down his spine.

And while Sessums himself, even at a very young age, seems well aware that effeminacy can be a source of good things, his mother quite explicitly tries to teach him this same lesson. After Sessums's father is killed in a car crash, his mother tells him that "I know people call you a sissy" and that "I know Daddy did a lot of the time," too (87). She orders Sessums to write the word *sissy* on a piece of her stationary and then makes him look at it, saying, "Now, whenever anybody calls you that again you remember how pretty that word looks on there. Look at the muscles those S's have. Look at the arms on that Y. Look at the backbone that lone I has. What posture, what presence. See how proud that I is to stand there in front of you. . . . Say it with Mommy. Sissysissysissy" (87–88).

In this way, Sessums's sissy memoir differs slightly from Doty and Talley's. Doty and Talley both write about their effeminacy opening doors to new and better, worlds, but they do not arrive in those worlds until adulthood. As both the description of the pleasure Sessums feels at being called a girl and the scene between Sessums and his mother make clear, Sessums is clear that effeminacy bestows benefits on him even when he is still a child. He writes less about his effeminacy giving him a new world and more about it giving him a new and privileged place within the world he was born into. In the "Author's Note" that precedes his memoir, Sessums says that his book is a "re-creation of my childhood and teenage years" that he has been able to write because "I *listened*. That's what most sissies do when we are children: We sit apart and listen" (n.p., emphasis Sessum's). With this statement, Sessums claims a paradoxical meaning for effeminacy. On the one hand, being a sissy sets a boy apart. But it also moves him into a special space, the space of the outsider-insider, the one who is both of a culture and able to see its flaws and shortcomings. What a sissy learns by virtue of being set apart is, presumably, worth repeating, worth listening to, otherwise there is little point for Sessums to publish a memoir at all. By his own accounting, effeminacy has expanded Sessums's imaginative possibilities; it has given him both the ability to observe and the ability to transform that observation into prose.

Read collectively, all three of these sissy memoirs—*Firebird*, *A.L.T.*, and *Mississippi Sissy*—reveal that both sides of effeminate paradox remain alive and well in contemporary US culture. Certainly many people still think of effeminacy as threatening; the ill treatment (ranging from relatively minor schoolyard teasing to more serious feelings of isolation to tremendously painful feelings of having disappointed parents) that all three sissy memoirists write about confirms as much. But each text also makes its own unique claims about how and why effeminacy is ultimately a privileged, positive state of being, one that confers special benefits and insights. In this sense they expand and intensify the smaller, more-often-neglected side of the effeminate paradox: fascinating effeminacy. By insisting that effeminacy has distinct, positive effects in their own lives, Doty, Talley, and Sessums—each in their own way—present themselves as flesh-and-blood, fully adult versions of McCullers and Capote's Sympathetic Sissies. Only in these very contemporary sissy memoirs, the Sympathetic Sissies do not die psychic or literal deaths. Nor are they supporting characters in someone else's narratives. They are, at last, center stage, speaking in first person and loudly insisting that effeminacy is something both powerful and powerfully good.

THE IT GETS BETTER PROJECT: POPULARIZING FASCINATING EFFEMINACY

While sissy memoirs do, discursively, expand and intensify the effeminacy as fascinating grotesque, it would be difficult to argue that the three sissy memoirs discussed here bring this message to an audience that could truly be called mass. Doty and Sessums's books were well reviewed, but literary nonfiction—especially literary nonfiction by openly gay men—is hardly the dominant form of media in the early twenty-first century. Talley, via the celebrity that his association with *Vogue* and his participation (as a judge) on the popular reality TV show *America's Next Top Model* provide him, is likely better known than either Doty or Sessums, but it would be difficult to argue that the publication of his memoir was a culture-shifting event. Fascinating effeminacy has long been a minority discourse, one much less publicized and argued-for across US culture than its flip side, threatening effeminacy. It would be difficult to argue that the three sissy memoirs discussed here have altered that dynamic on a mass scale.

But I want to conclude this chapter by arguing that the conception of effeminacy that sissy memoirs articulate has become much more mainstream in US culture and that here in the early part of the twenty-first century the two sides of the effeminate paradox are, if not equally weighted, more equal in terms of discursive force within the culture than they have been at any moment since 1940. More specifically, I argue that the sissy memoir's conception of effeminacy has been mainstreamed, by the It Gets Better Project, an Internet-based initiative whose goal is combat suicide among LGBT youth. The project's mission statement begins, "Growing up isn't easy. Many young people face daily tormenting and bullying, leading them to feel like they have nowhere to turn. This is especially true for LGBT kids and teens, who often hide their sexuality for fear of bullying. Without other openly gay adults and mentors in their lives, they can't imagine what their future may hold. In many instances, gay and lesbian adolescents are taunted—even tortured—simply for being themselves. . . . While many of these teens couldn't see a positive future for themselves, we can. The It Gets Better Project was created to show young LGBT people the levels of happiness, potential, and positivity their lives will reach – if they can just get through their teen years" ("What Is the It Gets Better Project?").

The project grew out of an online video that Dan Savage, a syndicated sex advice columnist and editorial director of Seattle's *The Stranger*, and his husband, Terry Miller, created in September 2010 in response to a rash of LGBT teen suicides ("What Is the It Gets Better Project?"). In their video, Savage and Miller address LGBT teens who might be considering suicide because of bullying at school and/or rejection (or fear of it) at home; Savage and Miller talk about how they themselves were bullied as teenagers but how "it gets better" in adulthood and how they have been able to find both happiness and acceptance as adults ("What Is the It Gets Better Project?").

From that initial video, the project quickly grew into an archive of over 10,000 user-created videos that have been viewed over 35 million times ("What Is the It Gets Better Project?"). Initially, these videos were from other LGBT adults, talking about their own experiences and urging bullied LGBT youth not to commit suicide, but very quickly people of all orientations joined in and made videos in support of LGBT youth. Many of these videos are from non-celebrities, but many celebrities have also contributed to the Project, including politicians (President Barack Obama, former Secretary of State Hillary Clinton, former Speaker of the House Nancy Pelosi), musicians (Adam Lambert, Ke$ha), actors (Anne Hathaway, Colin Farrell, the cast of HBO's *True Blood*), television personalities (Ellen DeGeneres, Stephen Colbert), the employees of major corporations (The Gap, Facebook, Google), and entire professional sports teams (The Boston Red Sox, The San Francisco Giants) ("What Is the It Gets Better Project?"). Given how popular the It Gets Better Project has become—stories from some of the submitted videos are being compiled for release in book form, and Google highlighted the Project in a television ad for its new web browser, Chrome, in May 2011 ("What Is the It Gets Better Project?")—and given the prominence and celebrity of many of its contributors, I want to make the case that the project's rhetoric represents one of the major modes in which effeminacy is currently characterized in US cultural discourse.

To be clear, the It Gets Better Project itself does not specifically mention effeminacy or any other type of gender nonconformity on the "About" section of its website. As the excerpt quoted from above demonstrates, the official language of the It Gets Better Project is largely focused on sexuality; the project's goal is to prevent the suicide of LGBT youth. Three of the letters in that acronym—L, G, and B—focus on identities that are based in sexual orientation. But the final letter in the acronym—T, for transgender—does tacitly acknowledge that youth can be bullied and tormented for gender nonconformity. And many of the user-submitted videos discuss being bullied for some type of gender nonconformity in middle or high school.

Savage and Miller's original, project-founding video does exactly this. Although Savage and Miller do not say the words *effeminate* or *effeminacy*, their accounts of the bullying they endured in high school both focus, implicitly, on the fact that they were effeminate. "I was picked on because I liked musicals," Savage says, "and because I was obviously gay" ("What Is the It Gets Better Project?"). Loving Broadway musicals is stereotypically considered to be a sign of effeminate homosexuality, and it seems unlikely that Savage was being "obviously gay" as a high school student by having sex with other boys in the hallways of his school. When he says that he was "obviously gay," he means, of course, that he was obviously effeminate. Effeminacy figures implicitly in Miller's recollection of his past as well. Miller describes being viciously bullied in high school; when his parents met with school administrators to see if the administrators could do anything to protect their son, the administrators told Miller's parents that "if you [Miller] look that way, talk that way, walk that way, act that way – then there's nothing we can do" ("What Is the It Gets Better Project?"). Although Miller does not specify what the administrators at his school meant by "that way," we can assume that they meant effeminacy, which was also understood to mean homosexuality. Miller's adolescent crime was looking and talking and walking and acting like an effeminate gay man, something that the administrators at his high school clearly thought justified the awful treatment he received at the hands of classmates.

Evidence suggests that Savage and Miller's experiences of high school are hardly unique. In 1989, a US Department of Health and Human Services report on youth suicide revealed that gay and lesbian youth make up 30 percent of all youth suicides (Talburt 118). And given the wide degree to which effeminacy is assumed to symbolize or signal male homosexuality, many of these suicidal gay teens were likely boys who had been bullied because of their effeminacy. Furthermore, not all gender nonconformity is treated equally. Pascoe says that her observation of butch lesbian high school students revealed that some young women actually gained prestige and status in the high school social order by dressing and behaving in ways typically ascribed to heterosexual male jocks (120–133). One butch lesbian student Pascoe observed found that her lesbianism and gender nonconformity "translated into popularity and extra support and counseling from the [school's] administration" because they were seen as "simultaneously charming and disruptive" but ultimately "nonthreatening to the existing gender and sexual order" that equated masculinity with strength and dominance and femininity with weakness (132). That is, school administrators and students might have found it unusual for a woman to be physically strong and to dress like a male athlete, but this lesbian student's masculine gender performance did not challenge the underlying cultural assumption that masculinity signals strength and competence. Effeminate boys, on the other hand, are a different story. Because they are biologically male, they are assumed, by default, to be masculine. When they fail to perform as masculine, the cultural assumption that maleness equals masculinity that in turn equals strength and competence is threatened. This is the alleged crime for which effeminate boys are so routinely ostracized, bullied, beaten up, or sometimes even killed.

To be fair, the It Gets Better Project is not specifically about effeminacy or even specifically about reaching out to gender nonconforming teens. But as the examples from the project's founding video hopefully make clear, both the project's creators and many of the people who have contributed to it have seen the bullying and abuse triggered by a boy's effeminacy as both one of the things that can drive a teenager to suicide and one of the things that the It Gets Better Project videos themselves are designed to help combat.

It is in this way that the rhetoric of the It Gets Better Project resembles the rhetoric of the sissy memoirs discussed above. Savage, in the founding It Gets Better Project video, tells LGBT teens, "It gets better, however bad it is now. It gets better and it can get great, and it can get awesome, your life can be amazing—but you have to tough this period of it out" ("What Is the It Gets Better Project?"). In saying this, Savage has essentially taken Doty's observation about queer boys being "simultaneously debased and elevated" and applied a chronology to it (106). Savage addresses LGBT teens and says, yes, you are debased now (teased, bullied, assaulted, cut off from seeing or knowing adult gay people who might show you that gays can lead happy, fulfilling lives), but later on, after high school, you will be elevated (it will get better, your life will be "great," "awesome," and "amazing").

Although Savage does not use the word *queer*, he has nevertheless expanded Doty's message so that its recipients include what we might broadly call queer youth, and he has separated the simultaneity of Doty's characterization of effeminacy into distinct chronological stages. In Savage's narrative of queer life, there is a period of early and terrible debasement that is later followed by a period of amazing elevation in adulthood.

And while Doty does say that the queer boy is simultaneously debased and elevated, elsewhere in *Firebird* he characterizes effeminate, gay adolescence in ways that mirror Savage's chronology. For example, Doty discusses his adolescent love of Petula Clark's song "Downtown." In the song, Clark advises listeners, "*When you're alone and life is making you lonely / You can always go—Downtown*" (qtd. in Doty 111, emphasis Doty's). Writing about what these lyrics meant to him as a teenager, Doty explains that "Petula says, *Listen, you can't fix anything yet, you aren't ready, your sadness and isolation cannot be solved, but there's something you can have which is full of promise, full of what's to come next*. Thus, she has proclaimed herself as every gay boy's friend; she sees us in our isolation and extends her song to us, proving her friendship by being the first to suggest that there's actually something we can do about our situation: get up and get yourself downtown" (111, emphasis Doty's). This is remarkably similar to the narrative of a gay life told in Savage and Miller's video and reveals another similarity between the sissy memoir and the It Gets Better Project: Both insist on escape, on getting away, on moving (even if only imaginatively) to another place, one where the rules that make you a mocked and reviled outsider will no longer apply.

This emphasis on other worlds is proof that the It Gets Better Project does engage with notions of the effeminate grotesque. Said engagement is implicit rather than explicit. I do not know of any It Gets Better videos in which the video-maker actually calls LGBT youth "grotesque," and I am sure that most of the people who have made videos for the site would consider the word *grotesque* to be an insult or a slur, the very thing they made their video in the hopes of protecting LGBT youth from. Nevertheless, just like the sissy memoir before it, the

It Gets Better Project does engage with both sides of the effeminate paradox. Its engagement with effeminacy as threat is the most obvious: the It Gets Better Project recognizes that all kinds of queer sexualities and queer gender performances (effeminacy certainly included) are seen in many places/contexts in US culture as the threatening grotesque. This is why sissy boys are disciplined; it is why Miller's high school administrators said they could do nothing for him as long as he walked and talked and acted "like that." The It Gets Better Project is clearly opposed to this, as well as to the pain and grief that it causes LGBT youth; the Project identifies the trope of threatening effeminacy (and the phobic reactions it triggers) as a contributing factor in LGBT youth suicide and as thus opposes it.

The It Gets Better Project, like the sissy memoir, also engages with effeminacy as the fascinating grotesque in subtle ways as well. First, it identifies LGBT youth as precious, special, and worthwhile. Just like the Sympathetic Sissies fiction discussed in Chapter One, the It Gets Better Project sees the silencing and erasure of effeminate boys (and indeed, all types of LGBT youth) via suicide as a profound loss for the world. Second, by advising LGBT youth to hang on until they can grow up and get away to a better world, the It Gets Better Project videos associate effeminacy (and indeed, all types of LGBT identities) with the idea of another world, a different reality. In this sense, they associate effeminacy with fascination, with hybrid modes of being that gesture to possibilities for human identity that are outside what is generally known. In the rhetoric of the It Gets Better Project, LGBT teens (including effeminate boys) need to get to a better world in order to be safe and happy; but, at the same time, LGBT teens are exceedingly precious and worthwhile because they already embody other "worlds," other gendered and sexed ways of being. This is why their suicides are so especially upsetting.

Barack Obama's It Gets Better video illustrates this rhetorical engagement with effeminacy as the fascinating grotesque very well. After beginning by saying the recent suicides of gay teenagers "breaks my heart" and that such things "just shouldn't happen in this country," Obama goes on to urge bullied LGBT teens to hang in there, to choose to survive (Obama). Obama tells bullied LGBT teens that they are worthy of respect and dignity and that America needs them to survive because "[w]ith time, you're going to see that your differences are a source of pride, and a source of strength. You'll look back on the struggles you've faced with compassion, and wisdom, and that's not just going to serve you, but it'll help you get involved and make this country a better place. It'll mean that you'll be more likely to help fight discrimination, not just against LGBT Americans, but discrimination in all its forms. It means you'll be more likely to understand, personally and deeply, why it's so important that, as adults, we set an example in our own lives and that we treat everybody with respect, that we are able to see the world through other people's eyes and stand in their shoes, that we never lose sight of what binds us together" (Obama).

While Obama is speaking to the broad category of LGBT teens, his message draws heavily on the tropes of effeminacy as the fascinating grotesque. Being queer (in terms of either sexuality and/or gender performance) will, Obama says, make your early life tough. But it will also transform you in a positive way, once you reach adulthood. Having being bullied for your queerness, Obama says, you will be more empathetic, not just to other LGBT folks, but to anyone who has faced discrimination. Your empathy will thus help the nation "fight discrimination." Obama's It Gets Better video thus not only draws on the rhetoric of the fascinating effeminacy, it amplifies it. Effeminacy (and other modes of queerness) will now not only benefit the queer individual, but also empower the nation as a whole. In this sense, Obama's message envisions a trajectory for queer lives that contains an end state that looks like that of Tony Kushner's nation-redeeming Healing Queens (discussed in Chapter Four).

In claiming that an effeminate childhood will make a boy empathetic to all forms of discrimination, Obama's video mirrors some of both Doty and Sessums's rhetoric about effeminacy. Doty is, of course, set apart from both his parents and peers by his effeminacy and he feels repulsed when his father, watching Dr. Martin Luther King Jr. on television, refers to him as "Martin Luther Coon" (93). And Sessums realizes that his effeminacy sets him apart and makes him a spy in Jim

Crow Mississippi when he hears white adults saying that "it's a sad state of affairs, ain't it, when you can't scare the coloreds no more and get away with it" (18). Hearing this come from the mouth of a white man who had personally been very kind to him after the death of his mother leads Sessums to view Mississippi as "a confusing brew of chicanery, malevolence, and kindheartedness," a world he, as a sissy, will stand apart from and report on (18). (Talley, on the other hand, grows up black in the Jim Crow south and hardly needs effeminacy to come to an awareness of southern racial injustice.) So while both Doty and Sessums talk about their effeminacy leading to personal insights about racial inequality in the United States, those insights remain personal and interior. Obama's It Gets Better video goes one step further, saying that queerness (defined broadly, but certainly including effeminacy) will actually benefit the nation as a whole and help it fight discrimination.

For queer people who grew up—as Doty and Talley and Sessums and so many others did, myself certainly included—experiencing their queerness as something wrong or bad, seeing and hearing the then-sitting President of the United States of America directly addressing LGBT teenagers and telling them that their lives are both worthwhile and nationally valuable, is amazing. But that does not mean that the It Gets Better Project has been without its critics. Needless to say, cultural and/or Christian conservatives have been outraged by the project.[3] But criticisms have also emerged from the left. Perhaps the loudest and most persistent line of criticism is one that goes something like this: why must we be resigned to the fact that queer childhood and adolescence must be awful? Or as blogger Zoe Melisa puts it, "There is actually no path to change in this vision. Promoting the illusion that things just 'get better' enables privileged folks to do nothing and just rely on the imaginary mechanics of the American dream to fix the world." For all that the It Gets Better Project critiques the bullying and isolation that stem from effeminacy (and indeed, from all forms of queerness) being seen as threat, its rhetoric does imply that queer kids being bullied is an inevitability, an unchangeable fact. Many queer people have, understandably, found this to be unacceptable; the Make It Better Project, which aims to "give youth and adults concrete tools they need to make schools safer for lesbian, gay, bisexual, and transgender (LGBT) students right now" is an example of a project that takes this critique as a call to action ("Make It Better Project: About").

There have also been other criticisms of the It Gets Better Project. Queer Asian blogger Jason Tseng says that the core idea of the It Gets Better Project is sound, but that its narrative about gay adulthood too easily glosses over the ways in which gay communities can themselves be discriminatory: "[T]he gay promise failed me," he writes. "I went from being ostracized by my straight classmates in high school to being ostracized by many gay white men in an urban enclave" (qtd. in Eichler). Tseng's comment is about racism in predominately white gay subcultures, but his mention of gay urban enclaves is also telling and points to another major criticism of the It Gets Better Project, namely, that its narrative is classist. The It Gets Better Project videos emphasize escape. Chiefly, this escape is implied to be temporal (queer youth must wait to grow up before they can escape harassment). But there is also an implied notion that escape will need to be geographical as well (queer kids can grow up, move away from small towns, and come to the big city, where they will be free and accepted). As Melisa points out, this feature of the It Gets Better Project videos means that they "tacitly reinforce the belief (especially rampant in queer communities) that the religious and the rural are more bigoted." The (admittedly limited) acceptance that Talley and Sessums report having found in their families—as well as the scholarship of Johnson and Howard—certainly proves that a simple "small town always bad for queers / big city always good" dynamic isn't true.

The kinds of geographical escapes (to college, to the big city) that are the implied solution of many It Gets Better Project videos also require money. Working-class queers may not be able to afford to move out of a home shared with parent(s) or extended families members. They may not be able to afford college. If one is presently being bullied for being queer or living in secrecy or fear for the same reason, how do things "get better" if one cannot get away to a new space? I have been arguing that the rhetoric of the It Gets Better Project videos is the same as the rhetoric of the sissy memoir. If so, then It Gets Better Project comes by its class-bias honestly.

What I mean is that in the sissy memoirs I have been discussing, all three of the sissy protagonist/authors are upwardly mobile, aspirational. Doty's father is an Army engineer, and while the family is by no means impoverished, what most excites and allures Doty is the world of high art: paintings by European masters, classical music, poetry. All of these things are the trappings of upper-class or "high" culture. When Doty says that his mother "taught me to love the things that would save me," these are the things he's talking about (171). He loves the fourth grade teacher who introduces him to the music of Stravinsky (and lets him dance to it) for the same reasons. Talley's life story is, of course, one of tremendous personal upwards mobility. Raised by a grandmother who worked as a janitor under Jim Crow, Talley goes on to earn a Master's degree from Brown University before eventually working at one of the world's most premiere fashion magazines, a job that enables him to have shoes and clothes custom-made for him in the finest couture houses of Europe. And while Sessums's parents were neither working class nor hemmed in by the injustices of Jim Crow, his sissy memoir tells a similar story: a childhood in Mississippi that ends with its protagonist/author moving away to New York City, where he will attend the Julliard School.

Noting this pattern lets us see that the sissy memoir's narrative of fascinating effeminacy depends a great deal on upward class mobility. Fascinating effeminacy beckons readers/viewers to other worlds; it shows them alluring alternatives to life as it is presently known. And in all three of the sissy memoirs discussed here, that process involves upward class mobility. Leaving and heading out to the big city does not make Talley or Sessums effeminate; likewise, Doty's embrace of "faith in the life of art" does not make him effeminate (188). All three protagonist/authors recall being sissies from the get-go. But their happy endings—the fascinatingly empowered end points at which they arrive in adulthood and which redeem the pain of having been seen, as a child, as threatening—require varying degrees of upwards class mobility. The same claim is implicit in the rhetoric of the It Gets Better Project videos.

Clearly, Savage's It Gets Better Project is not without its flaws. Nevertheless, it remains an important milestone in the ongoing evolution of the effeminate paradox in US cultural discourse. Although the It Gets Better Project does not focus specifically on effeminacy, its purview certainly includes addressing the pain that comes from being isolated, bullied, or assaulted because of having a non-normative gender presentation. The It Gets Better Project's enormous mainstream popularity demonstrates that the growing visibility and acceptance of LGBT Americans over the course of the twentieth century and the rise of a new communications technology, the Internet, have combined to help move a conception of fascinating effeminacy much further into the US mainstream than it ever had been before. Both Ablow's rage over the J. Crew toenail painting ad and the rash of gay teen suicides that inspired Savage and Miller prove that effeminacy as threat has certainly not vanished from US cultural discourse. Nevertheless, a conception of fascinating effeminacy—begun in McCullers and Capote's Sympathetic Sissies fiction, matured in James Baldwin's Truth-Telling Queens, personified in Liberace and the legions of Boys Who Sparkled in his wake, given national significance by Kushner's Healing Queens, personalized in turn of the twenty-first century Triumphant Sissy memoirs, and popularized by the It Gets Better Project—has now become a full-throated competing discourse, a means of defining effeminacy as valuable, which is no longer limited to a small subset of the gay and lesbian community.

CONCLUSION

"OUR MAKEUP IS TERRIBLE, BUT I LOVE YOU ANYWAY": WHY FASCINATING EFFEMINACY MATTERS IN THE TWENTY-FIRST CENTURY

Why does fascinating effeminacy matter? It matters because it reminds us all of one extremely important truth: our makeup is terrible.

Let me be more specific. Throughout this book, I have argued that some—although not all—modes of fascinating effeminacy are useful/valuable from a queer feminist political point of view precisely because when and where they appear, some modes of fascinating effeminacy grant effeminate men and boys the ability to present readers and/or viewers with a vision of a different world, a different arrangement of the "rules" and possibilities of sexuality, gender expression, and gender identity. And while it is tempting to speak of fascinating effeminacy or threatening effeminacy as though they were two entirely distinct things, they are not separate. They are always interconnected. In postwar US culture, effeminacy is almost always presented as the grotesque. Individual effeminate representations may emphasize one end of the paradox over the other, but effeminacy's threat is always rooted in its ability to fascinate, and the fascination it exerts is linked to its threatening nature. Because the trope of effeminacy as threat is alive and well, because so many people in the United States continue to see effeminacy as something weak or shameful or bad, moments of representation—either fictional or actual—in which a man willfully embraces effeminacy continue to be unusual. That which is unusual is remarkable. That which is remarkable has the power to fascinate. That which has the power to fascinate has the power to tell us a different story about our bodies, our gender identities, our gender expressions, and our sexualities.

So let's look, in some detail, at one particular example of contemporary fascinating effeminacy and the story it tells: Alaska Thunderfuck 5000's dance single "Your Makeup Is Terrible." Depending on your definition of reality, Alaska is either the drag persona of Pennsylvania-born artist Justin Honard (who took the inspiration for her name from a type of marijuana), or as she explains in the opening lines of the song, an alien who crash-landed on Earth after leaving "the planet Glamtron" (Alaska, "Your Makeup is Terrible"). After getting her "greetings and salutations"—including her catchphrase "Hiiiiiiiiiiiiiieeeeeeeeeeee!"—out of the way at the beginning of the song, Alaska wastes little time calling her listeners out. "There's an issue that has recently come to my attention," she speaks-sings, adding that "we need to discuss [it] right now" (Alaska). Emphasizing the seriousness of this issue, Alaska then repeatedly asks listeners, "Are you ready?" as the tempo of the song builds and builds (Alaska). Finally, as the musical tension crescendos, Alaska repeatedly tells her listeners, "Your makeup is terrible!" Immediately afterwards though, she softens the blow a bit: "But I love you anyway!" (Alaska, "Your Makeup Is Terrible"). At this point, other than the artist being a drag queen, the song seems be a typical boasting track in which an artist puts others down in order to elevate herself.

But then the song shifts, its tempo slowing down considerably. Alaska references the change in her lyrics, saying, "Oh my gosh! This is the really serious part of the song, do you hear that?" (Alaska, "Your Makeup Is Terrible"). At this point, Alaska, who had been confrontational, turns confessional: "You see, there's something I have to confess. You and I have a lot more in common than I thought. And there's something I need to bring to your attention right now" (Alaska, "Your Makeup Is Terrible"). After another several rounds of "Are you ready?" Alaska reveals her terrible secret, "My makeup is terrible!" and then begs for forgiveness, asking, "Do you love me anyways?" (Alaska, "Your Makeup Is Terrible"). So having condemned her listeners for having bad makeup and then having condemned herself for the same sin, the final lines of Alaska's song become communal: "Our makeup is terrible!" she opines, "but I love you anyway!" (Alaska, "Your Makeup Is Terrible").

If closing an academic study with an examination of the lyrics to a dance track written/performed by a drag queen seems silly, that's precisely the point. Fascinating effeminacy, at its best, reminds us that there is value in what lies outside the realm of the normal, the usual, and the serious. In this sense, my arguments about fascinating effeminacy's queer potential are indebted to Jack Halberstam's work—in *The Queer Art of Failure* (2011)—on children's animated films, another non-canonical, non-high art form of expression in which he locates radical potential for resisting hetero- and homonormativity.[1] In the specific case of "Your Makeup Is Terrible," the radical potential brought by fascinating effeminacy is Mikhail Bakhtin's conception of the grotesque. I discuss Bakhtin's theory of the grotesque in detail in Chapter Three, but to quickly recap: Bakhtin sees radical, transformative potential in the grotesque and locates its roots in the medieval European folk tradition of carnival, a festival in which the usual social order was temporarily inverted so that peasants could, at least for a time, mock and "rule over" the nobility and clergy to whom they typically owed unending deference. In Bakhtin's carnival-inspired conception of the grotesque, everyone in a community (regardless of rank or station) participates, which means that everyone in a community is degraded. But degradation, for Bakhtin, is not traumatic. It is transformational, in a positive sense: "to degrade is to bury, to sow, and to kill simultaneously, in order to bring forth something more and better . . . Degradation digs a bodily grave for new birth; it has not only a destructive, negative aspect, but also a regenerating one . . . it is always conceiving" (Bakhtin 21). Grotesque art, for Bakhtin, is radical because it "discloses the potentiality of an entirely different world, of another order, another way of life . . . [in grotesque art] the world is destroyed so that it may be regenerated and renewed" (48). Although Leo Bersani does not discuss Bakhtin in his now-infamous essay "Is the Rectum a Grave?," I see Bersani's argument there being related to Bakhtin's conception of the grotesque; Bersani says that the possibility that a man might want to be fucked anally and take pleasure from that fucking makes male-male anal sex a metaphorical grave for heteronormative masculinity. Considering that some men enjoy getting fucked (a sexual role that heteronormativity casts as exclusively female) scrambles the logic of heteronormative masculinity and demands that it be rethought, re-formed. This is precisely what Bakhtin says grotesque art does: it mocks, it pokes fun, it degrades. But it does so universally (obliterating hierarchies), and it does so with the intent of transforming and rebuilding in a new, more equitable way.

This is precisely the work done by Alaska's gloriously silly single. What begins as a performer positioning herself over her fans ("Your makeup is terrible!") morphs into a personal confession ("My makeup is terrible!"), which finally becomes a communal statement of both self-depreciation ("Our makeup is terrible!") and acceptance ("But I love you anyway"). With its tongue planted firmly in its cheek, Alaska's "Your Makeup Is Terrible" reminds us that we all create ourselves, that an ostensibly normal person's identity is no less constructed, crafted, and performed that the identity of a visiting alien drag queen. Even if a listener is not actually wearing makeup as they listen to the song, the song insists that they actually are wearing some kind of makeup, at least in a metaphorical sense. Alaska's lyrics reminds us that our identities are always both fabulous ("This face is my ID, motherfucker!" Alaska boldly declares in the song) and flawed and that both of those things are okay (Alaska, "Your Makeup Is Terrible"). Alaska herself, in a YouTube video describing the creation of the song, describes its music video—directed by Saša Numić—this way: "The music video shoot chronicles a young starlet's arrival to a crowded nightclub where she is to give a performance, but instead of giving a performance, she has a Britney Spears 2007 meltdown, and she eats a bunch of Tic-Tacs and then she shaves her head in the bathroom. Then in the middle, [legendary makeup artist] Mathu Andersen comes out of the darkness and he says, 'Your Makeup Is Terrible'" (qtd. in World of Wonder). Working in concert, Alaska's lyrics and video do for mastery, perfection, and self-satisfaction what Bersani suggests the rectum does for masculinity: shatters them. Reminding us that we're all in this together and that we'd best be able to laugh at ourselves, "Your Makeup Is Terrible" draws on both extreme ends of the effeminate paradox, reminding listeners/viewers that each of them is both a hot mess and a miracle. In this sense, the song is a particular piece of fascinating effeminacy that imaginatively (and with great humor and playfulness) scrambles the stories we thought we knew—stories about stable identity, about who exactly wears makeup, and about how competent/in control we are—and leaves us in want of new stories.

This is a good thing because contemporary US culture badly needs different stories about gender identity, gender expression, and sexuality. All too often, the dominant story about gender in contemporary US culture tells a tale of masculinity as a high-stakes, never-ending test where men must suppress their emotions, hide any evidence of their vulnerability, and display mastery of all things (including the bodies of women, gays and lesbians, and trans people) at all times in order to be men. In a related tale, contemporary US heteronormativity all too often continues to tell women that femininity must mean unending deference to men, an external appearance that is pleasing to men and achieved through unrealistic/unhealthy means and a maddening balancing act in which women must be attractive and sexually available but not too attractive or too sexually available. These narratives of heteronormativity are related. They both depend on a continual devaluing of femininity and anything deemed feminine. Together and at their most extreme forms they give us rape culture for women and a type of psychically toxic, entitled masculinity for men that all too often flies into violence when men's dominance is perceived to be questioned.[2] Like all norms, this form of heteronormativity perpetuates itself by incentivizing people in a given culture to feel advantaged by obeying it. Hence the rise of what queer historian Lisa Duggan has called "the new homonormativity," which she defines as "a politics that does not contest dominant heteronormative assumptions and institutions—such as marriage and its calls for monogamy and reproduction—but upholds and sustains them while promising the possibility of a demobilized gay constituency and a privatized, depoliticized gay culture anchored in domesticity and consumption" (179). Homonormativity demands that queer people fit themselves into heteronormative ideals, including ideals about gender expression; homonormativity is the reason that some economically privileged white gay men call for drag queens, leathermen, Dykes on Bikes, and other such alleged freaks to be removed from Pride Parade celebrations. Those calls echo Gore Vidal's work in *The City and the Pillar* (discussed in Chapter Two) and use the same strategy: if homosexuality is to be normalized, homosexuals must jettison gender nonconformity. Some modes of fascinating effeminacy have the ability to resist this line of thinking whenever and wherever it occurs, just as

James Baldwin's Truth-Telling Queens in *Giovanni's Room* resist Vidal's shaming of gender nonconformity.

In spite of the gains in mainstream visibility discussed in the previous chapter, I contend that effeminacy is still seen—in most of contemporary US culture—as threat. But again, what is threatening compels attention. And once an audience's attention has been grabbed, they can be told another story. That is the radical (feminist, queer) potential of some forms of fascinating effeminacy: they can, at their best, be a powerful force pushing back against both heteronormativity and homonormativity. Alaska's "Your Makeup Is Terrible" is a good example of this type of fascinating effeminacy, but that song in particular—which hit #1 on the iTunes Dance chart in June 2015—and Alaska's career generally both owe a huge debt to the television show *RuPaul's Drag Race* (Avery).[3]

Make no mistake about it: fascinating effeminacy in the United States currently has no louder megaphone (and no larger, more devoted audience) than those afforded by *RuPaul's Drag Race*. The show premiered on the Logo network—a cable network marketed toward LGBTQ audiences—in 2009. Since then, the show has aired eight regular seasons and one *All-Stars* season in which previously eliminated contestants returned to compete again. A second *All-Stars* season and a ninth regular season are currently planned (Wagmeister). The show has also earned three Emmy nominations: one for makeup in 2015, one for costumes in 2016, and one for "Outstanding Host" in 2016 ("Television Academy"). That hosting Emmy nomination acknowledges only one of the roles played by RuPaul Charles on the show. Creator, judge, star, host, and central mythological figure, RuPaul does it all on *Drag Race*.

Although the show features drag queens, it is itself a drag version of other reality shows popular among gay men, especially *Project Runway* and *America's Next Top Model*. Each week drag queen contestants participate in challenges—which have included runway walking, stand-up comedy, songwriting, singing, dancing, television hosting, puppetry, large group song and dance numbers, wet T-shirt contests, professional wrestling, and clothes-making—and walk the runway to show off their best interpretation of the week's given theme. On every episode, that week's two lowest performing queens (as determined by a panel of judges where RuPaul serves as ultimate arbiter) must "Lip Sync for Your Life!" in order to avoid elimination. The queen who delivers the weakest lip-sync performance is sent home, and, thus, each season whittles its cast down to a final winner, who is crowned "America's Next Drag Superstar." The show has inspired deep and passionate fandom and launched the careers of many contestants, including Alaska, who now tour the world performing, record albums, produce T-shirts, and host webseries on YouTube.

That said, the show has not been without its very vocal critics, both academic and popular. The most damning criticism of the show involves its use of language that many transpeople find hateful. Up until Season 6, a recurring segment on the show introduced a video clip of RuPaul (who would then provide a teaser for an upcoming challenge) with audio saying, "You've Got She-Male." That was changed in the wake of outcry after a Season 6 challenge entitled "Female or She-Male?" asked contestants to look at photos and determine whether the photo was of a ciswoman or a transwoman (Nichols). Many saw the "Female or She-Male?" challenge as part and parcel of RuPaul's long-problematic relationship to trans communities and transwomen (Sandeen). The show has also been criticized for its treatment of plus-size drag contestants (a plus-size queen has yet to win), as well as race. C. Winter Han, author of *Geisha of a Different Kind: Race and Sexuality in Gaysian America* (2015), says in an interview with *The Atlantic* that until Season 8 (in which Korean-American drag queen Kim Chi was a finalist to win the crown), "the Asian characters [on *Drag Race*] were more heavily racialized in ways the other contestants weren't, and more importantly, the show rewarded the Asian contestants the more they Orientalized themselves." And in an academic study of *Drag Race*, Sarah Tucker Jenkins makes an ultimately negative final view of the series, arguing that "although *RuPaul's Drag Race* does engage in some subversive behavior, it ultimately reinforces harmful hegemonic stereotypes" about trans women, body size, race, and effeminate men (v).

Many of these criticisms are valid. Trans people have a right to determine how they would like to be referred to, and *Drag Race*'s foot-dragging around getting rid of "she-male" and "tranny" from its episodes is shameful stain on the show's record. Han's analysis is also undeniable. But it is also worth noting that the show is, in fact, a show. It is a spectacle designed to make money. Yes, it is on a network marketed towards minorities. But being on TV at all means having to play some of the dominant culture's games. But I think Jenkins is far too quick to throw the metaphorical baby out with the metaphorical bathwater; her analysis discounts the paradigm-challenging work that *Drag Race* does, especially in terms of its depiction of effeminate men. In other words: a show can do good work and bad work at the same time. *Drag Race* has unquestionably done some bad work. But that doesn't mean that we can't acknowledge when and where it has also done good work.

To begin to think about *Drag Race*'s good work putting forward a mode of fascinating effeminacy that is helpful to a queer feminist politics, we need to begin by thinking about obvious artifice. While the show has had a few contestants come out as transwomen either on the show or after their time on it, most of the *Drag Race* competitors are cisgender men who dress up and perform a highly exaggerated form of femininity, and while the contestants are judged on the flawlessness of the feminine illusions they construct/perform on stage, the show itself makes no bones about the fact it deals in illusion and artifice. Much of the show consists of backstage footage where the contestants are either fully out of drag or only partially in drag, and all of the confessional-style shots used to narrate the show are taken when the contestants are fully out of drag. This open and frequent acknowledgement that drag is a carefully crafted illusion helps *Drag Race* present a wide range of femininities amongst both the performers' personae and the performers themselves. Just consider the name of Season 8's winner, Bob the Drag Queen; it is difficult to think of how drag's illusion—the truth that it is consciously crafted artifice—could be announced any more clearly. In emphasizing the artifice of drag so routinely, *Drag Race* helps hammer home the moral of a saying RuPaul himself turned into the chorus of his dance single "Born Naked": "we're all born naked and the rest is drag" (RuPaul, "Born Naked"). *Drag Race* subtly but constantly reminds its viewers that what one sees as natural and convincing and real (the drag looks on display in runway challenges) can, in fact, be an artfully crafted illusion created with wigs and makeup and foam padding. This imparts the lesson that all identities are created and crafted, even the "boy" identities that the contestants wear "out" of drag and which seem natural.

While the show's contestants are mostly effeminate men (plus a few transwomen), *Drag Race* presents a hugely diverse range of what exactly effeminacy might be. In terms of drag personae, the show highlights many different kinds of drag, and talk about "Fashion Queens" versus "Comedy Queens" versus "Big Girls" versus "Pageant Queens" (to name but a few types) is rife on Internet sites dedicated to fan discussion of the show. And then the performers themselves, out of drag, represent a diverse range of men (and transwomen) in terms of age, race, ethnicity, language, national origin, educational attainment, social class, and level of out-ness. Watching *Drag Race*, viewers see that BeBe Zahara Benet comes from Cameroon while Stacey Lane Matthews hails from rural Back Swamp, North Carolina; that Tempest DuJour is married (to a man) and has two young children while Derrick Barry is one-third of a romantic thruple; that Kim Chi is not out to his mother (as a drag queen) and has no plans to be, while Naomi Smalls's mother supports her son's drag enthusiastically; and that Willam can afford designer gowns while Chi Chi DeVayne came to the show in dire economic straights. In seeing these contrasts, *Drag Race* views are subtly but repeatedly told that drag and the men (and transwomen) who do it are not any one thing. And in the face of the effeminacy as threat trope, which tends to reduce effeminate men to thinly drawn negative stereotypes, this type of effeminate diversity is a very healthy thing for the show to be projecting into the wider culture.

Drag Race is also valuable because it reminds its viewers that effeminate gay men and their cultural practices have a history and that that history is worth study and celebrating. RuPaul's on-screen banter and some of the challenges that recur from season to season directly reference lines and concepts from the New York City house drag ball scene depicted in Jennie Livingston's documentary *Paris Is Burning* (1990). For example, a now-recurring challenge on *Drag Race* is called "Reading Is Fundamental!" which is a nod to *Paris Is Burning* that RuPaul acknowledges on air. In the challenge, contestants must "read" in other in the sense that "reading" is used in *Paris Is Burning*: a sly, witty insult about someone's appearance or personality that devastates the target while also wondering them if you've just insulted them or complimented them. Other episodes have featured gay "herstory" lessons about the Stonewall riots and the origins of Pride Parades. In addition to talking about collective gay history, *Drag Race* also highlights very individualized gay life stories. It does so by allowing its contestants space to speak frankly about the parental and familial homophobia they have experienced. From Kim Chi's resolute refusal to tell his mother than he does drag to Alyssa Edwards's tearful video reunion with the father who'd never previously supported him, *Drag Race* is one of the very programs on US television where audience members can hear frank truths about the terrible ways in which some families still treat children who are gay, trans, and/or gender nonconforming.

That said, *Drag Race* is not simply stuck in the past. One truly remarkable thing about the show is the way in which it provides many of its contestants with a future. Although RuPaul is always a shameless capitalist ready to promote his latest product at the drop of a hat, he has also been very generous in terms of creating opportunities for work and exposure for former contestants. They have guest-singing gigs on RuPaul's albums. They host webseries on the YouTube channel of World of Wonder, RuPaul's production company. The return to work as guest stars and hosts on specials RuPaul produces for Logo. They make appearances and sell merchandise at RuPaul's annual Drag-Con convention. And as Alaska Thunderfuck is perfect proof of, the exposure afforded by the show allows many of these performers to make a living doing drag. In this sense, RuPaul has taken my earlier claim that fascinating effeminacy can create new, imaginative worlds and made it literal. *Drag Race* and all of its related spin-off media ventures function as a real-life alternate universe, one in which effeminate men are adored as stars and their femininely coded skill sets (makeup, wig styling, fashion sense, etc.) are valued rather than mocked.

In this sense, *Drag Race* can be seen as the most intense and most widely seen distillation of many of the themes highlighted by many of the types of fascinating effeminacy in previous chapters of this book. Like Carson McCullers and Truman Capote's Sympathetic Sissies, RuPaul and the *Drag Race* queens bring an enlivening spectacle to an otherwise fairly dull world. Like James Baldwin's Truth-Telling Queens, they can sometimes appear absurd but on closer inspection one sees that they are among the few have the courage to live the truths of their lives as they see fit. And their tales of hardship and familial homophobia, when contrasted with their glittering onstage personalities make them every inch the Triumphant Sissies lauded in sissy memoirs. (The *Drag Race* queens are not marketed as alluring-but-sensitive romantic companions for women, so they are not Boys Who Sparkle like Liberace and Edward Cullen. And while RuPaul has, on several episodes, talked about the right to do drag as an American freedom, the show has yet to make the claim that its contestants are Tony Kushner-esque Healing Queens who can save the nation.)

Is *Drag Race* perfect? Absolutely not. Has it sometimes framed contestants in negative (transphobic, racist, fat-shaming) lights that seem to mirror, rather than critique, the dictates of the dominant culture? Yes, without a doubt. But art isn't created in a vacuum, and no one gets out of membership in a culture without internalizing some of that culture's dominant systems. Without excusing *Drag Race*'s errors, we can still acknowledge that the show has given fascinating effeminacy both its widest viewership since Liberace's heyday and one of its most progressive manifestations to date. RuPaul has done this not by ignoring the terrible ways in which effeminate men are often treated in the United States, but by embracing—and being smart about using—both sides of the effeminate paradox. For proof of this, look at RuPaul talking about his own slightly New Age, slightly punk sense of gender nonconformity's function in culture:

> Some people take identity very seriously. I don't. I choose to laugh at identity and play with it. I'll wear a suit or I'll wear a sailor's outfit. I'll dress femme. I'll dress butch queen . . . I'll do whatever. All of the experiences I've learned and every ascended master you've

> studied will say the same exact thing: Life is not to be taken seriously . . . [the function of drag has] been the same since the beginning of time when shamans, witch doctors, or court jesters were the drags . . . [drag's purpose is] to remind culture not to take itself seriously. To remind you that you are not your shirt or your religious affiliation. You are an extension of the power that created the whole universe. You are God in drag. You are dressed up in this outfit of a body, which is temporary. You are eternal . . . And this is a dream you're having. So don't get attached to it. Make love. Love people. Be sweet. Have corn dogs. Dance. Live. Love. Fuck shit up. (qtd. in Jung)

Hopefully, the paradoxes in RuPaul's speech are clear here. Note that he sees gender nonconformity's power lying exactly in the intersection of what I have been calling the effeminate paradox. The shaman and the court jester are freakish (threatening effeminacy), but their outsider status is precisely what gives them the power to critique and provoke (fascinating effeminacy).

For better or for worse—and often, it has been for worse—the effeminate paradox exists. It has proven extremely difficult (perhaps impossible?) to resolve: Sarah Schulman's *Rat Bohemia* (discussed in Chapter Four) is the only example of effeminate representation that does not engage the effeminate paradox that I came across in preparing this book. And so if we want change, if we want newer and freer cultural understandings of gender identity, gender expression, and sexuality, why not use what we have? As unpleasant (and all too often, deadly) as this current world can be to queers of all stripes, it is the world we currently live in. Any journey to some other "there" point necessarily starts "here." So if effeminate men and boys are going to be burdened with all of the negative consequences of threat, why not flip the script a bit and change the perspective from which we look at the effeminate paradox so that its fascinating aspects are played up? What I have tried to demonstrate in this book is in postwar US culture, many writers and performers and thinkers—many of them gay men, but ultimately people of all genders and sexualities—have been doing exactly for a long time and continue to do it. The problem isn't that folks interested in better treatment for effeminate men and boys haven't already been doing that work; the problem is that our scholarship about gender hasn't yet caught up to naming and honoring their glittery, sparkly, fascinatingly effeminate contributions to US culture. Hopefully this book is the first step in a larger critical project of doing exactly that.

In the meantime, while we wait on more work worthy of effeminacy's glittering loveliness, go and fix your makeup. It is terrible, after all.

NOTES

PREFACE

1. In *The Masculinities Studies Reader*, editors Rachel Adams and David Savran define this interdisciplinary field as "taking its lead from feminism" and "analyzing what has often seemed to be an implicit fact, that the vast majority of societies are patriarchal and that men have historically enjoyed more than their share of power, resources, and cultural authority" by "demonstrating that masculinities are historically constructed, mutable, and contingent" (2). But while linking the origins of masculinities studies to both feminism and lesbian and gay studies, Adams and Savran urge masculinities studies scholars to proceed carefully and remember that, unlike feminism and lesbian and gay studies, "masculinities studies analyzes a dominant and oppressive class that has, arguably, always been the primary focus of scholarly study" (7).

INTRODUCTION

1. For an excellent study of New Orleans bounce music, including so-called "sissy bounce" music, see Miller.

2. In saying that there is nothing new about American audiences clamouring for effeminate performers, I do not mean to disparage Freedia or Katey Red. To say that there is nothing new about American audiences applauding effeminacy is not the same thing as saying that there is nothing new at all about Freedia or Katey Red. They are powerful performers who have broken new ground. To see them is to want to watch them, to want hear them, to want to dance to their music, and that kind of presence is a rare gift indeed. Furthermore, openly gay, trans, and gender non-conforming rappers are, sadly, a relatively rare thing in hip-hop. And as profiles of Big Freedia make clear, she is an insanely hard worker, performing live five or six nights a week and often doing two shows at different venues in the same night. I very much admire the charisma, creativity, courage, and work ethic that she and other sissy rappers demonstrate.

3. Effeminacy has not always been near synonymous with male homosexuality. Alan Sinfield, in *The Wilde Century: Effeminacy, Oscar Wilde, and the Queer Moment* (1994), argues that the word effeminacy meant, in Shakespeare's time, a man being overly romantically invested in women (something akin to the contemporary slang meaning of "whipped" when used as an insult to indicate that a man has let his girlfriend or wife take control of their relationship). Sinfield contends that Oscar Wilde's infamous trials

for sodomy in the 1890s are what indelibly linked effeminacy and male homosexuality in the Western public imagination (his argument is that Wilde's contemporaries knew he was a dandy but were genuinely shocked to learn that he was homosexual).

4. In addition to Kimmel's *American Manhood*, other studies that describe late nineteenth-/early twentieth-century anxieties about American manhood include Bederman, Grant, Kasson, Kidd, and Rotundo. Gilbert has a good rundown of how similar anxieties functioned in the 1950s, and Pascoe is an excellent treatment of how these anxieties manifest themselves in the American high school of the early twenty-first century. For more on gay men's anxieties about effeminacy, see Hennen and Bergling.

5. Other examples of effeminacy as threat in American culture include (but are certainly not limited to) the following: In November 2014, a Tulane University football coach earned headlines when he punished two players for fighting by making them walk around the field together holding hands (Newport). In summer 2010, a South Florida karate school published two ads: in one, a young boy teeters awkwardly because he is wearing a bright red pair of adult women's high-heeled shoes; in the other ad, the same boy appears staring at himself in a hand mirror and messily applying bright red lipstick. Both ads are almost text-less; they allow the images of the boy to dominate and simply say "Karate Lessons" in one corner of the image (Towle). In *Sweet Tea*, a wide range of E. Patrick Johnson's gay African American oral history narrators report having grown up hearing the word *sissy* used as a derogatory term for a boy or man who was inappropriately feminine and, therefore, lesser than other, quote-unquote, real men. In a year and a half of observational field work at a California high school, sociologist C. J. Pascoe reports that she heard the epithet *fag* used countless times by students but saw a teacher or administrator reprimand them for this only once (38). In 2007, John Strausbaugh published a book-length rant castigating America for having become "a culture of fat, soft, stupid, fearful, whiny, infantile, narcissistic, fatalistic, groupthinking victims" and titled his work *Sissy Nation* (1). In February 2008, Lawrence "Larry" King—a 15-year-old boy who wore mascara, lipstick, and jewelry to school and who had announced to classmates that he was gay—was shot and killed in Oxnard, California, while he sat in a school computer lab. His murderer was a 14-year-old classmate (Cathcart). And Simmie Williams—a 17-year-old black gay man—was shot and killed in Fort Lauderdale, Florida, in the same month and year as Larry King; police say Williams was wearing a dress at the time of his murder (McCullum).

6. Hennen provides a superb overview of how effeminacy has been used a disciplinary mechanism and rightly reminds readers "the conception

of effeminacy is shaped in important but largely unacknowledged ways by whiteness" (39). This means that different racial identities are figured, in the cultural imagination, as possessing different levels of masculinity (or the lack thereof, effeminacy). Thus, in white racist thinking, black men are allegedly dangerously hyper-masculine, white men are allegedly "normal"/ unremarked/ideal, and Asian men are allegedly effeminate. For more on black writers and the question of effeminacy, see Reid-Pharr and McBride, "Straight Black Studies." For more on Asian Americans and effeminate stereotypes, see Eng; Han's *Geisha of a Different Kind*; and Wong and Santa Ana. For more on how stereotypes about effeminacy intersect with social class, see Sinfield and Chauncey. For more on how effeminacy has long been framed as un-American, see Greven's discussion of Andrew Jackson's presidency, Fielder's claim that the key American story is a flight from effeminacy, and Kimmel's *American Manhood*.

7. There are numerous examples of effeminacy-as-entertaining/empowering-spectacle in American culture. They include, but certainly are not limited to, the following examples: In 1955, Richard Wayne Penniman, recording as "Little Richard," had his first of several hit singles with "Tutti Frutti"; onstage Penniman's Little Richard persona vamped it up in sequined capes and women's makeup (White 248). In the 1980s, the members of all-male "hair metal" bands—such as Mötley Crüe, Poison, and Guns N' Roses—used teased hair, tight leather pants, and a terrific amount of makeup to sell records and bed scores of female groupies (Blush). In 1990, Madonna sparked a national dance craze with her hit single "Vogue," which took both its name and the inspiration for the accompanying music video from a style of dance created by effeminate black gay men in New York City's underground drag ball circuit ("Vogue [Madonna Song]"). Also in 1990, that same drag ball circuit became the subject of filmmaker Jennie Livingston's successful documentary *Paris Is Burning* (*Paris Is Burning*). Drag queen RuPaul Charles had a hit single "Supermodel (You Better Work)" in 1993, and his television show *RuPaul's Drag Race* debuted in February 2009 ("RuPaul"). Screaming queen Jack McFarland, played by actor Sean Hayes, was a popular supporting character on the sitcom *Will & Grace*, which aired from 1998 to 2006 ("Will & Grace"). Since at least 2000, several popular reality television series have featured effeminate men in prominent supporting roles. This includes "Mr." Jay Manuel and "Miss" J. Alexander on *America's Next Top Model* (2003–present), Tim Gunn on *Project Runway* (2004–present), and the entire five-man cast of *Queer Eye for the Straight Guy* (2003–2007) ("America's Next Top Model," "Project Runway," and "Queer Eye"). Finally, Fox's hit musical comedy series *Glee* (2009–2015), featured openly gay actor Chris Colfer

starring as effeminate gay teen Kurt Hummel, a role that earned him a 2010 Primetime Emmy nomination for Outstanding Supporting Actor in a Comedy Series ("Nominees List").

8. Of these writers, McCullers is the first to begin publishing major work, with *The Heart Is a Lonely Hunter* in 1940. All the others begin publishing during the 1940s, except Baldwin, who begins publishing in the 1950s. Tennessee Williams (born 1911) is also a part of this generation of queer US writers, although I do not discuss his work in this book.

CHAPTER 1

1. Segrest coins the phrase "vitalizing differentness" in a discussion of McCullers's *Ballad of the Sad Café* (1951). Specifically, Segrest is talking about Miss Amelia, the masculine, Amazonian café owner in that novella. Segrest argues that when Miss Amelia's "vitalizing differentness" is destroyed, that her town "withers into a wasteland" (25). Miss Amelia is herself certainly not an effeminate boy, but I think Segrest's phrase is illustrative of one of the major themes in McCullers's work. McCullers's fiction is populated with "freaks" and outcasts of all types: dwarves, mutes, Amazonian women, gay men, black intellectuals in the Jim Crow South, communists, and literal freak-show performers. McCullers consistently demonstrates a deep authorial sympathy for these outsiders, although she is careful to never naively suggest that the terms and conditions of their outsider-ness are the same. I agree with Segrest's reading of Miss Amelia's vitalizing differentness and the communal consequences of its destruction. I have borrowed the term and imported it into my discussion of effeminate boys in McCullers's work because I think McCullers also portrays effeminate boys as being possessed of a similarly vitalizing differentness.

2. Both men and women were susceptible to neurasthenia, but the disease's causes and implications were understood to be different for each gender. Bederman explains, "Whereas men became neurasthenics because the mental labors of advanced civilization drained them of the nervous energy necessary to build a strong, masculine body, women became neurasthenics when they tried to combine their normal function—motherhood—with the masculine, enervating intellectual demands of modern civilization. Neurasthenic women lacked the nervous force to fully participate in modern civilization because their reproductive systems, unlike men's, were a constant drain on their nerve force" (130).

3. Given this history, the Boy Scouts' history of discrimination against gays seems unsurprising. In 2000, the US Supreme Court upheld the Scouts' right to ban gays from membership ("US Supreme Court Rules Against Gay

Scout Leaders"). Thirteen years later, the Scouts allowed members (but not leaders) to be openly gay (Gast, Botelho, and Sayers). The ban on openly gay leaders was overturned in 2015 but only with a religious exemption clause allowing faith-based groups to continue to ban gay leaders in their troops. Also, the fact that an organization founded to prevent the creation and multiplication of sissies would also discriminate against gays is a testament to how deeply linked effeminacy and male homosexuality remain for many Americans.

4. Kidd notes that Twain's *Adventures of Huckleberry Finn* is usually excluded from lists of "Bad Boy" books "on the basis of literary superiority," but he goes on to argue against this classification, making a compelling case for the inclusion of Twain's novel within the genre (52).

5. *Penrod*, for example, "begins with the attempted sissification of the young protagonist by his mother, sister, and pageant director Mrs. Lora Rewbush" (Kidd 60). When Penrod makes a mockery of the pageant his mother wanted him to compete in by appearing onstage in coarse overalls, the event is framed heroically: Penrod has overcome the pernicious, sissifying feminine forces working against him and has confirmed, for readers, that no real boy wants anything to do with something as feminine as a pageant.

6. Gary Richards argues against reading John Henry's gender deviance as evidence of his homosexuality. While critics of McCullers as diverse as Mab Segrest, Louis D. Rubin, and Leslie Fiedler have all "problematically . . . presume[d] deviancy within a character's performances of gender to designate [that character's] sexual deviancy and thus largely disregard[ed] the absences of sexuality that McCullers includes with these figures," Richards points out that McCullers's male characters demonstrate a wide variety of combinations of sexuality and gender performance, sometimes conforming to but also often deviating from the medical/psychological homosexuality-as-evidence-of-gender-inversion model that was widely circulating at the time of her writing (183). From this, Richards concludes that McCullers understood that gender transitivity does not always (or only) equate to homosexuality. His close, careful reading of *The Member of the Wedding* thus forecloses reading John Henry as a prototypical gay man (due to a lack of textual evidence), while also re-emphasizing John Henry's status as a gender queer (due to an enormous amount of textual evidence). My arguments about John Henry build off of Richards's analysis, by acknowledging John Henry's queer (effeminate) gender performance, while also recognizing that there is insufficient textual evidence to make a determination about his sexual orientation.

7. On the question of Frankie's sexual queerness, I disagree with

Richards. Although he correctly identifies "Frankie's thorough naiveté regarding sexuality" throughout the book, he concludes by saying that because Frankie "has little or no perception of the intricacies of sexuality" that she, therefore, "fails to understand any of the transgressive nature of her scheme" to initiate a triangular relationship with her brother and his bride (186, 188). Richards acknowledges that this relationship that Frankie longs for would be simultaneously heterosexual (Frankie and her brother), lesbian (Frankie and his fiancé), incestuous (Frankie and her brother again), and non-monogamous (for all three partners), but his reading of her essentially says that she cannot be counted as a sexual queer because she does not understand the "transgressive nature" of her own longings. Thus, Richards reads Frankie in the same way that he reads John Henry—as someone whose gender performance is queer, but whose sexuality is virtually non-existent because her "sexual activities are . . . motivated more by the wish to appear adult than the desire to give and/or receive erotic pleasure" (187). Yes, Frankie's desire to become a member of the wedding is about a longing for community more than it is a longing for erotic pleasure, but the shape of this desire—the form of the fantasy that it takes—is decidedly queer. Richards's reading of Frankie also downplays the ending of the novel, where Frankie, now calling herself Frances, experiences "an instant shock of happiness" when she hears the ringing of the doorbell that signals the arrival of Mary Littlejohn, her new (and decidedly female) crush (392). Neither strictly heterosexual nor exclusively lesbian, Frankie's sexuality is thoroughly queer.

CHAPTER 2

1. Vidal originally intended the book to end with rape, but his publisher insisted on murder; the change from murder to rape in Vidal's revised 1965 edition is actually a restoration of Vidal's original intention for the novel. For more information on *The City and the Pillar*'s publication history, see Fone, 690–691.

2. The historians of sexuality discussed at length here—Chauncey, Howard, and D'Emilio—all work in US contexts. For more on how same-sex desire and behavior relates to identity in non-US contexts, see Cantú, Foster, Murray and Roscoe, and Schifter.

3. Chauncey's study focuses on New York City, but the mid-twentieth-century transition between sexual classification regimes was not limited to New York, the North, or even large urban centers. Historian John Howard, studying Mississippi from roughly the end of World War II to the dawn of the AIDS crisis, finds that "throughout the twentieth century, queer sexuality

continued to be understood as both acts *and* identities, behaviors *and* beings" (xviii, emphasis Howard's). Howard does not suggest that the normal man/fairy dichotomy Chauncey describes existed in mid-twentieth-century Mississippi, but his work does indicate that some men felt that having sex with men was an exterior sign of an interior essence called sexuality, while other men understood same-sex sexual encounters as isolated incidents of behavior that had little to do with their identity or lasting sense of self.

4. Unless otherwise indicated, all citations from *The City and the Pillar* are taken from the revised 1965 edition.

5. Clarkson presents a good overview of the academic version of this debate and its various players. Also see Savage, who talks about how repugnant he finds the term straight-acting and how he banned the (extremely popular) phrase from gay personal ads in *The Stranger*: "When a guy uses 'straight-acting' in his ad . . . He's saying that gayness, in and of itself, is unattractive, undesirable."

6. For more on the history of American writing concerned with male-male desire before the 1948 publication of *The City and the Pillar*, see Austen, Bronski, Fone, Gifford, Levin, and Slide.

7. For more on the reception of *The City and the Pillar* by gay critics and literary historians, see Austen: "Only with the publication of Vidal's *The City and the Pillar* in 1948 did there emerge a main character whose gayness was not camouflaged by his being too young, too old, sexually ambivalent, frightened, silly, or pathological. Though hesitant to admit it to himself, Jim Willard turns out to be definitively gay, and thus *The City and the Pillar* is the most forthright novel of the decade" (118); Levin: "Vidal's status made it impossible for critics to ignore this novel as they had previous ones in which homosexual behavior was central" (75–76); Adams: the novel's "'lurid' reputation assured it the status of a best-seller, thus making it one of the first homosexual novels to reach a vast audience" (15); and Fone, 690–691.

8. For a discussion of the ways in which same-sex desire had been highly visible (and often well integrated into wider heterosexual culture) in New York City as early as the late nineteenth century, see Chauncey, in particular, his twelfth chapter, which details how a vibrant and visible gay culture was systematically excluded from the city's public life beginning in the 1930s. For more on the history of gay and lesbian identity formation and the histories of American homophobia, see D'Emilio and Howard.

9. For an overview of Vidal's views on same-sex desire his now infamous claim that there are no homosexuals only homosexual acts, and his lifelong erotic fascination with twins, see Behrendt, especially 45–60.

10. This fight about whether Jim does or does not hate women is edited

out of the revised 1965 edition of the novel. In the revised edition, Jim and Sullivan's fight is extremely truncated. Sullivan says that "there is something wrong with two men living together, a man and a woman too, for that matter. Unless they have children, it's pointless" (178). Jim agrees, saying "We're too selfish," and the two men part ways (179).

11. In addition to Ross's reading of *Giovanni's Room*, which is contained in Dwight A. McBride's excellent edited volume *James Baldwin Now*, also see Ferguson; Henderson; Holland; McBride, "Straight Black Studies"; and Reid-Pharr.

12. The Harris essay I cite here was published under the name Trudier Harris-Lopez.

CHAPTER 3

1. The core of Meyer's *Twilight* saga consists of four young adult novels: *Twilight* (2005), *New Moon* (2006), *Eclipse* (2007), and *Breaking Dawn* (2008). My analysis of Meyer's work is focused on these four novels, although she has published other *Twilight*-related material, including a novella called *The Short Second Life of Bree Tanner* (2010) and *Life and Death* (2015), a retelling of *Twilight* with the main characters' genders reversed, so that the story becomes a tale of a human boy falling in love with a female vampire. In a *New York Times* article dated September 27, 2009, Jane Margolies reports that the four main novels combined have sold 70 million copies worldwide. The four main books have been turned into five feature-length films (*Breaking Dawn* was split into two films).

2. Connell's work that I cite here was published under the name R.W. Connell.

3. For additional feminist critiques of the *Twilight* saga's conservative sex/gender politics, see Berreca as well as Rosenberg.

4. Within the *Twilight* novels, Bella consistently emphasizes how Edward is a man out of time, how he grew up in a time when love was different, when people married younger, when people were more courteous, etc. Edward was born in 1901, but in his implicit conviction that the sign of manhood is restraint of one's passions, he actually adheres to a model of masculinity that Kimmel traces to the eighteenth and early nineteenth centuries, not the twentieth. Edward represents a type that Kimmel calls "the Genteel Patriarch," who at his best represents "a dignified aristocratic manhood, committed to the British upper-class code of honor and to well-rounded character, with exquisite tastes and manners and refined sensibilities. To the Genteel Patriarch, manhood meant property ownership and a benevolent patriarchal authority at home" (*Manhood* 13). Kimmel argues that while some of

America's founding fathers (Jefferson, Adams, Madison) represented this type of masculinity, it came—over the course of the nineteenth century—to be viewed as effeminate and outmoded in the United States. The attitude Edward displays towards Bella can be described exactly as the "benevolent patriarchy" of the Genteel Patriarch, and so while Edward might not have been viewed as effeminate during the American Revolution, in the early twentieth-first century United States he is decidedly effeminate.

5. Eventually re-titled as just *Queer Eye*, this series ran on Bravo for five seasons, between 2003 and 2007, and featured a team of five effeminate gay men who were dispatched to help "make over" the appearance and lifestyle of a straight man, in order to make him more appealing to his girlfriend or wife. While the cast members displayed many of the characteristics of sparkly effeminacy, they were always seen as asexual helpers who descended into the life of a straight man in order to improve that straight man's relationship with a female romantic partner. Thus, since the cast of *Queer Eye* were openly gay and not positioned as potential love interests for straight women, they cannot properly be called Boys Who Sparkle. If asked to name the precise role they played on the show, I would suggest the term "helper fairies." The helper fairy is a type that abounds on contemporary reality television. For other examples of the type, see "Mr." Jay Manuel and "Miss" J. Alexander on *America's Next Top Model*.

6. It is tempting to refer to openly gay singers with devoted female fanbases, such as Clay Aiken and Adam Lambert, as Boys Who Sparkle despite their open homosexuality seemingly preventing them from deploying the trope. For more on female fan reaction to Lambert, see Sales. Finally, it is interesting that American popular music (especially in the age of television) provides so many examples of Boys Who Sparkle, while canonical American literature provides so few. My tentative explanation of this fact is to guess that the exclusion of sparkly effeminacy from canonical American literature speaks to the presence of two separate, but overlapping, biases in literary canon formation: the bias against the popular and the bias against modes of cultural production that are perceived to be "for" or "about" women. Feminist scholarship has rightly done much to correct a lot of the second bias, but as the feminist critiques of *Twilight* suggest, there may not be much in sparkly effeminacy that is appealing to feminist writers and/or critics.

7. This chapter actually began with my desire to do just such a study. My idea was to find an archive of fan mail that female fans had written to Liberace and to have a close reading of that fan mail form the core of this chapter. Sadly, no such archive of fan mail seems to exist. The Liberace Museum in Las Vegas, Nevada, maintained no such archive and closed in October 2010

(Katsilometes). And if the fan mail that Winick studied for his 1962 article is still extant, I have been unable to locate it.

8. Each of the first three *Twilight* novels are narrated entirely from Bella's first person point of view. The fourth novel, *Breaking Dawn*, has a middle section that is narrated by Jacob Black, the werewolf; the rest of the novel is narrated by Bella.

CHAPTER 4

1. For more information on the debunking of Dugas-as-Patient-Zero, see Crimp's "Randy Shilts's Miserable Failure."

2. For more on male flight attendants, see Tiemeyer.

3. Bersani actually misquotes himself. In "Is the Rectum a Grave?" he discusses a crime in Florida where a family with three hemophiliac children who had contracted HIV from blood transfusions had their home burned down by angry and fearful neighbors. Trying to understand how even these (presumably) straight children could provoke what seemed like homophobic anti-AIDS violence, Bersani says that the knowledge of these children's HIV-positive status was enough to make their neighbors see them not as straight children but as "the infinitely more seductive and intolerable image of a grown man, legs high in the air, unable to refuse the suicidal ecstasy of being a woman" (212). Thus, when Bersani quotes himself in *Homos*, he changes "being" a woman to "taking their sex like" a woman.

4. Crimp accuses Shilts, who was himself gay, of internalized homophobia: "'Patient Zero,' the very figure of the homosexual as imagined by heterosexuals—sexually voracious, murderously irresponsible—is Shilts's homophobic nightmare of himself, a nightmare that he must constantly deny by making it true only of others. Shilts therefore offers up the scapegoat for his heterosexual colleagues in order to prove that he, like them, is horrified by such creatures" ("How to Have Promiscuity" 244).

5. For an example of an argument about gay male promiscuity that opposes Shilts's by arguing that promiscuity will save gay men rather than destroy them (because the sexual experimentation inherent in promiscuity will help gay men create and find satisfaction in newer, safer modes of sex), see Crimp's "How to Have Promiscuity."

6. While *Angels in America* is technically two plays, it is clearly Kushner's intention that the two plays be performed together. Thus, I refer to *Angels in America* in the singular, as a play not the plays.

7. Kushner does not explicitly specify Belize's racial identity, but context clues indicate that he is a black Latino. His last name, Arriaga, sounds Latino, while dialogue in the play—especially Belize's argument about politics with Louis in Act 3, Scene 2 of *Millennium Approaches*—makes it clear

that Belize identifies as black. For example, he tells Louis, "*You* hate me because you hate black people" (101, emphasis Kushner's). In the 2003 HBO TV mini-series version of *Angels*, Belize is played by Jeffrey Wright, who is African American.

8. The 1993 film *Philadelphia*, starring Tom Hanks as a gay male PWA and Denzel Washington as his initially homophobic, and later compassionate, straight lawyer typifies what Patton calls this "new citizenship paradigm."

9. Schulman has continued to explore the dreadful ways that some straight families treat their queer children in her nonfiction book *The Ties That Bind: Familial Homophobia and Its Consequences* (2012).

CHAPTER 5

1. When I began writing about Talley and his memoir, I absolutely assumed that he was gay. But the question of how Talley identifies is a tricky one. In 2007, he was ranked #45 on *Out* magazine's "Power 50," their list of the "50 Most Powerful Gay Men and Women in America." But in a June 2012 *Vanity Fair* interview, Talley says that he does not identify as gay; even though he has "had very gay experiences," he says he has only fallen in love twice, both times with women ("André Leon Talley on His Fashion Career").

2. For example, at the 2011 Costume Institute Gala (more commonly known as The Met Ball), Talley—who accompanied legendary *Vogue* editor Anna Wintour—wore bejeweled red loafers and a tuxedo under a bright bluish-purple caftan with a train so long that Jessica Morgan (one half of the fashion blogging duo The Fug Girls) described it as being "more dramatically be-tailed than your average wedding gown."

3. Users at Conservapedia, the conservative alternative to Wikipedia, describe the It Gets Better Project by saying, "It is noble to help troubled young people but it's wrong to deceive them. Dan Savage's video message is wrong. These teens need help, they need more, they need the truth. Mentally, it gets better by leaving homosexuality" ("It Gets Better Project").

CONCLUSION

1. Although I have not cited from it directly in this book, Halberstam's *Female Masculinity* (1998) is, conceptually, another huge influence on my thinking about gender nonconformity. This investigation of male femininity would not have been possible without the theoretical doors opened by his exploration of female masculinity. The book was published under the name Judith Halberstam.

2. For more on toxic white male masculinity, see Kimmel's *Angry White Men: American Masculinity at the End of an Era* (2015).

3. Justin Honard, as Alaska, competed on the fifth season of *Drag Race*,

which aired in 2013; he finished in the top three but lost the crown to competitor Jinkx Monsoon ("RuPaul's Drag Race"). He also competed on, and won, the second season of *Drag Race All-Stars* ("RuPaul's Drag Race"). The song title "Your Makeup Is Terrible" comes from a line Honard wrote for a *Drag Race* challenge in which the contestants had to design a fragrance and then shoot a television ad advertising that fragrance (World of Wonder).

WORKS CITED

Ablow, Keith. "J. Crew Plants the Seeds for Gender Identity." *FoxNews.com*. Fox News. 11 Apr. 2011. Web. 7 June 2011.

Adams, Rachel, and David Savran, eds. *The Masculinities Studies Reader*. Malden, MA: Blackwell, 2002.

Adams, Stephen. *The Homosexual as Hero in Contemporary Fiction*. London: Vision, 1980.

Alaska Thunderfuck 5000. "Alaska Thunderfuck—Your Makeup Is Terrible [Official]." Dir. Saša Numić. *YouTube*. YouTube. 9 June 2014. Web. 29 July 2016.

———. "Your Makeup Is Terrible." *Anus*. Sidecar, 2015.

"America's Next Top Model." *Wikipedia*. Wikipedia. n.d. Web. 1 Aug. 2011.

"André Leon Talley on His Fashion Career, His Weight Struggle, and His Sexual Past." *Vanity Fair*. 13 Aug. 2013. Web. 27 July 2016.

Angels in America. Dir. Mike Nichols. Perf. Al Pacino, Meryl Streep, Emma Thompson. HBO, 2003.

Austen, Roger. *Playing the Game: The Homosexual Novel in America*. Indianapolis, IN: Bobbs-Merrill, 1977.

Avery, Dan. "Alaska Releases Video for 'This Is My Hair,' Tops iTunes Dance Chart." *NewNowNext.com*. Logo. 23 June 2015. Web. 29 July 2016.

Bakhtin, Mikhail. *Rabelais and His World*. Trans. Hélène Iswolsky. Bloomington, IN: Indiana UP, 1984.

Baldwin, James. *Giovanni's Room*. 1956. New York: Dell, 2000.

———. "Preservation of Innocence." 1949. *James Baldwin: Collected Essays*. New York: Library of America, 1998. 594–600.

Bederman, Gail. *Manliness and Civilization: A Cultural History of Gender and Race in the United States, 1880–1917*. Chicago: U of Chicago P, 1995.

Behrendt, Jörg. *Homosexuality in the Work of Gore Vidal*. Hamburg, Germany: Lit Verlag, 2002.

Bergling, Tim. *Sissyphobia: Gay Men and Effeminate Behavior*. New York: Harrington Park, 2001. Print.

Berreca, Gina. "Five Reasons a Smart Middle Aged Woman Loathes TWILIGHT." *Psychology Today*. 15 Mar. 2009. Web. 27 July 2016.

Bersani, Leo. *Homos*. Cambridge, MA: Harvard UP, 1995.

———. "Is the Rectum a Grave?" Crimp, *AIDS* 197–222.

Beyoncé. "Formation." *Lemonade*. Parkwood and Columbia. 2016.

Big Freedia. "Big Freddie Kay Ready Feat. Katey Red." *Big Freedia: Hitz Vol. 1, 1999–2010*. Big Freedia, 2010.

"Big Freedia Explains Bounce Music, Ass Shaking +1." Dir. Will Colby. *Pitchfork.TV*. Pitchfork Media. 16 Jan. 2012. Web. 26 July 2013.

"Big Freedia Lays Out the Basics of Bounce." *All Things Considered*. National Public Radio. 27 Jan. 2013. Web. 26 July 2013.

"Big Freedia: The Queen Diva." Dir. Mark Zemel. *Pitchfork.TV*. Pitchfork Media. 14 Jan. 2013. Web. 26 July 2013.

Blush, Steven. *American Hair Metal*. Los Angeles: Feral House, 2006.

Bronski, Michael. *Pulp Friction: Uncovering the Golden Age of Gay Male Pulps*. New York: St. Martin's Griffin, 2003.

Brown, Erin R. "J. Crew Pushes Transgendered Child Propoganda." *mrc.org*. Culture and Media Institute. 8 Apr. 2011. Web. 7 June 2011.

Cantú, Lionel Jr. *The Sexuality of Migration: Border Crossings and Mexican Immigrant Men*. Nancy A. Naples and Salvador Vidal-Ortiz, eds. New York: New York UP, 2009.

Capote, Truman. *Other Voices, Other Rooms*. 1948. New York: Vintage, 1994.

Carr, Virginia Spencer. *The Lonely Hunter: A Biography of Carson McCullers*. Athens, GA: U of Georgia P, 2003.

Cassuto, Leonard. *The Inhuman Race: The Racial Grotesque in American Literature and Culture*. New York: Columbia UP, 1997.

Cathcart, Rebecca. "Boy's Killing, Labeled a Hate Crime, Stuns a Town." *New York Times*. 23 Feb. 2008. Web. 27 Aug. 2010.

Chauncey, George. *Gay New York: Gender, Urban Culture, and the Making of the Gay Male World, 1890–1940*. New York: Basic Books, 1994.

Clarke, Gerald. "The Art of Fiction L: Gore Vidal." Peabody and Ebersole 36–59.

———. *Capote: A Biography*. New York: Simon and Schuster, 1988.

Clarkson, Jay. "'Everyday Joe' versus 'Pissy, Bitchy, Queens': Gay Masculinity on StraightActing.com." *Journal of Men's Studies*. 14.2 (2006): 191–207.

Connell, R.W. *Masculinities*. 2nd ed. Berkeley, CA: U of California P, 2005.

Corber, Robert J. *Homosexuality in Cold War America: Resistance and the Crisis of Masculinity*. Durham, NC: Duke UP, 1997.

Crimp, Douglas. "How to Have Promiscuity in an Epidemic." *AIDS: Cultural Analysis, Cultural Activism*. Ed. Douglas Crimp. Cambridge, MA: MIT P, 1988. 237–271.

———. "Randy Shilts's Miserable Failure." *Melancholia and Moralism: Essays on AIDS and Queer Politics*. Cambridge, MA: MIT P, 2002. 117–128.

Dee, Jonathan. "New Orleans's Gender-Bending Rap." *New York Times Sunday Magazine*. 22 July 2010. Web. 26 July 2013.

D'Emilio, John. "Capitalism and Gay Identity." *The Lesbian and Gay Studies Reader*. Ed. Henry Abelove, Michele Aina Barale, and David M. Halperin. New York: Routledge, 1993. 467–476.

———. *Sexual Politics, Sexual Communities: The Making of a Homosexual Minority in the United States, 1940–1970*. 2nd Ed. Chicago: University of Chicago Press, 1983.

Dickey, James. *Deliverance*. 1970. New York: Delta, 1994.

Donaldson James, Susan. "J. Crew Ad with Boy's Pink Toenails Creates Stir." *ABCNews.go.com*. ABC News. 13 Apr. 2011. Web. 7 June 2011.

Doty, Mark. *Firebird: A Memoir*. New York: Harper Collins, 1999.

Dube, Rebecca. "The Mom of a 'Princess Boy' Speaks Out." *Moms.today.com*. *The Today Show*. 3 Jan. 2011. Web. 7 June 2011.

Duggan, Lisa. "The New Homonormativity: The Sexual Politics of Neoliberalism." *Materializing Democracy: Toward a Revitalized Cultural Politics*. Ed. Russ Castronovo and Dana D. Nelson. Durham, NC: Duke UP, 2002. 175–194.

Eddy, Chuck. "The Bands You Didn't See But Maybe Should Have, at SXSW 2011." *Rollingstone.com*. 20 March 2011. Web. 26 July 2013.

Eichler, Alex. "Critiquing 'It Gets Better Project' for Teens." *TheAtlanticWire.com*. *The Atlantic Monthly*. 8 Oct. 2010. Web. 28 July 2011.

Eng, David L. *Racial Castration: Managing Masculinity in Asian America*. Durham, NC: Duke UP, 2001.

Ferguson, Roderick A. "The Parvenu Baldwin and the Other Side of Redemption: Modernity, Race, Sexuality, and the Cold War." McBride. 233–261.

Fiedler, Leslie. *Love and Death in the American Novel*. 1960. Urbana-Champaign, IL: Dalkey Archive P, 2003.

Fone, Byrne R. S., ed. *The Columbia Anthology of Gay Literature: Readings from Western Antiquity to the Present Day*. New York: Columbia UP, 1998.

Foster, David Willaim, ed. *Chicano/Latino Homoerotic Identities*. London: Routledge, 1999.

Gifford, James. *Dayneford's Library: American Homosexual Writing, 1900–1913*. Amherst, MA: U of Massachusetts P, 1995.

Gilbert, James. *Men in the Middle: Searching for Masculinity in the 1950s*. Chicago: U of Chicago P, 2005.

Gleeson-White, Sarah. *Strange Bodies: Gender and Identity in the Novels of Carson McCullers*. Tuscaloosa, AL: U of Alabama P, 2003.

Grant, Julia. "A 'Real Boy' and not a Sissy: Gender, Childhood, and Masculinity, 1890–1940." *Journal of Social History* 37.4 (2004): 829–851. JSTOR. Web. 2 Sept. 2010.

Greven, David. *Men Beyond Desire: Manhood, Sex, and Violation in American Literature*. New York: Palgrave Macmillan, 2005.

Grover, Jan Zita. "Visible Lesions: Images of the PWA in America." *Out in Culture: Gay, Lesbian, and Queer Essays on Popular Culture*. Eds. Corey K. Creekmur and Alexander Doty. Durham, NC: Duke UP, 1995. 354–381.

Halberstam, Judith. *Female Masculinity*. Durham, NC: Duke UP, 1998.

———. *The Queer Art of Failure*. Durham, NC: Duke UP, 2011.

Han, C. Winter. *Geisha of a Different Kind: Race and Sexuality in Gaysian America*. New York, New York UP, 2015.

———. Interview by Spencer Kornhaber. "The Fierceness of 'Femme, Fat, and Asian.'" *TheAtlantic.com. Atlantic Weekly*. 19 May 2016. 29 July 2016.

Harris-Lopez, Trudier. "Slanting the Truth: Homosexuality, Manhood, and Race in James Baldwin's *Giovanni's Room*." *South of Tradition: Essays on African American Literature*. Athens, GA: U of Georgia P, 2002. 18–30. Print.

Henderson, Mae G. "James Baldwin's *Giovanni's Room*: Expatriation, 'Racial Drag,' and Homosexual Panic." *Black Queer Studies: A Critical Anthology*. Ed. E. Patrick Johnson and Mae G. Henderson. Durham, NC: Duke UP, 2005.

Hennen, Peter. *Faeries, Bears, and Leathermen: Men in Community Queering the Masculine*. Chicago: U of Chicago P, 2008.

Hepola, Sarah. "'Twilight' of Our Youth." *Salon.com*. 16 Nov. 2009. Web. 21 May 2010.

Holland, Sharon Patricia. "(Pro)Creating Imaginative Spaces and Other Queer Acts: Randall Kenan's *A Visitation of Spirits* and Its Revival of James Baldwin's Absent Black Gay Man in *Giovanni's Room*." McBride. 265–288.

Howard, John. *Men Like That: A Southern Queer History*. Chicago: U of Chicago P, 1999.

"It Gets Better Project." *Conservapedia.com*. n.d. Web. 28 July 2011.

"J. Alexander." *en.wikipedia.org*. Wikipedia. n.d. Web. 1 June 2010.

"Jay Manuel." *en.wikipedia.org*. Wikipedia. n.d. Web. 1 June 2010.

Jenkins, Sarah Tucker. Hegemonic 'Realness'? An Intersectional Feminist Analysis of *RuPaul's Drag Race*. MA Thesis. Florida Atlantic University, 2013. *Academia.edu*. n.d. 29 July 2016.

Johnson, E. Patrick. *Sweet Tea: Black Gay Men of the South, An Oral History*. Chapel Hill, NC: U of North Carolina P, 2008.

Jung, E. Alex. "RuPaul on How Straight People Steal From Gay Culture and Why Educating the Youth is a Waste of Time." *Vulture*. Vulture.com. 23 March 2016. Web. 29 July 2016.

Kasson, John F. *Houdini, Tarzan, and the Perfect Man: The White Male Body and the Challenge of Modernity in America*. New York: Hill and Wang, 2001.

Katsilometes, John. "Liberace Museum Closing: Final Day of Operation on Longtime East Tropicana Location Oct. 17." *The Las Vegas Sun*. 10 Sept. 2010. Web. 16 July 2011.

Kayser, Wolfgang. *The Grotesque in Art and Literature*. Trans. Ulrich Weisstein. Bloomington, IN: Indiana UP, 1963.

Kidd, Kenneth B. *Making American Boys: Boyology and the Feral Tale*. Minneapolis, MN: U of Minnesota P, 2004.

Kimmel, Michael. *Angry White Men: American Masculinity at the End of an Era*. New York: Nation, 2015.

———. *Guyland: The Perilous World Where Boys Become Men*. New York: Harper, 2008.

———. *Manhood in America: A Cultural History*. 2nd ed. New York: Oxford UP, 2006. Print.

Klein, Melanie. "J. Crew's Toenail-Painting Ad Causes Pink Scare." *Ms. blog*. *Ms.* Magazine. 13 April 2011. Web. 7 June 2011.

Kruger, Steven F. *AIDS Narratives: Gender and Sexuality, Fiction and Science*. New York: Garland, 1996.

Kushner, Tony. *Angels in America: A Gay Fantasia on National Themes*. New York: Theatre Communications Group, 1995.

"*Last Call with Carson Daly*: Big Freedia." *Hulu.com*. 29 Sept. 2010. Web. 26 July 2013.

Levin, James. *The Gay Novel in America*. New York: Garland, 1991.

"Make It Better Project: About." *MakeItBetterProject.org*. Make It Better Project. n.d. Web. 28 July 2011.

Margolies, Jane. "'Twilighters' Put Small Town in the Spotlight." *New York Times*. 27 Sep. 2009. Web. 17 May 2010.

McBride, Dwight A., ed. *James Baldwin Now*. New York: New York UP, 1999. Print.

———. "Straight Black Studies." *Why I Hate Abercrombie and Fitch: Essays on Race and Sexuality*. New York: New York UP, 2005. 35–58.

McCollum, Rod. "Simmie Williams' Murder: One Year Later, No Arrests, No Leads." *Rod 2.0 Beta*. 24 Feb. 2009. Web. 27 Aug. 2010.

McCullers, Carson. *The Ballad of the Sad Café*. 1951. *Collected Stories of Carson McCullers*. 1987. Boston: Mariner, 1998. 195–253.

———. *Clock Without Hands*. 1961. Boston: Mariner, 1998.

———. *The Heart Is A Lonely Hunter*. 1940. Boston: Mariner, 2000.

———. *The Member of the Wedding*. 1946. *Collected Stories of Carson McCullers*. 1987. Boston: Mariner, 1998. 255–392.

———. *Reflections in a Golden Eye*. 1941. Boston: Mariner, 2000.

Melisa, Zoe. "Why I Don't Like Dan Savage's It Gets Better Project as a Response to Bullying." *Tempcontremps.wordpress.com*. (femmephane). 30 Sept. 2010. Web. 28 July 2011.

Meyer, Stephenie. *Breaking Dawn*. New York: Little Brown, 2008.

———. *Eclipse*. New York: Little Brown, 2007.

———. *New Moon*. New York: Little Brown, 2006.

———. *Twilight*. New York: Little Brown, 2005.

Miller, Matt. *Bounce: Rap Music and Local Identity in New Orleans*. Amherst, MA: U of Massachusetts P, 2012.

Morgan, Jessica. "Met Ball Fug or Fab Carpet: Anna Wintour, with an Assist from ALT." *GoFugYourself.com*. The Fug Girls (Heather Cocks and Jessica Morgan). 3 May 2011. Web. 27 July 2011.

Muñoz, José Esteban. *Cruising Utopia: The Then and There of Queer Futurity*. New York: New York UP, 2009.

Murray, Stephen O. and Will Roscoe, eds. *Boy-Wives and Female Husbands: Studies of African Homosexualities*. New York: Palgrave, 2001.

Newitz, Annalee. "Why The Twilight Hate Has Gotten Boring." *io9.com*. 13 Apr. 2010. Web. 21 May 2010.

Newport, Kyle. "Tulane Coach Makes Players Hold Hands After Altercation in Practice." *Bleacherreport.com* Bleacher Report. 6 Nov. 2014. Web. 27 July 2016.

Nichols, James. "'RuPaul's Drag Race' to Refrain from Using 'Transphobic Slur' in Wake of Controversy." *HuffingtonPost.com. The Huffington Post*. 14 April 2014. Web. 29 July 2016.

"Nominees List: Complete Official 2010 Primetime Emmy Nominations." *Emmys.tv*. Academy of Television Arts and Sciences. n.d. Web. 9 May 2011.

Obama, Barack. "President Obama: It Gets Better." *YouTube.com*. White-House.gov. 21 Oct. 2010 Web. 28 July 2011.

Paris Is Burning. Dir. Jennie Livingston. Miramax, 1990. Film.

Pascoe, C. J. *Dude, You're a Fag: Masculinity and Sexuality in High School*. Berkeley, CA: U of California P, 2007.

Patton, Cindy. *Fatal Advice: How Safe-Sex Education Went Wrong*. Durham, NC: Duke UP, 1996.

———. *Inventing AIDS*. New York: Routledge, 1990.

Peabody, Richard, and Lucinda Ebersole, eds. *Conversations with Gore Vidal*. Jackson, MS: U of Mississippi P, 2005.

Pease, Donald E. "Citizen Vidal and Mailer's America." *Raritan* 11.4 (1992): 72–98.

Philadelphia. Dir. Jonathan Demme. Perf. Tom Hanks, Denzel Washington. Tri-Star Pictures, 1993.

Plaisance, Stacey. "Big Freedia Gets Own Reality TV Show." *Billboard.com*. 12 June 2013. Web. 26 July 2013.

"The Power 50: The Most Powerful Gay Men and Women in America." *Out* 15.11 (May 2007): 47–50.

"Project Runway." *en.wikipedia.org*. Wikipedia. n.d. Web. 1 Aug. 2011.

Pyron, Darden Asbury. *Liberace: An American Boy*. Chicago: U of Chicago P, 2000.

"Queer Eye." *En.wikipedia.org*. Wikipedia. n.d. Web. 1 June 2010.

Rechy, John. *City of Night*. 1963. New York: Grove P, 1984.

Reid-Pharr, Robert F. "Tearing the Goat's Flesh: Homosexuality, Abjection, and the Production of a Late-Twentieth-Century Black Masculinity." *Black Gay Man: Essays*. New York: New York UP, 2001. 99–134.

Richards, Gary. *Lovers and Beloveds: Sexual Otherness in Southern Fiction, 1936–1961*. Baton Rouge, LA: Lousiana State UP, 2005.

Rodgers, Richard, and Oscar Hammerstein II. *Carousel: A Musical Play*. New York: Knopf, 1946.

Rosenberg, Alyssa. "A Condemnation of Sparkly Vampires." *TheAtlantic.com*. N.d. Web. 21 May 2010.

Ross, Marlon B. "White Fantasies of Desire: Baldwin and the Racial Identities of Sexuality." McBride 13–55.

Rotundo, E. Anthony. *American Manhood: Transformations in Masculinity from the Revolution to the Modern Era*. New York: Basic Books, 1993.

Ryder, Katie. "White Music Fans Are Afraid of Difference." *Salon.com*. Salon. 1 Aug. 2013. Web. 1 Aug. 2014.

Ruas, Charles. "Gore Vidal." Peabody and Ebersole 85–99.

RuPaul. "Born Naked (feat. Clairy Browne)." *Realness*. RuCo. 2015.

"RuPaul." *en.wikipedia.org*. Wikipedia. n.d. Web. 1 August 2011.

"RuPaul's Drag Race." *en.wikipedia.org*. Wikipedia. n.d. Web. 29 July 2016.

Russo, Vito. *The Celluloid Closet: Homosexuality in the Movies*. Rev. ed. New York: Harper & Row, 1987.

Sales, Nancy Jo. "For the Love of Adam Lambert: Why Does Every Woman in America Want to Sleep With the American Idol?" *Details* Nov. 2009. *Details.com*. Web. 4 June 2010.

Sandeen, Autumn. "RuPaul Believes Trans People Should F***-Off if We Object to Being Called Tr***ies." *Shadowproof.com*. Shadowproof. 17 Jan. 2012. Web. 29 July 2016.

Savage, Dan. "Act Four: The Other Love That Dares Not Speak Its Name." *This American Life*. Chicago Public Radio, Chicago. 22 April 2005. Radio.

Schifter, Jacobo. *Public Sex in a Latin Society*. London: Routledge, 1999.

Schulman, Sarah. *Rat Bohemia*. New York: Dutton, 1995.

———. *Ties That Bind: Familial Homophobia and its Consequences*. New York: New P, 2012.

Sedgwick, Eve Kosofsky. *Epistemology of the Closet*. Berkeley, CA: U of California P, 1990.

———. "How to Bring Your Kids Up Gay: The War on Effeminate Boys." *Tendencies*. Durham, NC: Duke UP, 1993. 154–164.

Segrest, Mab. "Southern Women Writing: Toward a Literature of Wholeness." *My Mama's Dead Squirrel: Lesbian Essays on Southern Culture.* Ithaca, NY: Firebrand, 1985. 19–42.

Sessums, Kevin. *Mississippi Sissy.* New York: Picador, 2007.

Shilts, Randy. *And the Band Played On: Politics, People, and the AIDS Epidemic.* 1987. New York: Penguin, 1988.

Sinfield, Alan. *The Wilde Century: Effeminacy, Oscar Wilde, and the Queer Moment.* New York: Columbia UP, 1994.

Slide, Anthony. *Lost Gay Novels: A Reference Guide to Fifty Works from the First Half of the Twentieth Century.* New York: Harrington Park P, 2003.

Steinberg, Neil. "Gender Cops Know Nothing of Kids, History." *Chicago Sun-Times.* 19 May 2011. Web. 7 June 2011.

Sterling, Les. "J. Crew Makes Kids Gay? . . . Srsly?" *SeattleGayScene.* SeattleGayScene. 14 April 2011. Web. 7 June 2011.

StraightActing.com. April 2000. Web. 16 Dec 2009.

Strausbaugh, John. *Sissy Nation: How America Became a Culture of Wimps and Stoopits.* New York: Virgin Books, 2007.

Talburt, Susan. "Constructions of LGBT Youth: Opening Up Subject Positions." *Theory Into Practice* 43.2 (2004): 116–121. *Project MUSE.* Web. 5 Aug. 2011.

Talley, André Leon. *A.L.T.: A Memoir.* New York: Villard, 2003.

"Television Academy: RuPaul's Drag Race." Emmys.com. The Television Academy. n.d. Web. 29 July 2016.

Thompson, Anne. "Comic-Con: Costume Parade Reveals *Twilight* Backlash." *Variety.com.* 29 July 2009. Web. 8 June 2010.

Tiemeyer, Phil. *Plane Queer: Labor, Sexuality, and AIDS in the History of Male Flight Attendants.* Berkeley, CA: U of California P, 2013.

Towle, Andy. "'Man Up' That Sissy Kid of Yours—Send Him To Karate Class." *Towleroad.com.* Towleroad. 13 Aug. 2010. Web. 27 Aug. 2010.

"US Supreme Court Rules Against Gay Scout Leaders." *The Vancouver Sun.* 29 June 2000: A6. *LexisNexis Academic.* Web. 15 June 2011.

Vidal, Gore. *The City and the Pillar.* New York: Dutton, 1948.

———. *The City and the Pillar.* 1965. New York: Vintage, 2003.

———. Introduction. *The City and The Pillar.* By Vidal. 1965. New York: Vintage, 2003. xi–xix.

"Vogue" (Madonna Song). *en.wikipedia.org.* Wikipedia. n.d. Web. 1 Aug. 2011.

Wagmeister, Elizabeth. "Logo Renews 'RuPaul's Drag Race' for Season 9, Greenlights Reality Series from Kelly Ripa." *Variety.com.* Variety. 20 July 2016. Web. 29 July 2016.

Walter, Eugene. "Conversations with Gore Vidal." Peabody and Ebersole 3–15.

Watney, Simon. "The Spectacle of AIDS." *AIDS: Cultural Analysis, Cultural Activism*. Ed. Douglas Crimp. Cambridge, MA: MIT P, 1988. 71–86.

"What Is the It Gets Better Project?" *ItGetsBetter.org*. It Gets Better Project. n.d. Web. 25 July 2011.

White, Charles. *The Life and Times of Little Richard: The Quasar of Rock*. New York: Harmony, 1984.

"Will & Grace." *en.wikipedia.org*. Wikipedia. n.d. Web. 1 Aug. 2011.

Winick, Charles. "Fan Mail to Liberace." *Journal of Broadcasting* 6.2 (1962): 129–142. *Hein Online*. Web. 4 June 2010.

Wong, Sau-ling C., and Jeffrey Santa Ana. "Gender and Sexuality in Asian American Literature." *Signs* 25.1 (1999): 171–226. *JSTOR*. Web. 31 Aug. 2010.

World of Wonder Productions. "Alaska Thunderfuck's 'Your Makeup Is Terrible' on Let the Music Play." *YouTube*. YouTube, 15 July 2015. Web. 29 July 2016.

Wylie, Philip. *Generation of Vipers*. 1942. New York: Holt, Rinehart and Winston, 1955.

———. Interview by Mike Wallace. *The Mike Wallace Interview*. 12 May 1957. The Harry Ransom Center, The University of Texas at Austin, n.d. Web. 24 May 2010.

Yeager, Patricia. *Dirt and Desire: Reconstructing Southern Women's Writing, 1930–1990*. Chicago: U of Chicago P, 2000.

INDEX

www.ingramcontent.com/pod-product-compliance
Lightning Source LLC
LaVergne TN
LVHW050601110926
847619LV00018B/117